D0097907

623.82

KENDALL

COMPLETE BOOK OF BOAT MAINTENANCE
AND REPAIR $8.95

DATE DUE			
SEP 8 '81			
APR 15 '83			
SEP 12 '89			
NOV 1 '89			

AYER LIBRARY

THE COMPLETE BOOK OF
BOAT MAINTENANCE
AND REPAIR

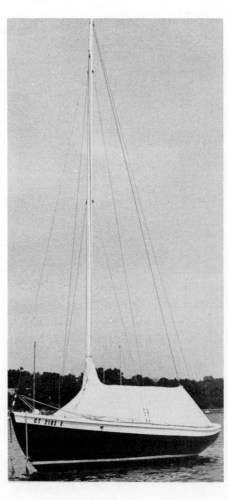

BOOKS BY DAVE KENDALL

The Complete Book of Boat Maintenance and Repair

Boating: Your Questions Answered

The Complete Book of

BOAT MAINTENANCE AND REPAIR

By Dave Kendall

DOUBLEDAY & COMPANY INC.

Garden City, New York   1975

Library of Congress Cataloging in Publication Data

Kendall, David A
    The complete book of boat maintenance and repair.

    Includes index.
    1. Boats and boating—Maintenance and repair.
I. Title. II. Title: Boat maintenance and repair.
VM321.K44   623.82′3
ISBN 0-385-04450-X
Library of Congress Catalog Card Number 70–150901

Copyright © 1975 by David A. Kendall
All Rights Reserved
Printed in the United States of America
9 8 7 6 5 4 3

DEDICATION

To Uncle Everett and "Peachy" (my first real boat-love);

To "Sky" and "Yare," who came later;

To Baba, Judy, Ginny, Sherry, Laurie, Whitson, and Margaret-the-Tadpole;

But especially to Matthew-Mug, who spent more hours in a hot and dusty boatyard before he was ten, than many people spend in a lifetime . . . just to keep his Dad company.

With deepest love and thanks.

ACKNOWLEDGMENTS

If I were to try to include every single person who ever helped me with an idea or a suggestion for this book, I'd have an acknowledgments section about the size of the service products directory you'll find elsewhere.

Even so, I would like to thank all the manufacturers of boating products who helped by providing information and material. I'd especially like to thank Charles A. Jones, editor and publisher of *Boating Industry* magazine, for his gifts of time and patience.

Contents

Author's Comment:

Your boat is uniquely an extension of yourself: it tells other people what kind of a person you are—or, at least, what kind of a person you want them to think you are.

This book contains the information you need to keep your boat in top condition. It will take you through all the necessary steps of fitting out, servicing during the season, and laying up the boat for the winter. I have written from the standpoint of a boatowner, as well as from that of the technical editor of a boating magazine. I have tried many of the things this book will advise you to do; I have worked on fiberglass, aluminum, and wooden boats. I hope you will find this work as satisfying and enjoyable as it has been for me.

DAVE KENDALL

THE COMPLETE BOOK OF
BOAT MAINTENANCE
AND REPAIR

1

So Now You Own a Boat! (or plan to)

Only a short distance from my home there stands a stately white clapboard home in an expensive and dignified area of the community. During the winters, the drives and paths are neatly shoveled; during the summer, the property is trimly manicured.

But during the weeks of early spring, this beautiful home stands disheveled, with lawn grown lank and weedy, storm windows still in place, and a million spring chores undone. The reason stands in the side yard: It is a twenty-seven-foot motorboat. Not a thing gets done to the property until that boat goes into the water.

Most boatowners are like that. Their cars can go unwashed, their homes unpainted, their wives unpermanent-waved—the major fruits of the boatowners' creativity can be seen in the condition of their boats. Resign yourself (better yet, get your wife to resign *herself*) to the fact that this will probably be true for you, too. With any luck at all, you can enthuse your family to some extent as well (see Figure 2).

If you already own a boat, new or used, you may want to skip over the next portion of this chapter to the section subtitled "Start with a Survey." It may be profitable for the rest of us to examine quickly some of the steps that go into the selection of a new boat.

Buying Your First *New Boat*

There's not much doubt that buying a new boat is rather like buying a new car. The steps you will take are similar: shopping for a model you like; picking the best dealer; getting the best price; financing; insuring; registering; settling warranty problems.

Figure 2

There are two things you may not have considered part of the process. They can be the most important factors in insuring you'll be satisfied with your purchase and investment.

First, look to see what the most popular types of boats are for families of your size in your area. Boating is one activity in which it pays to keep up with the Joneses. Then, if you decide to sell your boat (and it seems a pretty sure bet you will before too much time has elapsed), you will have a completely salable commodity and not an unsellable oddball.

Second, look to see which dealer has the best reputation in the area, both for sales honesty (*not* necessarily the dealer everybody says you can beat down farthest in price), living up to the obligations of his manufacturers' warranties, and good service. Be less concerned about the brand of boats and motors he carries. If he's a good dealer, he carries good products, or he wouldn't be in business for long. Chances are, you'll find this dealer will have just what you're looking for at a fair price. Remember, the dealer you're able to get that low-low priced deal from may have no service department and have no intention of making warranty adjustments.

Getting an adequately powered boat without having a red-hot you can't safely handle can be tricky. The manufacturers of the boats have an excellent rating system—these days, the Coast Guard and the Boating Industry Association certify the lines of most of these boat makers, and the certification plate affixed to the hull will be an essential guide to horsepower. Guess a little high. If you almost always have family and guests aboard, you will want ample power; this will actually mean better fuel economy than a lower-powered version and will avoid engine overheating and strain. If you almost always go out alone, you will be able to get away with less power, on the other hand.

By the way, there is a good rule of thumb for deciding whether or not you will need that optional extra fuel tank: Plan some typical excursions of the type you'll plan to make once you own the boat. Estimate the amount of time you'll need to get where you want to go. Then remember that a two-cycle outboard motor generally consumes one gallon of gasoline at full throttle for every ten rated horsepower. Therefore, if you have a 75-hp outboard, it's going to drink up *7½ gallons of gas every hour;* this is about the same fuel consumption for many 150-hp 4-cycle inboard engines. Plan your fuel reserves accordingly. It's no fun to have to stop at a gas dock every hour or so.

Whether to buy a fiberglass, aluminum, or wood boat is mostly a matter of taste, resale value, and the area in which you cruise. For example, fiberglass boats are popular in most open, coastal salt-water areas; they are relatively easy to maintain, are durable, and keep their resale value. Banks and insurance companies often provide for lower interest or premium rates for fiberglass boats.

On the other hand, in Midwestern lakes and streams areas, aluminum boats have gained outstanding popularity. They, too, are quite easy to maintain; the old myth about aluminum not withstanding the marine environment, even salt water, is long a thing of the past. Moreover, they offer performance and fuel-consumption economies because of reduced weight and horsepower requirements.

On some New England area lakes and coastal regions, wood still enjoys its stronghold as the most popular boatbuilding material. Wood hulls tend to need a bit more maintenance, but the techniques are simple and the materials inexpensive (neither is true for fiberglass or aluminum). For sound and temperature damping, wooden boats can't be beat. With proper care, they will last a good many years more than their owners' desire to own them.

Buying Your First *Used Boat*

Anyone who knows anything about depreciation knows that it seldom pays to buy anything new. Outstandingly good bargains in used boats and motors can be gained if you know just what you're doing. On the other hand, you can lose greatly in enthusiasm and investment in buying a poor used boat.

For example, it makes poor sense to pay premium dollar for a used boat that has obviously been used hard for water skiing, regardless of how good the boat-motor combo may look. Water skiing usually requires full-throttle running and often involves teenagers, who seem to have very little regard for the capabilities of the machinery they use. A used water ski boat alone may not be a bad deal, especially if it's fiberglass, as long as your dealer will make you a good deal on a new engine or a used one he's willing to guarantee in some meaningful way.

Perhaps the very best way to start in used-boat hunting is to visit a local boat broker in whom you have faith. Let the broker know you're not interested in dollars alone: You'll pay a fair price (which of course keeps the broker's commission—which *you don't pay*—high) for a fair boat in good shape. Tell the broker you will insist on a survey by your own surveyor. This is terribly important. Remember, you're only food on the table, shoes for the kids, and payment for the bills to the broker. He probably wouldn't sell you an outright lemon if he knew it was one. He's sure to recommend a surveyor who *won't* call the boat a lemon under any circumstances.

When you've found the boat you want, be prepared to plunk down a small (usually 10 per cent) downpayment as "earnest" money—subject always to an "okay" from your own surveyor. Go to a neighboring town to get your surveyor, even though it may mean paying his travel time and expenses. For obvious reasons don't pick on a surveyor who's also a broker. Be prepared to pay from ten dollars to fifty dollars for the survey, depending on the value of the boat (be prepared to pay much more if an expensive major yacht is involved). (See Figure 3.) Also be prepared to be on hand when the survey is made—hang over the surveyor's shoulder and ask lots of questions. He won't like it for sure; he may

Figure 3

even specify you may not accompany him on the job. Don't you believe it! It's your money being paid to survey a boat in which you'll make a major investment in time and money; you have every right to watch that the project goes well. One more thing about surveyors: You may note that the survey report will probably try to disclaim any responsibility for any mistakes the surveyor may make. He can't do it. The courts have held that a person cannot sell his expertise and then disclaim responsibility for being an expert.

The survey report may well show up certain deficiencies in the boat's condition. Don't be overdismayed. After all, you've paid him to tell you what's wrong, not just tell you good things about the craft. Determine if you can talk the owner into making repairs (which he will guarantee) at the agreed price. If you can't, try to get him to reduce the price enough at least to split the difference on repair costs with you. If that's unsuccessful, forget the boat and move to something more dependable.

The survey report will probably not include a report on the condition of the boat's engine or engines and/or sails, if applicable. You will have to have a mechanic look at the engines (remember, many boatyards and marinas won't permit service personnel from rival establishments on the premises) and will certainly want to take the sails to a sailmaker for his evaluation of their condition. Engines that have been salt-water cooled will surely rust out before they wear out. If an engine's ten years old, it's pretty close to the end of its useful life, even if it has been "rebuilt" (usually new rings, valves, points, plugs, condenser, carburetor, etc.) recently. This will be true for the rebuilt engine the boatyard may try to sell you as a low-cost replacement: The important thing is how long has the engine been used in salt water, not how many times it has been tuned up.

Start with a Survey

So now you own the boat of your dreams. You may also be somewhat disillusioned at this point. That lovely shiny paint finish may turn out to be a great, thick coat of paint applied by many former owners to cover scars and defects. That new-boat aura may have blinded your eyes to less-than-perfect finishing techniques. You've just found out the stuffing box on the inboard engine's propeller shaft leaks, the fuse blew the very first time you tried to use the running lights, and the brand-new compass is so inaccurate that you landed a mile and a half from your destination the first time you tried night piloting. Calm down, relax, it's not yet time to man the lifeboats!

Even though you may have had your used boat surveyed by the best in the business—even though that new boat just came from the showroom—you will want to start with a survey of your own. Here's how to go about it.

Plan to devote some leisurely study to the project—say an entire Saturday morning. You'll certainly find that "pottering about the boat," as the Britons term this type of project, is rewarding and fun, anyway.

Figure 4

To do the best job, equip yourself with a loose-leaf notebook filled with an ample supply of paper. What you're going to do is to create a maintenance log, just as many people prepare a log-

book of their cruises. Basically you will want to create a record of
the service you put into your boat, how much time it took, how
much money it cost, even the types of products used and their
performance.

If your boat is a new one, you're both starting from scratch. You
may wish to divide the maintenance log into sections. For example: for the hull exterior (known as "topsides") surfaces from the
deck to the waterline; for the hull's exterior bottom surfaces; for
the deck and the deck hardware; for the interior and cabin area, if
that's applicable to your size boat; for the engine, battery, controls,
propeller, etc. (you may need another similar category for sails,
spars, and rigging if appropriate); and a final section for the mis-
cellaneous equipment roster, to include such items as life preservers, compass, anchor, anchor lines, fenders, cockpit and bunk
cushions, etc. In this final section, for example, you will want to
keep careful record of the dates on which your fire extinguisher
was tested and/or recharged as required by law.

You will want to go over your new boat from stem to stern,
working in each section to categorize what equipment is on hand,
when it was bought (some may be new, others may be brought
from formerly owned boats), what service was provided (bottom
paint by date it was put on and brand, for instance) by the dealer.
Also note any areas where the construction, finish, or design of the
boat seems to be deficient by your standards. You may want to
call instances of construction and finish deficiencies to your dealer's attention for a warranty adjustment; you will perhaps want to
alter the craft's layout slightly to meet your needs.

Continue to maintain the service log throughout your entire
period of ownership. When you are ready to trade the boat in on
another new one or sell it in a private sale, the fact of your having
kept the log bespeaks a seamanlike, orderly way of doing things. It
will certainly be a good trading tool when working with a dealer
on a trade-in; the log will be a real selling advantage for the dealer's salesman, for example. Any private owner will want to know
"what's been done" to the boat; here's your way to document your
careful ownership, as well as support your insistence on getting a
fair used-boat price for your pride and joy.

If your boat is a used one, the maintenance log should have been
started long ago. Chances are it wasn't, so you'll have to do the
initiating. Organize it the same way as for a new boat. You'll

probably find lots of things with which to fill the pages—jobs that need to be done, jobs that should be done sooner or later, and jobs you'd like to get at.

Bear in mind the sure fact that there'll always be jobs you'll want to do to your boat. Keeping note of them in this maintenance logbook is the only way you'll ever be able to plan to do them as part of a meaningful schedule.

On the subject of making even minor alterations in your boat's layout, remember that the designer planned it the way it is for good reason. He had in mind the boat's weight distribution and trim as she sits in the water. He knew how she would behave when running, given certain factors of weight distribution. It's quite true that wedges and trim tabs can go a long way in correcting improper running trim in a powerboat. It's also true they're problematic to install and use properly, not to mention the cost. No similar device exists for an improperly balanced sailboat.

Moreover, layout is always a matter of livability. How easily can you move about the boat when it's under way? How can an enclosed area be properly lighted and ventilated? You will want to use your maintenance logbook to note proposed changes in lockers, stowage, and living space. Then live with the present layout for at least a season. Try to learn why the designer laid the boat out *his* way and not yours. You will probably find his way was better, especially if yours is one of the older, semicustom boats. The layout was probably close to perfect for the amount of space involved to begin with; subsequent owners will have made minor alterations that will have refined, rather than altered, the boat.

Using the Service Log

To gain maximum use of your maintenance log, you should probably re-establish it annually. That means you should create a new section for each section of the boat each year.

When, for example, you have tried a new bottom paint or a new type of varnish, log the amount of product you used and how much it cost; at the end of the season, record your reactions to its performance.

You may well find that a "sale price" bottom paint may save you one third the cost of painting your boat with a comparable amount of moderately priced paint. On the other hand, you may also find that the boat will absolutely require a midseason haulout and repainting because the low-cost paint just didn't protect against marine growth underwater. In such a case, you will have spent one third *more* than you would have spent for the somewhat higher-priced finish. This is not necessarily bad. If, for instance, you don't mind spending the additional money because it means a lower expenditure in each of two payments, rather than a bigger initial lump sum, then you should go for the lower-priced product. Don't forget to figure in the cost of haulout, however, your additional labor, and any loss in efficiency, not to mention use of the boat (while it was hauled) in your computations.

If you use your boat for business entertaining at all, the service log seems a sure-fire way to document expenses for income tax deductions. Don't forget to include copies of all paid invoices, which you might want to staple to the appropriate log sheets. The time and effort spent in keeping with the log will be returned manyfold in enabling you to buy maintenance products in more exact amounts and cut wastage. It will also help you determine, from past experience, what investment you will need to plan for upkeep and replacement parts. Moreover, if you notice that your replacement rate seems much higher than the norm, there may be something you're doing wrong; a change in technique could save you a lot of money and down time.

A maintenance log will also enable you to put chores in their proper priorities. For example, a friend of mine recently spent half a weekend red leading the bilge of his wood boat. The time was late spring, when both he and his boatyard were champing to get his boat in the water. Both bottom and topsides remained to be painted; the deck was halfway through a resurfacing job. The point is that in the forty-three years of her existence, his boat had never had her bilges painted. It wasn't a necessary job, it was just one he had planned to do "someday." The logical day and year was not the one he picked, with basic prelaunch chores screaming to be done. The other half of the weekend, by the way, was spent in painting the cockpit—a chore that could have been done when the boat was afloat. And so it goes. Keep a careful maintenance log and you won't fall into this type of trap.

A maintenance log will also help you visualize your work schedule in a new, different, and delightful way. It will point out times when there is no maintenance going on, yet which could be handily used to get ahead of the traditional schedule.

Why wait until spring, for instance, to remove the old paint from your boat's bottom? You may not wish to repaint until spring, but the old paint can be stripped off the moment your boat's taken from the water in the fall. Perhaps it's too cold to paint in the wintertime, but it's certainly not too cold on many sunny February weekends to do some sanding. Without a million other guys clamoring for the electric outlets and getting in your way, the boatyard can be a rewarding place to be during *clement* winter weather. Of course, you can always bring home the floorboards to be sanded and painted in the basement. Much ondeck and interior painting can be left to be done after the boat's been launched; actually, that's better time, since there's less chance of dust and dirt's being blown into wet paint offshore.

Some boatowners don't believe you've lived until you've spent two twenty-hour weekend days laboring in a ninety-degree-plus boatyard under a broiling June sun, finished up the chores by your car's headlights, then had to walk home because the engine wouldn't start. I've done just that, and I don't agree. The rest of this book will be devoted to telling you how to avoid this trap of boat ownership, how and when to do your work in a simple, effective, productive manner, to get the most fun and pleasure from your boating hobby.

Good luck!

2

Spring Maintenance: The Hull

So now the winter is over and the moment of truth is at hand. It's sink or swim with you and your new boat. There she sits under her winter cover; the snows are melting and time's a-wasting. Let's get at it.

The first thing you've got to do is make it possible to work on the boat while at the same time protecting her from collecting rainwater, which could freeze and do damage during cold spring nights. It will be of great importance, on the other hand, to be able to get at the outside surfaces, especially the bottom and topsides, as soon as the weather's clement.

To partly uncover your boat, you'll find there are several methods; you may well develop others of your own as well. The cheapest and easiest way is to loosen the bottom edge of the cover on either side of the boat. Roll it up like a window shade to the deck line, using a number of cheap one-by-two's on either side to core the roll.

When you roll the cover up, roll it *in* rather than out. This will avoid creating a water-trapping gutter inside the roll. When the cover's been rolled up high enough, clip it temporarily at each end, canvas to canvas, with spring-clip clothes pins. Now you're free to work on the exposed portions. At the end of the workday, simply pass a series of lines around cover and boat like a big package; this will hold the cover down and leave the topsides exposed. At the end of the work weekend, if any high winds can be predicted, it might be well to unroll the cover and refasten it in the conventional manner. There is one mitigating factor: If your boat is a wood one, you will find that it helps to swell the hull prior to launching if rain is allowed to sluice down the topsides and bottom. This means leaving the cover rolled up. The risk involved (of wind getting under the edges of the cover itself) may well be worth it.

The second method of partially uncovering is to utilize some new clips made by the Grifolyn Company. These are called Versa-Ties (they go with the Grifolyn line of Versa-Tarps, which will be discussed in the section on fall covering) and are sold in a plastic pouch pack at plastics supply outlets; ask your local builder or building supply house where you can get them, or contact Grifolyn directly at the address you'll find in the service materials directory elsewhere in this book.

The Versa-Ties fasten in a unique manner to avoid your having to make holes for tie-down grommets. This means you can put a row of Versa-Ties at the bottom of each side roll of the cover when you've completed the window-shade procedure. Then the rolled cover itself can be fastened down securely without your having to use that not-so-secure expedient of packaging, as in the first method.

Doing a good job on your boat follows the old discipline: Work from the bottom up. The outside of the hull is the most important part, and the bottom is the most important segment of that part. After all, consider that if your boat's topsides aren't pretty, the boat will probably function well enough, especially if it's a fiberglass or aluminum boat. If the bottom doesn't receive proper attention, however, you'll suffer poor performance and poor fuel economy all season long, perhaps for as long as you own your boat.

Bottom Paint: Fiberglass Boats

When a fiberglass boat leaves its dealer's showroom, if the bottom hasn't already been painted, it may well be covered with wax. Even an older fiberglass boat's bottom surfaces may have waxy substances still present. Here's where they come from and what to do about them.

When a fiberglass boat is built, its hull is shaped in a mold. To ensure that the hull will part from the mold, the builder utilizes a "parting agent" with which the mold is sprayed. One of the components of the parting agent is wax.

The types of gel coat (outer surface) resins used by many boatbuilders for their fiberglass boats are "air inhibited." That means they don't cure readily when exposed to air. The reason for this is that the gel coat is usually the side of the boat against the mold: there's the whole thickness of the hull wall between the gel coat and the air. If air were required for curing, the outer surface would never cure at all until it was taken from the mold; some initial curing is obviously essential.

However, if a boatbuilder were to wait until the boat's gel coat was absolutely cured, his molds would be tied up for an impossible length of time. Since molds are expensive, this would boost the price of new boats beyond all reason, and you and I would never be able to consider buying one. It's a vicious circle. That's why the resin materials suppliers came to the rescue of all of us—boatbuilders and buyers alike—with a type of resin that contains a waxy substance. When the boat is taken from the mold, curing of the gel coat is enabled to continue (as it must) by this waxy material, which continues to migrate to the surface of the gel coat resin. It keeps the gel coat airtight and lets it cure completely. Even when the migrating wax is removed from the boat's surface, it may be replaced by more wax from within the resin material; that is the function of the wax, after all, to be continually self-renewing. It may take years for this waxy material to dissipate itself by coming to the surface, where it is removed by you. Then the gel coat should stop curing; this prevents it from becoming brittle from overcuring.

Both the parting agent and the migrating wax will be present in varying amounts on the gel coat surfaces of a new boat; at least the migrating wax may well be on the bottom surfaces of a used boat. Both types of wax must be removed before painting, or the paint will fail to bond with the boat and flake, peel, or strip away to leave the bottom unprotected.

Sanding is essential to preparing the surface of your boat's bottom for painting. If one of the reasons you bought a fiberglass boat was to eliminate the need for sanding and paint, accept right now the fact that you are stuck with this procedure, at least until marine science develops and markets an in-the-resin antifouling protection (it's in the works right now).

The important idea in painting the bottom of a fiberglass boat is to be methodical and follow the directions of the paint manufacturer. For top performance, antifouling paints should be applied at least once a year in northern coastal areas. In southern waters, you will want to repaint as often as necessary to keep the bottom clean—once every six months perhaps, or every three months in far-southern, near-tropical areas.

Cleaning the bottom area also will help to remove wax, dirt, and old paint films. At least wash down with a solvent such as mineral spirits, acetone, white gasoline, or alcohol. Mineral spirits offer a number of safety advantages, and they are recommended for this reason.

A *primer* will be needed if you plan to paint with one of the traditional alkyd (oil-based) copper or copper/bronze antifoulers. The primer should certainly be of the same manufacture as the paint you intend to use, or at least be one recommended by the manufacturer of the bottom paint. The manufacturer's directions should be followed strictly.

Traditional bottom paints continue to offer a number of important advantages to fiberglass-boat owners. One of the most vital is price: They are comparatively inexpensive. In addition, they offer excellent hiding and covering characteristics. However, they do need to be replaced with reasonable frequency, because they are usually of the exfoliating type (that means they flake off). In fact, this is the way these paints achieve high antifouling results. The marine organisms cling to the outer flecks of paint, the organisms get too big and heavy, and the organisms and paint flecks flake off together, leaving clean paint. Often, authorities conclude these paints do not offer the high growth-kill characteristics of modern antifouling systems. Certainly there is no contention that these are not slick, racing-surface paints.

Modern synthetic antifouling paints offer excellent surfaces as well as protection from marine growth. Early varieties of these vinyl- and epoxy-based antifoulants were difficult to apply. However, the trend is toward treatment of fiberglass-boat surfaces with materials that offer high efficiency in growth kill as well as ease of application: the vinyl-based paints, for example. These paints do tend to be high in cost, however, and application requires some finesse. Most important in application is the understanding that it is difficult to blend edges if the painted edge is not completely dry or completely wet. A semidry edge can tend to lift if you brush out too much. It's usually recommended that you work steadily and quickly, completing one whole side of the boat if possible (depending on the size of the boat, whether or not you can turn it upside down to work on it, and how much cradle-crawling you have to do, of course) before you take a break. The primary rule is *be careful* not to brush out too much. Try, rather, to lay the paint on with a full brush. Some skill at lacquering would be handy, since some of these paints use a lacquer-thinner base and behave similarly. Organotin bottom paints are unusually effective in this category (see the following section on aluminum boats).

The number of coats you apply will depend strictly on how often you scrub your boat's bottom and/or beach her to clean and touch up the bottom paint. The application of two coats, however, is usually a good rule of thumb for an exfoliating bottom paint of the traditional variety; this paint has the very important advantage of removing itself when its work is done. Enough paint is essential to make sure you don't get down to bare hull as you scrub the boat during the season. With the nonexfoliating synthetic paints you will certainly want to use two coats the first time you paint the bottom from the bare gel coat stage. One additional coat each spring should do the trick, though several coats should be put on scuff areas such as the bottom of the keel area, the skeg in a small dinghy or outboard, the bottom of a sailboat's centerboard, and the very bottom of the bow. It's especially important if you beach your boat often to picnic or swim. With the synthetic paints, all painting should be done at the beginning of each season, except for any midsummer touchup. With the alkyd traditional paints, one coat should go on in the fall, and the second coat should be applied no more than an hour before launching in the spring. The traditional paints must be either literally wet or no more than tacky when they're put into the water for best results. This is not necessary with the synthetics, many of which can be applied days before launching.

Bottom Paint: Aluminum Boats

Marine organisms make no distinction among types of materials used in boatbuilding. They grow on fiberglass and wood boats as well as on aluminum. However, there are certain essentials involved in providing antifouling paints for aluminum boat use. Most important among them is that metal-containing antifouling paints, improperly used, can do great damage to an aluminum boat.

When aluminum is placed in contact with dissimilar metals commonly used in all types of marine applications, it may be attacked by galvanic corrosion. This is literally the creation of minute electrical currents and is the same as that taking place in a typical boat or automobile storage battery. It causes severe corrosion when aluminum is coupled to copper or copper-bearing alloys, for example. It has been found that this type of corrosion is much more severe when a bimetallic couple (aluminum with copper, for example) is immersed in salt water than in fresh water or just exposed to a marine atmosphere. This is because salt water is a better conductor of electricity than fresh water or moisture-laden air.

Cleaning is the first step in preparing an aluminum boat's bottom surfaces for antifouling paint. According to the Marine Aluminum Committee of the Aluminum Association, "cleaning can be accomplished by the use of household detergent and warm water, followed by thorough rinsing." You may also use regular household abrasive cleaning powders if you find them necessary to remove caked dirt. As well, a light surface abrasion with medium coarse emery cloth may aid paint adherence, though heavy sanding is neither recommended nor needed.

When the bottom paint accumulations become too thick on an old boat, you may use an organic paint remover with complete confidence. The committee cautions, "removers with a caustic base should never be used." When the hull has been cleaned, the surface should be washed thoroughly and mechanically abraded with either the household cleanser or emery paper, or both where necessary. It is vitally important to remove all dust and grit and to dry the hull thoroughly. It goes without saying, I hope, that you will try to work in as dust-free an atmosphere as possible on a dry, warm day.

Surface preparation is step No. 2 in painting a new aluminum boat or one from which all paint has been removed. Obviously, if you have cleaned and lightly sanded and have a good, viable paint surface, you may now paint.

However, bare aluminum must be chemically prepared to ensure top-paint adherence. Here's how you go about it.

The two satisfactory types of surface preparations for aluminum are either a wash primer or a conversion coating. Both are single-coat paint systems designed to provide a clingy type of surface for subsequent coats of bottom paint.

A *wash primer* is most effective when it is applied over an acid-etching cleaner. Only a single application is necessary, and the manufacturer's directions should be followed as carefully as possible.

A *conversion* coating is as readily available from your marine or paint supply store as is the wash primer. It accomplishes the same end as a wash primer but by means of a chemical reaction with the aluminum surface. Like the wash primer, a conversion coating may either be brushed or sprayed onto the boat. A single application is all that's needed. It is essential that both systems—wash primer and conversion coating—*not* be used on the same boat. Again, follow manufacturer's instructions to the letter. If you do and the job goes wrong, you have cause for complaint. If you don't and you botch the job, you have only yourself to blame, and the manufacturer will properly tell you so.

Of all antifouling paints, those containing the treatment called TBTO or tributyl tin oxide have proven to be the most compatible with aluminum, according to the Marine Aluminum Committee. These are based on organo-tin compounds. They are quite effective as antifoulants, and may well provide protection for the entire season. An additional benefit is that the antifouling activity of the organo-tin antifouling systems seems to extend to scratched portions of the surface. This effect is caused by leeching of the protective coating onto bare adjacent portions by the very action of the seawater itself! This characteristic seems to be applicable to organo-tin compounds only.

Not to be used are antifouling paints containing mercury in any form. The mercury cannot be prevented from forming an amalgam that will destroy the aluminum. Read the label on the can of any antifouling paint you propose to buy, and ask all the questions to which you need answers; it's your boat.

Paints that can be used include those with heavy metal toxicants such as copper oxide, arsenic, or lead compounds. It is, however, of vital importance that they be applied only over two or three coats of a compatible barrier paint such as zinc chromate. The zinc chromate and antifouling paint should extend high enough up the hull, especially on the transom, so heavy loading of the boat will not expose bare aluminum to salt-water immersion with the copper bottom paint. Antifouling paints may be applied directly to boats with factory-applied cosmetic paint on bottom surfaces, providing that paint is in good condition. It is important to be sure that the antifouling system will be compatible with the factory-applied paint.

Outside the Hull: Topsides

Maintaining your wood boat in the spring is more than cosmetic. It is necessary to prevent leaking, general deterioration, and even rot. There are four general types of wooden craft involved: *carvel,* or smooth-planked, boats; *lapstrake,* or step-overlapped planked, boats (sometimes this type of construction is referred to as "clinker built"); *plywood* (either sheet or molded) boats; and *strip-planked* boats. Of these four types, only the first two should do any leaking when they're first launched in the spring; actually, the lapstrake boat shouldn't leak much or for very long.

Your *carvel-planked* boat will almost certainly leak some when she is first launched. This is perfectly natural and to be expected; it doesn't mean you've bought a lemon. Here's why the leaking occurs:

Any wood plank will swell laterally when it becomes water-soaked. Your boat's builder calculated the amount of swelling that would take place, taking into consideration the thickness and width of your boat's planking, and positioned the planks accordingly. If the boat was well built, the edges of the planks were beveled so that the back, or inside, edges just touched when the planks were dry. The outer edges of the planking might then be anywhere from a quarter to a half inch apart. This created an open seam, which he primed with white lead, filled with caulking cotton to a carefully determined density halfway to the outside edge, then topped off with a puttylike caulking compound. The compound and cotton weren't stuffed into the seam *too hard,* or too densely, because they would then not be soft enough to permit the planking to swell. The purpose of the open, cotton-and-compound-treated seam is to give the planking something to swell against to seal out the water.

This spring you must ensure that there remains caulking cotton and compound in the seam, as well as that they remain soft and pliable, or else you will be plagued with a leaking boat all season long. This is especially true of the bottom of the boat and should be done while you're preparing the boat for the water.

Even if the caulking is reasonably soft and pliable, you will often find that there are areas where it has hardened and chunks have dropped out. These areas will leak: depend on it. You must

Figure 5

replace the seam compound there, using a putty knife to work the compound well into the opening, or a caulking gun to force the compound in under pressure (see Figure 5). While you're about it, plan to "pay" the seams as well to prevent excessive early leaking. Paying is the process of working some compound into even tiny open areas in the seams. These tiny cracks in the seams are perfectly normal and occur when the caulking and planking dry out together over the wintertime. The planking shrinks as it dries and the seams open up; the compound becomes hard (sometimes even brittle) as it dries and loses the elasticity that enables it to cling to both sides of the seams while still filling the open portion.

There are a number of different types of compounds you can use to pay and fill seams. The traditional seam compound has an oil base like a putty. Before applying it, you should use a primer to fill the pores of the wood and prevent premature drying of the compound (see Figure 6). Red lead primer or the traditional copper-bottom antifouling paint will work well as a seam primer. Linseed oil should work well, too. Follow any directions the manufacturer of the caulking compound you're using may have provided.

Figure 6

If you're using traditional oil-based compound and a copper antifouling paint primer, I suggest you may want to mix just a bit of the antifouling paint with the compound to thin it for best seam penetration as well as to give it antifouling properties of its own.

If you decide you are willing to spend a bit more money to get a more long-lasting job, you may want to use a silicone-rubber-based caulking compound. These come in caulking tubes and are applied with a "gun" to force the compound well into the seams. The silicones do an excellent caulking job because they dry to a naturally resilient rubber that has extremely good adhesive qualities. This means that the caulking will cling to both sides of the seams as well as stretch out in between. Before you apply one of these primers to any bare wood, however, you should use a primer of a special type sold by the compound manufacturer; it's well worth the additional slight cost, because the compound itself is quite expensive, and you don't want to waste the time and money you've invested. If the seams are completely filled and you're just doing touch-up caulking, you will not need to use the primer.

How do you know how much caulking to put in? If the seams are just open the width of a drying-check (crack), simply pay them with a caulking gun or putty knife. If the old caulking has dropped out, renew the caulking to the same level. At all costs, even if you are repairing a known leak area, don't stuff the seam chock-a-block full. This will keep the seam from swelling completely and create new leaks all along the length of the seam several feet fore and aft of where you've done the stuffing. Instead, try to use a better caulking compound than was used previously, with better adhesion and elasticity to keep the water out. If you plan to do your touch-up caulking with silicone-rubber compound over an oil-based variety, make sure the two will be compatible; check with the local marine dealer for his advice, or consult the manufacturer of the new compound.

Recaulking a boat really comes under the heading of "repairs" and will be covered at a later time in the chapter on repairs.

A word of real caution may be important at this time: Caulking can be a dangerous business. It may be better to do too little than too much, which can seriously damage your boat (see the chapter on repairs). Some custom-built carvel-planked boats were not caulked at all but were so carefully constructed that complete swelling would close the seams tightly, wood-to-wood. A boat of this type *should never, ever be caulked under any circumstances.*

Your *lapstrake*-planked boat requires reasonably little caulking, if indeed it requires any at all (see Figure 7). It certainly does not require caulking cotton, and only a little compound, preferably of the soft, silicone-rubber variety, to prevent minor leaks. A lapstrake-planked boat is not meant to be caulked, since the overlapping of the planks and the constant-wood-to-wood contact serve to prevent leaking. Caulking will only force the planking wider apart and create leaks. Moreover, a lapstrake boat is often fastened together

Figure 7

with clinch nails or rivets through the thin overlapping portions of both planks. Caulking could cause the plank overlaps to split away and require replanking!

Your *plywood* boat requires no caulking at all. Obviously a plywood hull of the molded variety was fashioned in one piece and has no seams. A plywood hull built of sheet stock has a few seams, but these were permanently sealed by the builder during construction. If your boat leaks at one of these places, it will require a reasonably important repair, and you should turn to the chapter on repairs.

Your *strip-planked* boat has some unique advantages. Though built of wood, it is now seamless and is a unified structure. It was built up to specification of thin square-section planks (often ⅞ inch by ⅞ inch), which in the better boats run from bow to stern the full length of the hull without joints. The planks themselves were securely fastened together both with a high-grade waterproof glue and mechanical fastenings (usually boat nails), and the whole structure is a highly integral, strong, light, seamless one. There should not be any leaks in the structure, at least through seams that could require planking.

Almost any antifouling paint will do for almost any type of wood hull so long as it is carefully applied according to the manufacturer's recommendations. The general types include the traditional oil-based paints with metallic compound poisons. These are generally the copper and copper-bronze paints, which largely rely on exfoliation to provide the desired antifouling effect.

An exfoliating bottom paint has minute metallic flecks, which cling only tenuously to the bottom of the boat and each other. When a marine organism begins to grow on the bottom of your boat, the weight of the organism causes the flecks of paint to "let go," carrying with them the fouling element. This exposes new flecks of paint to ongrowing organisms. For traditional wood boats that are not used at extremely high speeds, the copper-based paints are excellent. They tend to be relatively inexpensive (that's "relatively," now) and do their work well. Moreover, the very exfoliating nature of the paint system prevents a too-great buildup of paint thickness over the years. Providing you don't use excessive amounts of paint each spring, you should enjoy reasonably long intervals between complete paint-removal jobs.

Synthetic bottom paints include the vinyl-based, epoxy-based, and organo-tin paint systems. Concentration is on high growth-kill achievement. These paints are not exfoliating types and are excellent for planing boats, fast sailboats, and trailered boats where the paint needs to resist scuffing. Application of the paints over a wooden hull can require complete removal of other types of paints previously used, as well as preparation with special primers.

The exfoliating paints should be applied in the springtime literally just as the boat is being prepared for launching. For maximum effectiveness, the paint should be no more than tacky. Complete drying and skinning over minimizes effective exfoliation. Careful sanding is about the only real surface preparation necessary; the *surface* should be dry prior to paint application, as well as clean and grease-free.

The synthetics can be applied a considerable time prior to launching without impairing their effective growth-kill characteristics.

Again, careful sanding is necessary as well as, in some cases, use of a primer coat, which is relatively simple to apply.

Fiberglass boat topsides require only cosmetic work. Long-term accumulation of dirt and stain over the wintertime usually calls for some reasonably harsh cleaning and cleansing methods. These are completely covered in the sections on dirt and stain removal under in-season maintenance of fiberglass surfaces.

If these procedures won't restore color and gloss to the boat, it may well be necessary to do some painting. Some special paints (epoxy-based) for fiberglass use are expensive and exacting to use. Follow the manufacturer's directions carefully to avoid your having to do the whole job over again.

Here are some tips to remember. You will obviously need to ensure that the surfaces are clean, dry, and grease- and wax-free. The wax may have been applied as a protective and beautifying coat or it might well be in the fiberglass resin itself (see the section on bottom-painting fiberglass boats). In any case, it must be removed by use of solvents and by careful sanding. All gloss must be dulled on the surface prior to the painting procedure.

Some paints require some special temperature considerations, both for the atmosphere and the mix itself. You're stuck with atmosphere temperature unless you can move the boat indoors. Wait for the proper day or you *will* be sorry. Temperature of the mix can be maintained easily. Usually, the mixture wants to be chilled, and this can be accomplished by floating the can in a shallow basin of ice water. In either case, follow the recommendations of your paint's maker.

Because fiberglass is such a smooth-surfaced material, most paints will not want to cling to it. For an alkyd, or oil-based paint, you will probably need to use whatever prime coat the paint manufacturer recommends. For an epoxy-based paint, you won't need the primer, but a special brushing technique may help.

When you paint anything, the tendency is to stroke the "long way," that is, with the long axis of the surface. This means that for a boat, you tend to brush along the fore-and-aft axis of the topside surfaces. With an epoxy paint it may be necessary to eliminate the tendency of the paint to sag by stroking up and down. If the paint sags before it has cured, you will only make matters worse if you try to brush out the sags. Like lacquer, the half-cured epoxy paint will only "lift" and create a real mess; wait until the paint has cured, then start again from the beginning. Additives for these paints are tricky to use. For example, while you may thin a regular oil paint, you will not want to use a "thinner" in an epoxy paint. The thinner is called a reducing agent and is used for clean-up. Instead, however, you may want to use a retarding agent. This will help you keep a wet edge for proper blending of areas by slowing the paint's curing at that point; it does not seem to measurably increase the over-all curing time of the paint, however. Again (these paints are *so* specialized), follow the manufacturer's recommendations explicitly.

Repainting should not be necessary on an annual basis, as it is with a wood boat. Instead, you may find that careful waxing and treatment of a painted fiberglass surface will cause it to stay fresh and glossy for an extremely long time. You may need to repaint only every other, or perhaps even third, year.

Aluminum boat topsides should require very little maintenance for the forthcoming season launching. If your boat isn't painted, you don't need to paint it, and I don't recommend painting. It is a time-consuming, though not difficult, process. Moreover, it shouldn't be necessary. A good cleansing solution of detergent and water should get most of the winter dirt easily. Any staining can be eliminated with harder detergents or solvent cleaners.

If you go at the business of cleaning your aluminum boat's natural finish too hard, you will remove all the natural oxide coating, which protects the aluminum against dirt and corrosion. Most aluminum-boat owners don't object to the not-unsightly dulling "patina" of oxide on their craft. It is not unlike the patina that forms on fine sterling silverware from use and cleaning, as well as oxidation.

If you don't like the oxide coating, by all means remove it chemically with a strong solvent cleaner and by buffing; an extremely fine wet sandpaper will do an excellent job for you. Then use a good quality boat wax to prevent additional oxidation. This wax will probably have to be stripped and replaced from time to time as the film is worn away or fails and oxide starts to form.

Many aluminum boats today have been factory painted and may need some repainting to keep them fresh looking. Like fiberglass, this is a material that needs only cosmetic attention, however; painting for the sake of preservation is not necessary.

The steps for painting aluminum have been carefully outlined in the section of this chapter devoted to preparation for application of a bottom antifouling paint. If your boat's paint is in good condition but has simply dulled, you may treat that surface as you would any paint that needs renewing. Otherwise you will need to follow the careful steps for preparation, cleaning, and precoating the metal prior to painting.

According to the marine aluminum manufacturers, the very best type of paint for final aluminum coating is bake-dried enamel. Unless you have some pretty specialized equipment in your basement, it won't be possible for you to bake-dry your boat. If you're interested, however, only in the finest possible job, contact your local sports car agency for the name of a local autobody shop with experience in painting aluminum bodies. It may well be possible to trail your boat to such a shop and have them spray and bake your boat. The job could well be worth the cost in looks and durability of the finished paint surface.

Wood boat topsides all should be finish-coated in the spring. Providing you did your fall preparation and prime coating well, you will need only to do a thorough sanding job, and a light one at that, before your topsides are ready for a good finish coat.

The proper finish coat for a wood boat can be one of the traditional alkyd paints, a polyurethane paint, or an epoxy. The amount of time and money as well as your personal inclinations are the factors in deciding.

If you have only a modicum of handyman experience, then use an alkyd paint. The ease of application as well as the reduced cost will appeal to you. Gloss, resistance to chalking, hiding (the ability to "cover"), and color retention will be excellent, too. Use a special marine filler compound or one of the epoxies to fill any nicks and gouges you weren't able to catch last fall when you did the prime coating.

You can pay the topside seams just as you did the bottom seams, and very effectively, too. It will be helpful if you "tint" your seam compound to match the boat's topside color (use some of the topside paint, of course), and apply the compound smoothly with a putty knife. Then, immediately before the compound hardens or cures, dress the seams with paint. The brushing action and the paint will smooth all imperfections in the surface of each seam and blend it with the planking. When this seam-dressing paint coat has dried and has been lightly sanded, flow on two light finish coats of high-gloss marine enamel, sanding lightly between coats and wait-

Figure 8

ing the length of time the paint maker recommends before applying the second coat. Brush the paint out carefully; the result will
be a smooth, glistening surface that should help its gloss and color
well throughout the season.

At the waterline, it is often attractive to apply a boottop stripe that
will set off, and contrast to, both bottom paint and topside paint
colors. My own boat, for instance, has dark green topsides, a dark

red (the traditional copper-bottom-paint color) bottom, with a broad white boottop. You can buy special boottop paint for this purpose; it has some antifouling qualities to resist marine growths and staining at the waterline; it is somewhat harder than a conventional bottom paint to withstand the hard waterline-area scrubbing during the season.

If your hand is a steady one, you will perhaps prefer to "cut in" your waterline area and/or boottop stripe by hand with a full small brush. A good painter can do an excellent job, and I recommend this technique for the highest quality.

If your hand is less than steady, you will probably want to make a mechanical delineation before painting by using masking tape. If you use this paper tape, do it carefully; masking tape is no cure-all for being sloppy. Burnish the tape edge thoroughly with a hard, rounded tool such as the back of a screwdriver with a wood or plastic handle. This prevents paint "creep-back" under the edge of the tape. It also may create some lifting of under paint when you remove the tape, so be prepared for a little touch-up. To minimize the chance of paint creeping under the tape edge, brush away from, not toward, that edge and use a relatively dry brush at the very edge of the tape; be especially careful where the tape crosses seams or irregularities. Remove the tape immediately when the paint has become tacky; this will help prevent more than necessary bonding of the tape adhesive with the underpaint. Wherever possible, tape the upper edge to minimize the chances of runs over the tape.

You may really doubt your ability to create an attractive waterline even with masking tape. In this case, you'll be pleased to know that there is a plastic tape "instant waterline," which needs only to be pressed on. It's one of those self-adhesive tapes with a peel-off back. Adhesion, even on high-speed powerboats, is reported to be good. When the waterline gets to looking scruffy in a year or two, or if you change boat colors, just peel up the old tape and apply new.

Outside the Hull: Decks and Brightwork

Maintaining a fiberglass, aluminum, or painted wood surface is much the same for any part of your boat. There are some important considerations in deck maintenance, however.

For example, it's quite possible that the owner of a wood boat might find that his boat's deck and deckhouse surfaces were covered with fiberglass. In this case, he would use traditional wood-boat spring maintenance techniques on the topsides and fiberglass-boat clean-up procedures on the decks and deckhouses. The owner of a

Figure 9

fiberglass boat, on the other hand, might find that his boat had a teak deck. He would use the normal fiberglass techniques on his boat hull but quite different programs for the decking.

Teak decking became especially popular during an era when yachting was the sport of the well-to-do and there were plenty of deck hands available to keep the teak spotless. While teak *needs* relatively little maintenance to preserve it as an excellent deck material, most owners do a good deal of maintenance to keep it looking attractive.

Teak that has been untreated or allowed to weather does acquire a lovely, silvery patina; this patina is supposed to be attractive and, in truth, is extremely appealing on the appropriate type of boat. Unfortunately, it also stains easily. Stained or weathered teak can be renewed by applying a bleach cleaner and an oil coating, which will prevent further staining or oiling. Like paints, teak preparations should be applied according to the recommendations of the manufacturer.

Many older wood boats still have canvas-covered deck surfaces. Surprisingly enough, the more paint you put on a canvas deck, the less protection you have. A lightly painted canvas deck maintains its flexibility and offers good protection; a thickly painted one cracks because the heavy coating is brittle—too brittle to work with the movement of the boat. Then water seeps through the cracks and starts in to penetrate the wood surface underneath. A leaking canvas is worse than no protection for a wood deck; it allows moisture in, but usually prevents it from drying out. Rot and major structural replacement are the inevitable results.

On some fiberglass boats and wood ones, too, owners will find some deck or deckhouse surfaces made of vinyl. Colored vinyl requires very little maintenance other than cleaning. The color can, of course, be changed by using one of the "tints" described in the chapter on spring maintenance of equipment, specifically life preservers and upholstery.

Wood-grained vinyl also should require little maintenance other than a good washdown. Patterns of the wood grains include traditional deck plank-and-seam patterns that are embossed with a wood texture and raised seams. Most cleaners can safely be used, though any abrasive that could tend to "cloud" the surface would be bad. Most petroleum-based thinners are safe to use, though I'd certainly recommend testing the cleaner on a patch of the vinyl that is usually out of sight (as opposed to the middle of the cockpit, for example). Acetone definitely cannot be used on vinyls, however; it cleans them very well, removing even the printed-on grain!

Varnished wood is called *brightwork;* the term does not apply to highly polished brass, bronze, or chromed fittings. The use of some brightwork aboard any boat can certainly enhance her value and appearance. The use of too much will make her difficult to keep.

The traditional spar varnish that is used for brightwork, as well as many of the synthetic varnishes (epoxies and polyurethanes), tend to be softer than the varnish used for an inside surface. This is to enable them to keep gloss and transparency even under severe weather and handling conditions.

Perhaps the key to good varnishing is hard sanding and gentle application. The hard sanding prevents excessive varnish buildup over the years and makes it unnecessary to use hard removal methods such as the use of paint and varnish removers. It is almost axiomatic that disk sanding techniques aren't very good for bright-work; they tend to leave semicircular scratches and minute groov-ing in the wood, which show up dramatically once the first coat of varnish has been applied. Instead, a flat sander will create a smooth, flat surface, which is ideal for varnishing. Sanding each season should remove most of the previous varnish down almost to fresh wood. The alternative is eventual cracking of the overthick varnish coat, water seepage that blackens the underwood, or even rot; to cure this you'd have to remove all old varnish, bleach the wood chemically, restain it, fill and prime it, and varnish it. Sound like a major undertaking? You bet it is, and it's not worth it for a purely decorative thing.

Careful annual sanding will keep the varnish under control. Two coats of good-quality varnish carefully flowed on with a full brush should follow the sanding. Don't mix the varnish, it doesn't need it; and especially don't shake the can! Shaking and mixing create air bubbles that will still be in the varnish when you've finished with the brightwork. Careful flowing with the brush (don't even wipe the brush excessively) and "licking" to eliminate bubbles will create a beautiful job.

Varnishing is one of those rewarding chores that show all the hard work you've put in. Guests always "oh and ah" over varnish. It is also a job that can just as well be done after the boat's been

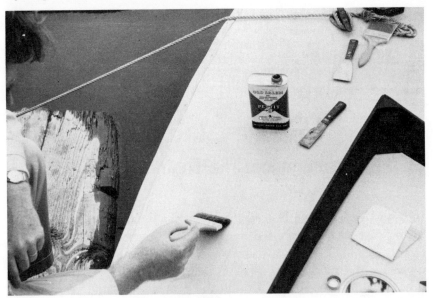

Figure 10

launched. At any rate, a still, cool day with sunlight seems important to outside varnishing; be careful not to varnish too late in the day, when it is likely to "dew" before the varnish is completely dry. This will certainly cause the varnish to haze, and you'll have the whole job to do over again.

A word of warning may be valuable here: Painting or varnishing on *any* flat surface on a too-damp day or in the evening just before dewfall will cause flatting of the gloss and require redoing (see Figure 10). Excessive thinning of oil-based paints, or thinning with the wrong stuff, will also cause flatting.

3

Spring Maintenance: The Engine

It would be reasonably easy to give you detailed instructions on taking care of both inboard and outboard marine engines. I could readily get hold of the instruction manuals for all types of engines by make and model and reprint them. The trouble is that by the time I write the material, Doubleday publishes it, and you read it, the motor makers will have done us in. They'll have changed models, and the information will be immediately obsolete.

Besides which, unless you are a factory-trained mechanic, you shouldn't do too much fiddling around with a marine engine. I can't stress too highly the safety aspects of this. If you have been following the outboard motor market, you know that the motor firms have been doing some potent research to increase the efficiency of their powerplants. This means they've been aiming at a very high-performance standard and achieving it.

Remember when your outboard was a relatively simple little two-cycle engine? Remember when the carburetor was the simplest type of fuel-metering device possible? Remember when, if the little kicker didn't run, it was almost invariably a case of fuel-line clogging or fouled spark plugs? I have a very mechanical-savvy friend who claims that if your two-cycle motor doesn't run satisfactorily, it's almost without doubt a spark plug problem. Replace the plugs and try again. If it still doesn't start, replace the plugs still another time. With simple outboards that was, and remains, excellent advice. With the not-so-simple V-4s, V-6s, or 6-in-lines, we have now in the upper ends of the horsepower ranges, it's at best an expensive procedure; at worst, it won't even begin to solve a problem caused by sophisticated carburetion and capacitive discharge ignition systems.

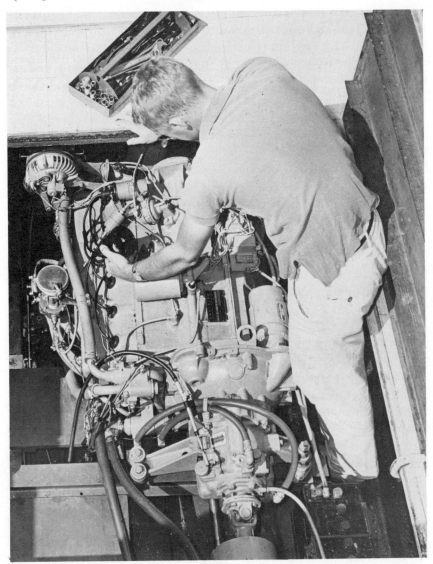

Figure 11

A two-cycle engine is just what its designation implies. It's designed to operate on a very gutsy power principle that says there is a power thrust every second passage of the piston. A two-cycle engine sucks in its fuel charge, not through a manifold pipe, but into the crankcase. Each time the piston rises to the top of the cylinder, it creates a vacuum in the crankcase behind it. That sucks in a fresh fuel charge, which waits for a downward stroke of the piston to be detoured into the cylinder.

The two-cycle engine relies on that fuel charge to carry with it minute particles of lubricating oil; it does not have a sump of lubricating oil in the crankcase. The oil coats the moving parts of the engine, and some of the oil finds its way with the fuel charge into the combustion chamber in the cylinder head. There it is burned with the fuel. That's why the two-cycle engine tends to emit a bluish smoke when it is running; that is why the spark plugs tend to foul up (though not so much so if your outboard is one of the current ones with capacitive discharge ignition system and high-voltage, resistor-type spark plugs). Under usual operating conditions, when the motor is running fast, a high temperature is achieved in the combustion chamber, and the oil is burned off. When you idle your engine for prolonged periods, though, some of the lubricating oil is deposited on the spark plugs and it interferes with their firing efficiency.

Summerizing your outboard motor is really a matter of constant preventive maintenance. This means you should make a regular and thorough inspection, or have someone competent to do so make it, to prevent problems. The time you and/or your mechanic spend in this preventive maintenance procedure will be repaid by uninterrupted time and fun afloat. If you are not a competent mechanic, if you would hesitate to delve the innards of your auto's engine compartment, *stay the hell out of your outboard motor's cowling.* There are things you still can and must do as an owner, but making maintenance examinations or doing important service jobs aren't among them.

Here, according to the service experts at the Mercury motor-making firm, are certain springtime servicing recommendations for the *handy* boater (see Figure 12).

First, the cowling should be removed and the outboard motor cleaned thoroughly, including all accessible powerhead parts. You can use a solvent for this, or if you protect ignition components such as distributor, coil, plugs, and leads, the type of emulsifying agent known as "Gunk." You brush or spray Gunk on, let it sit long enough to turn greasy deposits into a kind of soft, gray soap, then flush everything away with a garden hose (preferably hooked up to a warm-water faucet). You should take special care to make sure you don't slop water into the carburetor intakes or leave it puddling in the housing to cause rust. The engine can then be coated with an aerosol spray rust and corrosion preventive.

Then the spark plugs should be removed and the shaft rotated (by hand or with the starter—keep your hands away from the spark plug lead-wires while you're cranking, or you'll get a beauty of a

Figure 12

Figure 13

shock). This will loosen and remove any oil deposits that may have formed in the cylinders and crankcase during the prolonged winter storage period. If your motor has a manual starter rope, check it for wear at this time, too.

Owners of outboards equipped with electric starters should have their batteries tested and recharged before using. Some owners invest in one of the very small, plug-in trickle chargers and leave their batteries hooked up all winter long. It's not a bad idea, but remember that any live battery creates hydrogen gas. Be sure the rig is in a cool, dry spot that is well ventilated and well away from open flames (such as in the furnace room) or sparking relays and switches.

Another important step is the inspection of spark plug leads for damage or deterioration, particularly where insulation comes in contact with metal parts. The spark plug electrodes are another important thing to check. Under very ideal circumstances, plugs may be reusable, in which case you should reset the electrode gaps to

the manufacturer's specifications. Be very careful when you replace the spark plugs not to get them cross-threaded. This will
damage the threads in the cylinder block with all sorts of dire results. After seating the individual spark plugs fingertight on their
gaskets, a half-turn more with a wrench will usually be enough to
tighten them. Any more might strip the threads or cause the wrench
to slip and crack the procelain insulators. Be sure to reconnect each
spark plug lead-wire to its proper plug. This should be readily apparent from the natural "set" and length of the wire, but if it isn't
and you didn't bother to note the plug wire arrangement before
making disconnections, trot down to your local outboard motor
dealer for advice. At the very least, you may be able to take a look
at another outboard of the same make and model to regain the
proper sequence.

Now, check all fuel lines and fittings for possible damage or loose
connections. If the fuel tank is rusty, sand the rust down to a viable metal surface and touch up the metal with an aerosol spray
can. Many people spray in a light film of oil when they lay up an
empty fuel tank in the fall. If you are one of them, pour in a half
gallon or so of raw gasoline and slosh it around well (see Figure 14)
to loosen and wash away any oil film that could later clog a fuel
fitting or line.

Some people store fuel tanks full of gasoline. We'll review that
practice and its alternatives later in the chapter on fall lay-up, but

Figure 14   Figure 15

suffice it to say that now, in the spring, that fuel is *not usable*. The major fuel corporations admit that gasoline does not store very well. That means it only stores for about three or four months before it begins to turn gummy. While this can be minimized by using a product (additive) called "Sta-Bil" at lay-up time to prevent gumming, if that hasn't been done, you *must* remove and get rid of winter-stored fuel before you try to start your engine for the first time (see Figure 15). It isn't a bad idea to use a product like "Gummout" in the tank, either, just to make sure that varnish-causing gum doesn't hang on in the system somewhere. At the same time, clean and check the fuel filters on the engine and in the fuel tank.

Now you should refer to the owner's manual for your motor's individual lubrication points, and lubricate the engine as directed. A grease fitting located under the swivel bracket is often overlooked (see Figure 16). You should use a good-quality marine grease.

Before you replace the cowling, check your outboard thoroughly for loose, damaged, or missing parts.

Now lubricate the lower drive unit with the special gear lubricant recommended especially by the manufacturer. After removing the vent and filler hole screws and gaskets (check your owner's manual for the location of these), add lubricant through the filler hole and

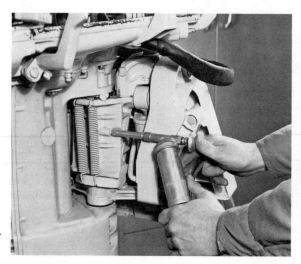

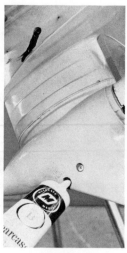

Figure 16   *Figure 17*

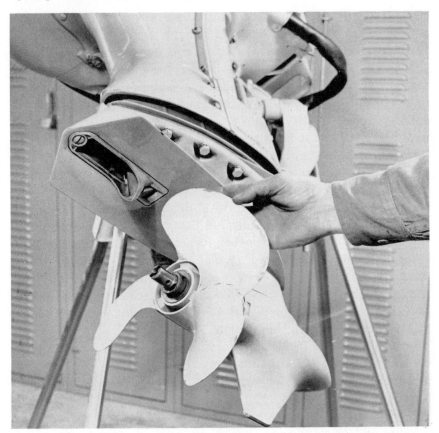

Figure 18

keep adding until lube starts to squeeze out the vent hole, which is usually above the filler (see Figure 17). Before you replace the vent screw and filler hole screw, you should make sure the gaskets under the screw heads are back in place. This is especially important in salt-water areas. Otherwise, water may leak past the threads into the gear housing.

You should, while you're messing with the lower unit, check the water inlet ports and the telltale opening (where water comes out in a small stream to indicate the water-cooling system's working) to make sure the cooling water flow to and from the engine is unobstructed.

Remove the propeller now and inspect the blades for cracks or bends, and have a look for possible hub damage (see Figure 18).

You can trim up nicks and burrs with a file, but you should remove as little metal as possible to avoid severely unbalancing the prop. This will greatly reduce its efficiency, add measurably to fuel consumption, and make passengers in the stern specially miserable because of vibration. You wouldn't run a car on a defective tire; give your outboard motor the same consideration. Before you reinstall the propeller, lubricate the prop shaft splines with a waterproof grease. It's important in salt-water operation because it makes removal of the prop easier in the fall or later in the season.

A word of caution may be important. Before you start fooling with the prop, remember that you've just finished tuning up the engine. Like all modern outboards, it should start easily. Take the wise precaution of placing a block of wood between the anticavitation plate and the prop whenever installing or removing the propeller shaft nut. It will prevent accidental starting.

Finally, if your rig has remote controls, check that the cables operate freely for safety and efficiency. Lubricate the linkages. If they don't function smoothly and without undue binding, better take the matter up with your dealer.

To complete your personal service make-ready operation, retouch any damaged or scraped painted surfaces. A clean, well-preserved outboard denotes a careful owner; it could be especially important at trade-in time.

If you think your carburetor is dirty, or the magneto points need cleaning and/or setting, do the job according to maker's specs or, better yet, let your qualified outboard mechanic do the job.

Summerizing your inboard engine is often a rather involved process. Remember, an outboard motor was brought into a cool, dry storage place for the winter. Your inboard engine or engines have just spent the winter being alternately frozen and bathed in condensed moisture; they required a lot of work to winterize them. Now you're going to have to undo all you did in the fall (see Figure 19).

Inboard engines are traditionally based on automotive blocks. Remember the four-cycle automotive engine in a 1939 car? It was simple to maintain properly, even if it was a V-8. If it was a six-cylinder block, almost anyone felt that was just a step away from the old Model T and Model A Fords; and after all, the farmers used to maintain and repair *those* motors with ease.

Now take a look at the four-cycle engine in your 1975 car! If it's

Figure 19

a V-8, it enjoys a sophisticated engineering unheard of thirty years ago. Even if it's a "six," it combines more performance and less weight than anything on the market before World War II. Both have pollution-control equipment built right in. This is exactly what has happened to inboard marine engines. They are sophisticated, highly engineered power-packages.

Look under the hood of your car. Would you plumb those complicated depths even to do a tune-up? If you *would,* read on. If you shudder at the thought, let a good, able mechanic do the job for you. Yes, you *should* learn something about those engines in your boat, but not at the expense of their dependability and your fun and safety for the season ahead.

Basically, your four-cycle gasoline marine engine provides a power thrust or stroke at every fourth piston movement. It sucks in fuel through the carburetor or bank of carbs, and intakes through a manifold and series of valves. Similarly, it exhausts burned fuel gases through another set of valves and a second manifold. Fuel is ignited by a spark plug, which is timed by the distributor to fire at just the right moment. Lubrication is provided at high pressure by an oil pump that pushes lubricant through a rather complicated system.

For many years, pleasure boats have been traditionally cooled by intaking seawater, passing it through the engine's water jacket, and exhausting the hot water. In salt-water areas, this has been a costly process. There are two basic reasons:

First, sea-salt water has corrosive qualities all its own. In addition, unless the flow of cooling salt water is kept fast, the salt begins to settle out and cake in crevices in the cooling jacket, creating hot spots in the engine. Keeping up this high-flow rate means that the cooling water is passing through the engine faster than it should; the engine never gets a chance to heat up properly.

Second, because of this running-cool proposition, fuel is improperly combusted inside the engine. An excess of water is created, in addition to the fact that engine efficiency is poor to begin with. The water finds its way into the crankcase, where it interacts with elements in the lubricating oil to form acid. The acid attacks the engine parts as it is carried through the lubricating system.

Because of these two engineering situations, sea-salt water-cooled marine engines have had relatively short lives. They are being rusted away by the salt water from outside. They are being corroded away by the acids from inside. One source indicates that the life of a sea-salt water-cooled marine engine can be calculated to be from five to ten years.

Modern marine propulsion engineers have countered by providing heat exchangers and keel water-cooling devices and combining them with closed-systems fresh-water cooling. Marine engine life is dramatically extended this way.

Here's what you should do, according to the Graymarine Corporation, to establish a proper spring maintenance program for your inboard engine.

If you have stored your boat with its fuel tanks full, you *must* drain down all stored fuel before you try to start the engines. There is a product called Sta-Bil, that will reportedly eliminate gumming, but without it gasoline can only be stored for about three to four months before it begins to create gum. Unprotected gasoline should never be run through an engine, since it causes varnish deposits to form in the carburetor or carburetors and on valves.

The engine should be cleaned thoroughly using a solvent or the emulsifying agent called "Gunk." Gunk will brush on or can be sprayed from an aerosol container. It causes greasy deposits to be emulsified into a soft, gray, soapy substance, which you then flush away with a water hose. In older wooden boats, it would be well to check to determine whether the Gunk will remove necessary oil from the caulking compound in the bilge and garboard seams; in this case, solvent should be used, and care should be taken that it isn't slopped into the bilge. If you use a solvent, make sure that all hatches are open, the boat is well aired, and that no one is smoking or using a flame nearby. Consider using mineral spirits.

Remove the distributor cap and lightly oil (a drop or so) the wick that rubs against the camshaft under the rotor. Put another drop on the breaker-arm pivot point, and wipe the cam lightly with just a trace of lubricant such as Vaseline or Lubriplate. It's well not to overlubricate. Clean and adjust the breaker points at this time if they need it and you know how. Your service manual will give you the point setting.

Change the oil in the crankcase, preferably after you've completed any tune-up chores—replacing spark plugs, cleaning the carburetor, etc.—and the engine has run long enough to be warm. In most cases, you will have to pump the engine oil out of the sump using a pump provided on the engine or a separate pump. Refill the crankcase with fresh oil according to the manufacturer's recommendations (probably SAE 30 weight) to the high mark on the engine dip stick. Don't overfill, and don't forget to check the oil level again after a few minutes' running. Change the oil filter canister. You should have changed transmission oil in the fall; if you didn't, do the job now while you're still dirty from the crankcase oil change.

Check the carburetor flame arrester to make sure that the air passages between the little flame-quenching plates are free from oil and lint. If they're clogged, remove the filter and wash it in solvent.

Reconnect any water-line connections you may have opened for the winter, replace the lower drain plug in the block if you removed it, and check the coolant level in the cooling system if you have a heat exchanger.

Now ventilate the entire bilge and engine space thoroughly before initial startup. Check the water flow as soon as the engine is running satisfactorily. If the boat is already afloat, remember to open the water intake seacock valve! If your boat is still unlaunched, provide some cooling water flow before start-up actually takes place. It would be better not to connect the engine water intake line directly to a garden hose, since the pressure forces water through the engine, whether or not the water pump is actually working. Remember that a boat with a keel cooler should not be run unlaunched.

Summerizing your fuel system is mostly a matter of making sure it's clean. Resign yourself that you're going to have to "waste" some gasoline to do this. Under the sections on inboard and outboard engine summerizing, it was noted that gasoline stored all winter long will not be suitable for use in the spring. Gasoline just doesn't store longer than three or four months very well. Gum deposits form in the tank and find their way into the engine, with subsequent carburetor and valve problems resulting. Moreover, gum tends to shake loose just when you most need your engines, during bad and stormy weather. Then the jouncing of the boat agitates the fuel in the tank, the sloshing fuel picks up gum and dirt, and the foreign particles find their way through the lines to clog filters and carburetor jets.

If you want to do a really good job, or if the tank on your used boat is pretty foul, remove it and take it to the local radiator-cleaning firm. For safety's sake, remove all tank fittings and fill the tank with water and allow it to stand for a while. This will displace any explosive fuel fumes. The radiator-cleaning shop will use a solvent and a jet of live steam to flush loose any deposits in the tank.

You might have been smart enough to do this job over the winter, so now let's assume all you have to do is install the tank and check the filters, lines, and fuel shut-off valves. Use some dry-gas solution with the gas to cut condensate problems.

When you install the tank, or on a sort of biennial (every other year, not twice a year) basis, you may wish to take the fuel lines apart and blow them out as well as redo the joints so you're sure everything's tight. That's the time to make sure the system meets recommended engineering practices. The Boating Industry Association publishes an excellent set of recommended engineering practices for builders, and you may wish to follow suit. For example, the practice as it relates to fuel filters notes that fuel filters should be designed for periodic servicing. They should be provided on the inlet side of fuel pumps and may be mounted either to the engine or to an adjacent boat structure. They should be resistant to salt water, alcohol, and stale gasoline.

According to the association, fuel tanks should be located in dry, well-ventilated compartments. Preferred locations are above cockpit floors, where any possible leakage will be readily apparent to you and your passengers. Contact between the tank and adjacent boat structures should be limited to the necessary supports to permit maximum circulation of air. Tank-supporting surfaces and hold-downs should fasten the tank securely and should be insulated by nonabrasive and nonabsorbent material. Deck fill plates should be located as far as practicable from ventilators. They should be placed where spillage will flow overboard. Flexible fuel-fill piping should be of fabric or fabric and metal-reinforced neoprene, grounded to tank and engine. An overboard tank vent should be provided to permit the discharge of fumes and prevent them from flowing into the boat or through ventilators. Flexible fuel lines should have an inside diameter of at least $\frac{5}{16}$ inch, while a $\frac{3}{8}$-inch outside diameter copper tube is required. Fuel lines should be made up with a minimum of connections. Where rigid fuel lines terminate at an engine connection, a section of flexible line should be provided with sufficient slack to absorb engine vibration. Deck fill plates should be grounded through the fuel tank to the boat's bonding conductor or common ground point. Adequate ventilation as required by the Coast Guard should be provided for both the engine and fuel tank compartments.

Summerizing your electrical system is not unlike the procedure you use for the fuel system. Basically, you want to insure a constant flow of electricity.

Regular ship's power will come from your batteries, and they should be well charged at the beginning of the season. Since battery power is direct current, it will be a relatively simple job to insure that all circuits have tight, clean connections. If any copper contacts have turned green with verdigris, take them apart, scrape them shiny, and reconnect them tightly. A blob of Vaseline or grease over the connection will protect against corrosion in the future.

If you are in doubt about your boat's battery or batteries, have your dealer check them cell by cell to make sure they're capable of holding a charge. When your engines are started for the first time, you will want to insure that the ammeters show some charge. If they don't and/or they fluctuate wildly, the problem could be inside your voltage regulator (this is the device that prevents you from overcharging your batteries; briefly, it works on a sort of electrical pressure system). When the batteries are empty of electricity, there is no back pressure against the generating system, and the voltage regulator permits current to be poured into the batteries as fast as it's made. As the batteries fill, there develops a back pressure; it isn't so easy to push in more electricity. The input slows. When the batteries have been fully charged, they "push back" against the generator as hard as it pushes against them. The excess electricity is shunted away to "ground" and dissipated. As the batteries lose current, it is replaced. If the regulator points stick, current may run through to ground at all times. Then you'll need to burnish the points or perhaps even replace the regulator.

Summerizing your drive system is easy if you have a conventional inboard engine. Then it will be necessary for you to change the oil in the transmission and check the props (see Figure 20), struts, and shafting. If your prop has been nicked or banged up, have it rebalanced and straightened by a shop that has a dynamic prop-balancing machine. Check the prop strut to make sure it's not loose or bent out of line. Finally, check your prop shaft for possible bending; to do this, mark on the boat's rudder, just aft of the prop shaft nut, the place where the shaft's center line points. Then turn the shaft ninety degrees to determine whether or not the new mark moves up or down, or stays in the same place. Keep moving the shaft and remarking every ninety degrees. If the mark stays true, the shaft is true; if it jogs much up and down, have the shaft straightened.

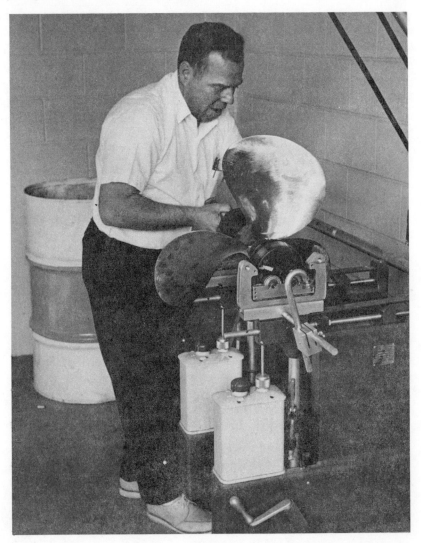

Figure 20

Finally, when the boat is afloat, check the stuffing box to make sure the packing isn't permitting a leak. Run the boat a short distance and recheck. Of course, if you have a wood cruiser with a conventional inboard engine, you will have disconnected the shaft; it will need to be reconnected after the boat has completed swelling in the spring after launching.

If your boat is an inboard/outdrive, you should have removed the entire drive unit—or better yet, have had your dealer remove it—last fall. Reinstallation and lubrication of the unit should be to the manufacturer's specifications. If you don't have a complete set, don't try the job. Remember your I/O shifts, steers, and pumps cooling water from that unit. Most important, of course, are the water-tight seals, which must be perfect to prevent boat and unit leakage.

4

Spring Maintenance: Equipment

Not the least of getting boat and motor ready for the spring season is the business of equipment maintenance. The obvious lessons of regularity in preventive procedures apply here, too.

Sails and Rigging

To a sailor, sails and rigging are the engine of his boat. They are the most commonly used motive power. They deserve important maintenance if they are to perform satisfactorily throughout the season.

A sailboat mast and rigging are never, or almost never, stored in place. The usual procedure is to take mast, boom, and standing and running rigging apart and store them separately, most often in a "spar shed" at a boatyard, where the mast and boom can be supported under cover and the wire rigging can be stretched out limply alongside (see Figure 21).

Now it is time to ready the rigging for the season. When the mast has been "stepped" or replaced in the boat, everything at the top is going to be high in the air and, for practical purposes, not readily accessible. Masthead fittings, mast tangs for attaching stays and shrouds, and pulleys for halyards should be checked, lubricated, and tightened where necessary before mast stepping. This is the time at which the rope or wire halyards are rove through their blocks ready for use.

Old-time sailors know that using the same piece of line for the same job, over and over again, season after season, put heavy strains on certain places—the spot where the halyard passed over a pulley

Figure 21

or cleat, for example. At these spots, the line was, and is, apt to fray and eventually fail. The sailors "freshen the nip" of such a line. This simply means to swap the line end-for-end or to slightly alter the length of the line so the strain falls at a different spot.

Sails should have been washed and stored carefully last year. Before they are first bent on at the beginning of the season, you will want to go over them very carefully. The best way is first to check the seams and batten pockets. Do this by holding the sail up to a strong light bulb. You'll be able to see if the stitching holes are elongated or the stitching is frayed or worn. Also look to see if the seizings on sail track slides have been frayed. This will be the first area where the sails will fail in a heavy wind, just when you need dependable performance most.

Life Preservers and Cushions

Life-preserving vests and cushions, along with certain types of upholstery aboard many boats, are usually made of vinyl. This plastic is an easy one to care for, and usually a good detergent solution will do the trick.

However, let's for a moment assume that you've just painted your boat a new color or the upholstery and cockpit seat cushions are getting shabby. It is possible to freshen vinyl colors, as well as change them, with several preparations on the market. They are called tints.

Involved is the use of a special vinyl cleaning solution that is provided in the tinting kits. Then the surfaces of the cushions or upholstery are tinted with a special coloring material. Not a dye, the tint seems to penetrate the vinyl and create a new, long-lasting, and durable color surface. The cost for these kits is minimal, much less than the cost of new vinyl upholstery or cushions. On many power boats, the convertible tops and side cushions are also vinyls and can be tinted just the same as the seats to match the boat color.

The Anchor and Chain

You wouldn't start off in your car after it hadn't been used for an entire winter, without first checking the brakes. The anchor and chain as well as the anchor line are of vital importance in making your boat stop and stay when and where you want it to.

A main mooring usually is made up of a heavy anchor and chain, which makes up all but the last few feet of the mooring "rode." All shackles should be wired shut so they cannot unscrew and let your boat loose. If main mooring line, the final few feet of the rode, is nylon rope, it should be checked carefully for chafing and wear incurred last year. If you use manila line, renew it before the mooring is placed so you have the maximum safety factor available.

The secondary anchors and lines should be made up and kept ready for use as part of one of the first activities of your boating season. An anchor stowed below in a locker or crammed under an engine somewhere is simply useless in an emergency. Place anchor chocks on the foredeck where the "hook" can be securely lashed and kept ready for use. The anchor doesn't need painting but should be carefully cleaned of corrosion and sand. A spray corrosion-preventive will make the anchor a somewhat more attractive fore-deck accessory. The best way to keep anchor line handy is to hang it in the cockpit within easy reach. The coil of rope should be "stopped" or tied with a light line at intervals to keep it neat. The stopper line should be made fast in a slippery, or bow, knot for easy releasing in an emergency.

The Trailer

If you trail your boat from waterway to waterway, you had better do a careful job of commissioning it for the season (see Figure 22). The most important component of the trailer is the running gear. Included are the bearings and hubs, which should be greased after the winter lay-up. Tires that were stored indoors

Figure 22

Figure 23   *Figure 24*

during the night should be inflated to the proper tire pressure and reinstalled. The wheel lug nuts should be tightened to between fifty and fifty-five foot-pounds of torque for safe operation.

The trailer lights should be washed out with fresh water, and the lens seals should be replaced. The contacts inside should be cleaned and coated with grease or Vaseline so they will not corrode. Trailer brakes should be blown out with an air hose if possible to remove any sand or grit, which could score the inside of the brake drums. The coupler should be lubricated for easy operation and painted if necessary to prevent any rusting. Finally, trailer rollers should be lubricated, and any rust spots on the frame should be touched up to prevent corrosion (see Figure 23). The first time your boat is remounted on the trailer, you should carefully check the bunk and roller adjustment for proper support to your hull (see Figure 24).

Miscellaneous Equipment

The galley stove on your boat will provide a lot of dependable service if it's carefully checked in the spring. A pressure alcohol stove has almost no moving parts to get out of order, so the most important maintenance factor will be cleaning the tank, tank filter, and pump. The burners have small holes that will clog very easily if you do them with a soap pad. You will probably want to fill and light your stove immediately after you finish cleaning it to make sure all orifices are clear. Pressurizing the stove and lines is the best way; heating the stove will evaporate any lingering moisture and burn off any soap on the burners.

Freshening the ice box is a necessary chore if your food isn't to smell musty all season long. Your wife can tell you the best way to do this is with a mild solution of bleach and water along with a healthy follow-through with detergent and hot, hot water.

Water skis are pretty simple affairs, but they may well need sanding and varnishing or painting. The bindings are often aluminum alloy-framed, and adjusting screws will corrode and bind up if not kept clean. One of the spray lubes or a dressing with light machine oil will keep screws turning freely. Rubber foot cups don't need much in the way of service, though you can use a rubber dressing (it's sold for auto tires) to freshen gloss if you want. Unfortunately, the tire dressings I know about are all black, and you may not want that. Be advised.

If you have a separate fuel tank for an outboard, or if you carry an emergency can, you will want to make sure that it's ready for the season. Dust and dirt don't go well with gasoline in a carburetor, so be sure to rinse the tank thoroughly. A good procedure is to put a gallon of gas into the tank and add some "Gummout," which will tend to dissolve any deposits left from the winter. Don't try to use this rinse gas, but dispose of it carefully.

5

Season Maintenance: The Hull

If the motto for spring maintenance is "work up from the bottom," it is just the opposite for the maintenance you do during the boating season. You will almost surely want to work from the top of the boat downward (see Figure 25). There are some pretty good reasons for this.

Few of us live in a wilderness. That means that power houses, shoreside construction projects, nearby highways, etc., all contribute to the suspended dust and dirt in the air. In my community

Figure 25

a railroad power station spews forth quantities of what is termed "fly ash." Whether it's ashes or soot, dust, dirt, or blown sand, a fair amount's going to be deposited on your boat's top and decks. It will be your job to remove it.

And remove it you should, because dust and sand are abrasive substances. So whether your boat is fiberglass, wood, or aluminum, whether your decks are gel coat resin, paint, or vinyl fabric, fine abrasive tracked about will dull gloss, contribute to color fading, and create unattractive chalking.

Even more, loose dust and dirt will heap itself in little drifts any place it is allowed to do so. These drifts become compacted with rain wetting, and become extremely difficult to remove without damaging the surface or necessitating the use of a really harsh detergent.

Finally, rain will wash loose dirt and dark-colored dust in streaks down your boat's topsides. That may be picturesque for a tramp steamer moored in a South Pacific port, but it doesn't do much for your image as a boat keeper in your home port. The best preventive is to continually loosen and flush these deposits away with floods of warm, sudsy water and a soft deck swab or sponge. You should follow up immediately with a similar treatment to the topsides to make sure that they don't streak from the action of the cleansing agent. This type of procedure is recommended (though simply flushing with a stream of fresh water is better than nothing) similarly for deposits of salt crystals, which are as abrasive and cutting as sand.

Here's where the conservationists among you are probably ready to begin writing heated letters about flooding things away with oceans of suds. Yes, I share your feelings completely. Have you ever traveled a river surfaced eighteen inches thick with a carpeting of detergent suds? I have, and it's an unpleasant experience.

But warm, *soapy* water should be safe enough, because a mild liquid soap like Ivory Liquid is biodegradable. That means nature can chemically break down the soap and cleanse the water of residue. Obviously, soaps do leave a film if they are not promptly and thoroughly rinsed away. Where greasy films or deposits of oily soot are involved, it may prove necessary to use a detergent (see Figure 26). It's a pretty tough proposition to have to catch any sudsing or run-off from boat washing, so the best that I can recommend is to head for open water and carry enough fresh water with you to do

Figure 26

the rinsing job away from the marina or protected waters. Low-sudsing detergents, even biodegradable ones, are available, happily, though there are times, to my mind, when only the airy, bubbling action of real suds will seem to do the job of gently loosening dirt without surface damage.

Cleaning and Waxing: Fiberglass Decks

Figure 27

Keeping the deck of your fiberglass boat clean, shiny and color-bright is going to be one of the most vexing chores of boat owner-ship (see Figure 27)—not hard, that is, just exacting and sometimes troublesome. The reason, of course, is simple if you stop to think about it: You expect to repaint or do major surfacing care to the deck, deckhouse, cockpit, and other similar areas of almost any other type of boat, perhaps on an annual basis. You have been conditioned largely by early advertising for fiberglass boats to think that you will have to do little or nothing to maintain your fiberglass deck in like-new condition for an extended period of time, perhaps even for the life of the boat. It isn't so. The longer you do nothing to keep your fiberglass deck in good shape, the harder you are going to have to work to make it presentable again. If you start from the beginning, the boat will continue to look nice for an indefinite time.

If you get any boat dirty enough, she will need cleaning. A fiberglass boat is no exception, though she does start off with the advantage that maintenance is a strictly cosmetic operation. It is just a question of knowing the right "out" for the "damned spot."

The MFG Boat Company has offered some excellent advice for fiberglass-boat owners. What it has to say bears repeating.

First, consider the problem you are going to have if your boat is berthed in a protected salt-water area, particularly near a marsh that is popular with the local sea gull population. Boats make fine perches for fish-watching and spotting gulls. Moreover, the decks of fiberglass boats are good hard spots on which to crack the shells of mussels and crabs. You'd be surprised how much damage a mussel shell can do dropped from about fifty feet!

The worst aspect of sea gulls perching on your boat will be the certainty they're not boat-broken; you're going to have to do the clean-up. Bird droppings are unpleasant at best. Much of the matter may be flushed loose and washed over the side with a deck swab, that sudsy solution of mild soap, and a stream of water from a hose. However, the caked-on matter may require that a household detergent or very mild cleansing powder be used for complete removal. Unfortunately, it isn't recommended that you attack deposits of hardened droppings with a scraper. Even a plastic scraper of the type used on auto windshields or home freezers will be liable to scratch the pigmented gel coat. If the droppings come loose easily, you may find that a troublesome stain will persist. A mild solvent or stain remover may be necessary.

Naturally, all such cleaning should be followed by a washdown with clear water and waxing of the spots where the cleanser was used.

Dust and dirt blown offshore by the wind usually can be flushed from a gel coat surface with mild soap or a quality boat-soap and water. Unfortunately, simple flushing with cold water just won't remove deposits of dirt from the tiny crevices and corners. That sudsy solution will be necessary, followed again by a clear-water rinse. Soap probably will not remove wax the first or second time it's used, though it will eventually, and rewaxing will be required.

Beware of using harsh detergents, which will certainly remove (or strip) some of the wax protection from the surface. These really harsh superdetergents may well remove the oxidized gel coat itself. There are times when this will be a desirable thing to have happen. Know it will surely happen, however, and plan to have to rewax after use of such a detergent.

Cleaning and Waxing: Fiberglass Topsides

Surface algae grow readily on the waterline areas of all boats. Oily scum and grease streaks accumulate at even the cleanest of marinals and harbors. Characteristic of powerboats and of sailboats with integral fuel tanks is a streak of fuel stain under the tank vent fitting.

Oil, grease, and algae stains can involve a more-than-usual clean-up job, depending on how long they have been allowed to accumulate. Left for a protracted period, they may actually penetrate the gel coat surface of a boat. Further, since these stains recur in the same waterline area, under the same vent fitting, over and over again, repeated heavy cleaning tends not only to dull the gloss, but also reduce the gel coat and make what's left susceptible to further staining. It is another maintenance vicious circle that you've got to break.

If your boat is moored or berthed in the water (as opposed to being dry sailed or kept on a trailer), a washdown using a household detergent with a mild bleaching action may be the only cleansing procedure that will do the job—providing it's done frequently enough. The trick is to get at the topsides frequently; teaching the kids to help, and using a long-handled brush or swab, take away some of the major-project aspects of topside cleaning.

Trailered, car-topped, and dry-sailed boats should be wiped off with a fresh-water-wet cloth while the hull surfaces are still damp. Scum and other growths and stains are easiest to remove immediately after the boat is pulled from the water, and before they have dried and "set" in place. Because the boat isn't in the water unless it's moving and being used, this type of wet-cloth wipedown should be enough to keep the topsides and waterline (not to mention decks and bottom surfaces) clean except for an occasional application of soap and water.

For stubborn waterline stains on your fiberglass boat, however it's kept, you will find that stern measures are needed. Certainly strong detergents, perhaps even cleansing powders or soap pads, will be required. After continued staining and cleaning, it may actually be necessary to use an ultrafine wet sandpaper to restore color and surface gloss. It should be remembered that these hard and harsh *cleansing* (they are more than just *cleaning*) methods do remove part of the gel coat surface, which will need to be replaced sooner or later.

There are, today, special cleaners for oil and grease. Benzine, gasoline, or mineral spirits may be used to cut oil and grease, too.

A thorough flushing of the surface and waxing of the affected areas should follow all these stern cleansing methods, both to discourage susceptibility to future staining and to bring up the color and gloss.

The best of all maintenance is, of course, preventive: It keeps dirt and stains from accumulating. Waxing is the key word here. The frequency of a thorough wax job depends on how much the boat is used and under what circumstances, and the type of wax employed.

Once-a-year waxing is a very poor minimum. If that's all you can manage, be sure to supplement it with touch-ups following drastic cleaning and cleansing. Once every month of the boating season may well be too much of a good thing, especially if the heavy wax accumulation tends to absorb stain itself and yellow, thus *creating* maintenance problems rather than solving them.

The happy medium depends on the amount of time you have to give, the amount of dirt and mess your boat accumulates on the topsides, and the heroic cleansing you do that tends to remove old wax. I would suggest about twice a season on the general topside area and perhaps once a month (preceded by *heavy* cleansing and wax stripping each time) along the waterline.

Even before a fiberglass boat ever touches water, she should be washed with mild soap or quality boat-soap, using a soft cloth, thoroughly rinsed, and polished with high-quality paste wax. Special boat-washes are available that are light-colored or white so that following two or three applications, discoloration does not occur or is kept at a minimum. This prelaunch waxing helps to preserve a boat's sheen and color besides helping to slough off the dirt from the very beginning. Stiff-bristled brushes should not be used on new boats, anyway.

If shine is not restored and dirt not removed by a mild wash and rinse, you should move along by steps from stern, to sterner, to sternest cleansing methods, listed in order from 1 through 5.

Method 1. Scrub with a household cleanser with a very mild abrasive action, rinse, and wax.

Method 2. Apply a high-quality marine fiberglass cleaning agent in either liquid or paste form. Basically, this cleaner is a mild rubbing compound. The job can be minimized by the use of a sheepskin buffer driven by an electric drill or polisher if you have the power capability at hand and there is no danger of electrocution. Rinse thoroughly to remove all traces of grit, wash with mild soap, rinse thoroughly again, and wax.

Method 3. Apply a regular rubbing compound followed by rubbing with marine fiberglass cleaning agent. It is necessary to continue rubbing the regular compound until the material practically dries up and disappears. It should be tried first in an unobtrusive spot, since it can leave a hard-to-remove stain on some surfaces. If this treatment has done the job you want, rinse thoroughly, wash with mild soap, rinse again, and wax.

Method 4. Most drastic of the cleansing methods is the sanding down of the boat surface with wet-and-dry sandpaper of the finest grit. This should be done by hand so that a minimum of topside gel coat is removed. It is a procedure especially useful on older fiberglass boats with dark-colored gel coats that have chalked, dulled, and faded. Since the treatment will leave a dull surface, it should be followed by the application of a rubbing compound, then a marine fiberglass cleaner. As with all the methods, the final steps involve thorough washing, rinsing, and waxing.

Method 5. If your boat still looks "patchy," even dirty, areas of the underlamination are showing through the gel coat. It's time to paint. Painting methods are covered in the section of fiberglass repair, since this procedure need not be a regular one: It is the process of making a cosmetic repair.

You will almost surely find that many fine scratches, even some little nicks, will be "compounded out" in the process of heavy cleaning. Deeper nicks, scratches, and blemishes also are covered in the section on making repairs to fiberglass boats. The procedure is simple and relatively easy if you follow directions. It is extremely rewarding, since the repairs become part of the basic structure.

Painted Wood Surfaces

The in-season care of any painted surfaces is similar to that of fiberglass. The major effort is to keep the surface clean without damaging or abrading it through overharsh cleansing methods. A mild household detergent will do the harshest job necessary if it's done often enough. An even milder liquid soap such as that used at home for dishwashing will be excellent as long as any lingering soap film is very carefully and thoroughly flushed away.

The areas of heavy dirt accumulation will be on flat deck surfaces, especially near toe rails and trim or decorative strips. Here, a fresh-water hose and a deck brush used once a week will probably do most of the cleaning that needs to be done.

On the topsides, thorough rinsing is the key. The most that will accumulate will be salt crystals if you boat in a tidal area, with an occasional scuff from a float or another boat. The scuff can be "compounded" smooth with a mild cleansing powder. The salt crystals should be kept clear with a fresh-water hose and a soft brush.

Topside refinishing during the season may well be necessary for a painted wood boat if major blemishes occur; these are damage to the paint surface only, not that requiring major repair to the boat structure. The procedure for a paint touch-up is basically to get the surrounding area completely clean, sand throughly, and fill any nicks or dents with filler compound. A light paint coat will then prevent excessive penetration of the wood by moisture during the balance of the season. A proper refinishing should be part of the surface preparation for painting as you undertake the job come fall. Refinishing for a fiberglass or aluminum boat will probably not be needed unless the blemish is extremely unsightly. In any case, unless it constitutes structural damage, it should not be repaired until the boat is out of water and the job can be done properly.

Painted aluminum and fiberglass further require only general cleaning similar to that given a painted wood surface. Removal of dirt, salt crystals, and bird droppings will keep the paint glossy and color-fresh. General cleaning procedures also are outlined in the section on season hull maintenance of fiberglass boats.

Teak deck maintenance will be required because most boatowners find the silvery weathering patina that this wood acquires unattractive. Of course, the application of some sort of wood pore sealer will keep the teak from absorbing additional stain. In the section on spring hull maintenance, you will find a description of the procedures on bleaching, cleaning, and oiling teak; in the service products directory you will find a list of manufacturers of teak brighteners and treating preparations.

Teak decks can leak just as any seamed structure can. The cause

Figure 28

is usually drying out in the direct rays of the summer sun during hot, dry weather. If the deck only leaks during these times, you can easily fix it by carefully locating the leaking seam, then doing a little touch-up seam caulking with one of the black silicone rubber seam compounds to match the existing seam compound. Carefully mask both edges of the seam to prevent any slopover onto the seam, and be careful where you set down your tools and compound; the black is awfully hard to get up.

If your teak decks leak all the time, you'll have to do a repair job, and you should check the later section on repairs. It's a pretty tough job to do afloat.

Vinyl and canvas deck surfaces should be treated similarly in that they are both highly susceptible to damage from sharp—not *hard*—objects. A pointed anchor, the end of a spinnaker pole, a sharp toy in the hands of a youngster, all can damage such a deck surface. Surprisingly, being soft, the vinyl and canvas decks resist damage from hard objects very well; they have sufficient "give" and resiliency to take a great deal of punishment.

Cleaning these two types of decks is very similar. You use a thorough cleaning agent, only that amount of mechanical cleaning (brushing or scrubbing) needed to get the dirt off and no more, and rinse completely.

Repairing a vinyl or canvas deck is necessary immediately. Usually, these have been applied over wood undersurfaces, and it will be necessary to prevent water from seeping in. A good canvas repair can be made with a canvas patch glued into place and feathered out at the edges, then painted. A proper repair will involve cutting out the damaged portion completely and carefully inserting a carefully fitted piece, which should be mechanically fastened at the edges. The same procedure should be used for a vinyl deck, except that the patch need not be painted.

Plywood decks could require some special techniques. Often the surface of painted or varnished plywood will check in an over-all "mud-cracking" pattern. This is a sign that the surface is paint sick; all paint or varnish should immediately be removed. The surface should be carefully primed and then repainted.

It is important that a checked plywood deck not be left to weather any longer than necessary. The checks or cracks do allow moisture to seep through into the plywood. While most boat plywood is "marine" grade and is laminated with waterproof glue, the intrusion of water can contribute to the start of rot (see Figure 29). This is one major task that should be undertaken whenever it is noticed, even at the cost of using up a midseason weekend.

Unpainted marine aluminum should require almost no maintenance during the season. It will acquire a natural patina of oxide, which actually serves to protect the metal from corrosion and stain-

Figure 29

ing. Normal cleaning agents such as detergents and soaps that are nonabrasive will work well without removing the natural patina.

In normal service, the hull is likely to be scratched and nicked. These can be sanded smooth using a very fine-grade wet sandpaper or emery paper. The sanded area will then, of course, be extrabright. It can be left that way to reoxidize, or the entire boat could be cleaned to match. Waxing will provide some protection for the cleaned surface, but the waxing should be repeated periodically. Cleaning and waxing are not needed, even in a saltwater environment, to protect marine aluminum alloys from corrosion. Marine aluminums do not include copper but instead are magnesium and manganese alloys that are highly corrosion-resistant.

Varnished Wood Surfaces

Varnished wood must be kept clean, but it requires little or no actual maintenance during the season. Even the cleaning should be mild and careful to avoid scratching the bright varnish gloss. The best cleaner by far for varnish is fresh water and a chamois, which will remove all film and dirt along with water and salt spotting. The chamois should be continually rinsed in fresh water to prevent smearing dirt around. Because marine spar varnish is soft by nature to enable it to withstand the weather, it doesn't require waxing. In fact, waxing tends to dull and smear the wax shine and should not be used at all.

Metalwork

Keeping most kinds of marine metal surfaces clean is relatively easy. Marine aluminum and stainless steel railings and hardware, for example, require no special cleaners, though any common cleaning agent used for cleaning brass, bronze, or copper will work well for stubborn stains and discoloration. Chrome plating is easy to clean with an ordinary metal cleaner; it should be kept free of salt deposits to prevent pitting of the chrome plating and corrosion of the undermetal. Brass, bronze, and Everdur are easy enough to clean with Brasso or Noxon but extremely difficult to keep clean. Most boaters let them oxidize.

6

Season Maintenance: The Engine

Once, when I was a boy, I developed a powerful attraction for a lovely young blonde in my school class. I thought it would be great fun to take her for a ride aboard my outboard-powered skiff. It took a long time, but I cranked up my nerve and asked her to join me the following Saturday morning for a spin. Wonder of wonders, she accepted.

I made every preparation I could think of. I brought the skiff in from her mooring and washed her inside and out. I made several minor repairs so the boat would help me give the best impression of myself.

The Saturday morning dawned golden; it was one of those few-times-a-season days when everything seems perfect; the temperature comfortable, the air tangy, the sky cobalt, the water calm with a bright little breeze to keep you comfortable. My fair young friend arrived, looking especially fetching, I thought. I ushered her to the beach, aboard the boat, and pushed off. There and then my romance came to an ignominious, greasy, angry end: The damned motor wouldn't start. I'd checked everything but the right thing, the motive power. That's when I learned the lesson of the importance of in-season engine maintenance.

Outboard Motors

Outboards used to be messy things at best; an outboarder couldn't go boating like a gentleman. He was always covered with oil and gas, always hot and bothered from tinkering with the kicker. Times have changed.

Today's outboard is ultradependable, quiet, and comparatively economical. High-performance engineering is rapidly creating an engine that will soon be as efficient and economical as a four-cycle mill.

The principal problem with two-cycle outboards has always been their tendency to foul spark plugs; this means that if your outboard doesn't have the new high-voltage capacitive-discharge ignition and resistor spark plugs, prolonged idling can create real problems for you. The lubricating oil so necessary to the life of the engine doesn't completely burn off conventional plug electrodes at idling or trolling speeds and tends to coat them to prevent proper firing. The result is an engine that becomes progressively harder to start and will one day let you down, as mine did me (for the same reason) by refusing to start.

Of course, avoiding prolonged idling or trolling is one way to accomplish a type of preventive maintenance. The old saw goes, "An outboard is either being run wide open or it's turned off." That's pretty much true, and it's no terribly bad thing for the motor. Modern motors are built to run continually at high speeds, though not necessarily *always* wide open. It does keep them free of oil deposits.

In the old days, we used to mix a half pint of outboard oil (any good-grade, four-cycle oil would do) per gallon of gasoline. If you're still doing it, you're going to have fouling trouble quickly. The modern outboards are made to be run with a much, much higher fuel-to-oil ratio: currently about fifty to one, fuel to lube. The oils recommended are ashless, high-film-life types that are much more efficient and do less fouling. In addition to not running your motor at constant idle, make sure your fuel-to-oil mixture is *precisely* that recommended (see Figure 30).

Many fuel docks offer premixed fuels in different ratios. If you take care in ordering, you'll always get the right mix for your motor. If the fuel station you patronize doesn't offer "two-cycle gasoline," there are a couple of important rules to follow when mixing your own.

At a dock, always remove the tank from the boat if possible before filling; this is obviously not possible with integral tanks. Remove the cap, open the tank vent, and run about a gallon of gasoline into the tank before adding the proper amount of oil for the amount of gasoline you intend to take aboard. This will provide immediate dispersal of the oil, an important point in mixing.

Figure 30

If you plan to take aboard an appreciable amount of fuel, or if a high proportion of oil is required for your motor, it will be best to alternate the additions of oil and gasoline to assure complete mixing.

Water and the gears on your boat's outboard don't mix. At the periodic intervals recommended by the motor maker, perform the lube-fill check recommended for spring and fall. That is, you should remove both the filler and vent screws with their washers from the lower unit. Put the nozzle of the lubricant tube into the lower filler hole and squeeze in the special lubricant until old lube appears at the upper vent hole. It is entirely possible that some water may leak into the unit. The addition of new grease will displace that water and force it out the vent hole. Replace the vent and filler screws and washer securely. I recommend that, before the screws be removed, in fact, you suspend a small tray or basket below the outboard's lower unit. This will catch the screws if you drop them. Obviously, the outboard's lower unit must be tilted up to perform this test.

If you have trouble starting your outboard in wet weather, it is entirely possible that part of the high-tension ignition current is "leaking" away across the film of dampness inside the motor shroud. During dry weather, it's possible to prevent this by application of one of the silicone aerosol spray preparations especially designed for waterproofing the ignition systems of cars and boat motors. In the old days, when Pyrene fire extinguishers were allowed, the Pyrene spray would dry out an outboard's damp magneto. Now Pyrene extinguishers are properly outlawed (sprayed on hot metal in a closed space, the carbon tet solution creates phosgene gas), and other types of extinguishers should not be used.

The business of *having* to rinse an outboard motor regularly in fresh water is a thing of the past (see Figure 31). Lots of people

Figure 31

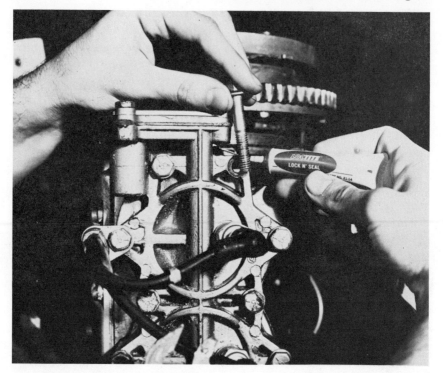

Figure 32

still do it, though new metals prevent destructive corrosion in salt-water use. A fresh-water rinsedown, however, of the motor cowl and exterior surfaces, as well as the interior, will keep your powerplant clean and attractive.

The problem of what antifouling paint to use can be difficult. Most outboard motor lower units are made of aluminum alloys these days. That means that a mercury-based bottom paint should never be used, a lead or copper-based paint used only when a proper barrier coat has been applied, and damaging electrolysis prevented at all costs. Organo-tin bottom paints are available in colors that will match both boat and motor and provide maximum antifouling protection without danger of damage. For a more detailed review of aluminum painting procedures, check the section on spring hull maintenance.

Loose or leaking threaded parts on outboards can be eliminated by the use of a new locking compound (see Figure 32). Loctite, the compound comes in a special kit with a tube of locking compound and a spray can of cleaning solvent. The compound is a polymer plastic that self-hardens in the threads of assembled fasteners. Disassembly is routine with ordinary tools, according to the maker.

Inboard Engines and Outdrives

Because the lower unit of an outdrive is very similar to that of a large outboard motor, the maintenance effort is similar. Regular lubricant checks should be made and should include the upper gear chamber.

Most inboard engines are based on automobile engine blocks. The type of maintenance they require, therefore, is pretty much the same. Most four-cycle inboard engine problems seem to come from dirty or clogged fuel filters, lines, or carburetor jets.

Keeping the input fuel filters clean should be a program of continuing maintenance. So should checking input water lines for seawater-cooled engines. If there is a seawater filter it should be checked often to prevent sand, silt, and weed from getting through into the cooling jacket. With a conventional inboard engine, which is seawater cooled, and with many seawater-cooled outdrive installations, the hot, cooling water is exhausted through the engine exhaust piping directly overside. If your engine has a cooling system thermostat, the inflow of water will be delayed until the engine has heated up partially. If there is no thermostat, the water will flow through immediately. In either case, as you run, make periodic checks of the cooling water stream out the exhaust fitting at the stern. If the stream stops or diminishes measurably, stop the engine to avoid overheating. Check all intake lines to make sure they're free.

Engine drive and control components have lubrication points, which are indicated in the owner's manual. It is necessary to service these on a scheduled basis to prevent a failure afloat.

Careful control of engine rpm is important too. One expert reports that an automotive engine is designed to run only one hundred hours at full throttle before a major breakdown occurs (that is, one hundred hours of continuous running, by the way). You seldom run your auto engine at full throttle, so its life is dramatically lengthened to many, many thousands of miles of trouble-free driving.

If, on the other hand, you run your inboard wide open every time you take her out, you are shortening the engine life at a frightening rate. Close attention paid to the manufacturer's recommended cruising rpm, considering the weight of your boat and load, as well as type of prop, will give you lots of hours of trouble-free running.

Sample Parts List—Outboard Motor

Many motor makers provide you with a small kit of parts and a manual to help you keep your engine running. Here's what you should carry at all times:
Several spare spark plugs of the proper type and gap
Tube of gear case lubricant
Tube of general lubricant
Spare can of fuel-mix oil
Spare can of ignition waterproofing spray
Minimum set of tools including:
   Adjustable wrench
   Spark plug wrench
   Screwdriver
   Pair of pliers
   Plug-gap setter
Spare shear pin for your motor, if applicable
Spare propeller nut cotter pin
Spare propeller nut
Space propeller (if you boat in rocky, debris-laden shallows)

Sample Parts List—Inboard Engine

In addition to your owner's manual, there are a number of spare inboard parts you should carry, especially if you venture far from home. If you need instruction in installation methods, ask your local dealer for help; tell him you want to know how to make emergency adjustments.

Several spare spark plugs of the proper type and gap

Can of crankcase oil

Can of general lubricant

Can of waterpump grease if appropriate (check to see whether your engine's water pump is equipped with grease cups)

Can of ignition waterproofing spray

Spare set of points for the distributor

Spare ignition condenser and coil

Spare distributor cap

Spare ceramic element for fuel filter

Spare propeller

Spare propeller nut

Spare fuel pump

Minimum set of tools including:

Adjustable wrench

Spark plug wrench

Several screwdrivers of different sizes

Pair of pliers

Pair of vise-grip pliers

Plug-and-point-gap setter

Trouble-shooting Your Engine

Usually, lack of ignition or lack of fuel (or both, rarely) is the cause of hard starting or of nonstarting. Here are some things to check:

Motor won't turn over and won't start. Could be a dead or weak battery; check and recharge or replace. Check for loose or corroded battery connections; check cable connections at terminals. Clean, reclamp, and coat with grease or petroleum jelly. If the terminals are all right, check the ignition switch for loose contacts or defective switch (short across the terminals to see if the switch is bad). The starter and solenoid may be faulty due to having been wet from bilge water, on an inboard engine; from wet weather on an outboard.

Motor will turn over but won't start. This also covers hard starting or nonstarting, too. Electrical difficulties could be suspected. Check all ignition connections, including improperly set point gap, accidentally grounded high-tension lead, etc. The plugs may be dirty or improperly set. Check for a cracked distributor cap and also to see if the carbon contact inside the distributor cap is broken or missing. Poor carburetion may be a problem, too. Check, of course, first to see if you have gas in the tank. Running out is embarrassing, but it's not tragic. Check to make sure the fuel line isn't pinched in any way; that's an easy thing to have happen with outboards, especially. If you have an inboard, look to see that your fuel line doesn't pass close to an exhaust line or extra hot part of the block, which could cause the gasoline to vaporize and create a fuel-stopping

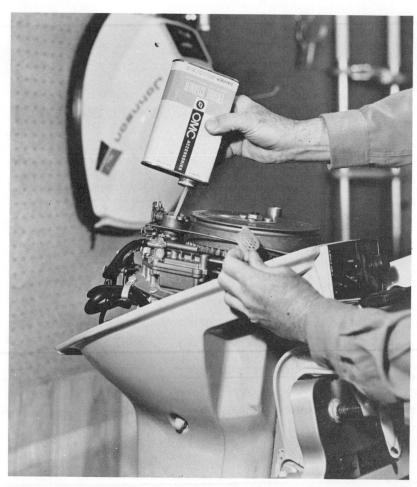

Figure 33

vapor lock. Blow back through the fuel line and check the fuel filter. With an inboard, you can check to see fuel is reaching the carburetor by removing the flame arrester, then working the throttle linkage; fuel should squirt up into the carburetor venturi area. If the engine has automatic choking, make sure the choke butterflies are closing and are free to move. To see if fuel is getting to the cylinders, remove a spark plug to see if it is moist. If there is no trace of fuel, the carburetor adjustment could be bad or the float valve could be jammed upward in the "closed" position. Tap the side of the carburetor bowl and check the jets for clogging. If fuel is leaking from the fuel pump cover, this is a sign the fuel pump diaphram is ruptured, and the pump should be replaced; this is an inboard engine problem.

Motor misses at high speed. The spark plugs may be fouled; check them. Spark plug insulation may be cracked, or a wire may be shorting out near the block. The ignition breaker point spring may be weak, or there may be a fuel blockage. Backfiring through the carburetor is always a sign that insufficient fuel is coming through; run through the carburetion and fuel system check above.

Motor idles roughly and unevenly. A spark plug wire may be loose, so check them all with the engine stopped. The carburetor idling adjustment may be out, too. The plugs may be defective or fouled; you can check while the engine's running by purposely shorting the plugs, one by one, with an insulated screwdriver. If the engine idle roughens even more with a plug shorted, that plug has been firing properly; if the engine idle remains the same with the plug shorted, the plug is bad.

Guide to making a quick ignition-system check. First, remove a lead from a spark plug and hold it about a quarter inch from the cylinder head. Turn the engine over with the ignition switch on. You should get a nice, fat, juicy spark. Make sure *you* aren't part of the ground, though, or you'll get a shock; hold the wire by the insulation. If the spark is hot, check the plugs to see if they're okay. If the spark is weak or missing altogether, the trouble is in the distributor (inboard or four-cycle outboard such as a Homelite) or the magneto (two-cycle outboards). Check the magneto or distributor points if you can to determine if they are clean and shiny. In an inboard engine, the points may be stuck or welded together, and this is a sign of a burned-out condenser. Replace the condenser and clean the points carefully, then gap them.

A general rule. It is important in trouble-shooting that you understand generally how an engine runs. If you don't, all the tips in the world are meaningless gobbledeygook. If you do, only make one adjustment at a time so you don't lose track of what might be wrong. Of one thing you can be reasonably sure: If your engine has been running well and suddenly malfunctions, the likelihood is that the problem is simple and not complicated at all. Complicated internal problems such as poorly adjusted valves, bad rings, loose bearings, etc., show symptoms long before breakdown. Keep in mind the principles on which your engine runs. Try one remedy at a time, based on those principles. Proceed in a logical, orderly fashion, and you're almost sure to find the problem.

7

Fall Maintenance

Most knowledgeable boatmen agree: The fall isn't the end of the old boating season, it's the beginning of the new! That means that if you're smart, you'll begin your preparatory work for the new boating season as soon as you take your boat out of water. Don't forget, of course, that you've got to cover the boat, too, and protect it from the ravages of the winter. I have a friend who only covers his boat's cockpit to prevent its filling with snow. The rationale he follows is that the deck surfaces should be able to take a certain amount of punishment, and that amount is no worse than the summer sun, sand, and salt dish out.

My friend is wrong. To begin with, the summer is at best three and a half months long; the winter season is almost three times as long. Moreover, ice crystals cut and score just as severely as salt crystals or sand; high winter winds add to their abrasive action. The moral of all this is: You should cover your boat if you care about protecting your investment and the amount of work you've put in.

Fiberglass and Aluminum Boats

The most important step you can take in readying your boat for the winter and the new boating season to follow is to get it thoroughly cleaned (see Figure 34). The season's dirt and stains haven't "set" yet, and a good, thorough scrubdown will do the job. You don't have to be concerned about water pollution with your boat out of water, so use a high-sudsing detergent and plenty of good, hot water along with a brush to get into the crevices. The idea is

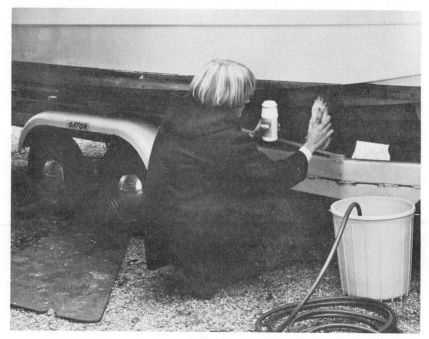

Figure 34

to scrub loose as much grime and stain as possible so you won't have to abrade it off (with sandpaper or the like) next spring. Of course, abrading stains will remove some of the gel coat or the paint as well as the gloss and color.

To me, the principal advantage of a fiberglass or painted aluminum boat is that you shouldn't have to paint or pull extensive maintenance for regular activity. This means you shouldn't remove any more of the outer surface than is absolutely necessary during the cleaning process. On the other hand, it is possible to *enhance* the appearance of your boat by taking off some of the dulled gel coat or oxidized paint.

I guess what I'm trying to point out is that there is a fine line between *cleaning* the boat thoroughly and gently with detergent suds, and *knocking hell* out of the surface with industrial-grade solvents and cleansing agents. The heavy-duty cleansers will save you some elbow grease now, but you'll pay for it later when you have to replace the paint or paint the gel coat to make the boat look ship-shape again.

Figure 35

When you've gotten *all* stains and dirt off, and absolutely not before, wax the hull and deck surfaces thoroughly (see Figure 35), to provide the maximum protection against the ravages of the winter. Some boaters extend protection to chromed surfaces, too, with a brush-on vinyl coating created especially to harden into a film that can then be peeled loose in the spring. It's a good product, especially if your boat has a number of chromed accessories. The manufacturers usually indicate that these vinyls won't hurt painted or gel-coated surfaces. Perhaps the most important thing to remember about fiberglass and aluminum hull preparation is a combination do-and-don't. For your own later sake, *do* get all dirt and grime off as gently as possible; *don't* wax over any dirt or grime that might be left on the surface, in the interest of getting the job done quickly. It will be terribly hard to get all that winter-hardened wax off, then get at the dirt again in the spring.

This is the time, of course, to make the great strides in getting the last vestiges of marine growth off, too. If the bottom is still fouled, get all the barnacles and grass off, even those little, hard, calciferous barnacle "feet." Sand the bottom thoroughly and, perhaps, put on a coat of antifouling paint right now.

All-Wood Boats

If the preparation on a fiberglass or aluminum boat was important, the fall maintenance of a wood boat is doubly important. It is necessary for protection as well as appearance. A scrubdown is important, of course, and you can use the harshest type of detergent or abrasive cleaning powder. The idea here is to get all the dirt and oxidized paint off as quickly, thoroughly, and easily as possible; it's a different philosophy from that which you'd use if your boat were fiberglass or aluminum. Your advantage won't last, however, because you've got to use your energies in another way (see Figure 36).

When your boat's painted surfaces are thoroughly cleaned, they've got to be thoroughly sanded as well. You should do the bottom, topsides, painted decks, deckhouses, any exterior painted

Figure 36

surfaces. Use a medium and then progressively finer grades of sand-paper to do the best job of surface preparation you possibly can.

A lot of you are surely asking why you're expected to do this kind of work in the fall. There are a couple of reasons why I recommend doing it now rather than waiting until spring.

First of all, the paint has just been heavily cleaned, and its outer portions are likely to be soft and chalky. This is the time when sanding is easy, productive, and rewarding. If you wait to sand until the spring, the paint may have completely failed, however, from exposure to the elements. It may require a lot *more* preparative work.

Second, the boatyard shouldn't be crowded with workers on fall weekends. You won't have much competition for the available water faucets or electrical outlets. You won't experience that frustrating line-voltage drop you get in the spring as sander after sander is used. Finally, the weather tends to be cooler, and you're working comfortably (remember, you heat up as you work) without rivulets of perspiration blinding you.

Last, and certainly not the least, you will have all this work *done* in the spring. After all, spring's when you want to be boating, not slaving. Fall's the season when you're pretty well resigned to having the boat out of water. Don't be too misled by the temptations to leave the boat in to enjoy those "sparkling fall days afloat." With leaf-raking and family expeditions to get Hallowe'en pumpkins and cider in the country, you have little enough time to do your fall chores, let alone continue a summer pastime. Too often those sparkling days turn into gray ones with lowering skies and icy winds. Then you're stuck with doing next to no fall maintenance, covering the boat in the first snowstorm of the season, and pulling your mooring with frozen hands. Better to haul the boat a bit early, get her in good shape for the winter and the new season, enjoy your fall activities (how about those football games, for instance!), and do your sailing early in the spring when the weather really *is* nice and there are less chances of hurricanes.

If your boat's painted surfaces have that heavily rounded, putty-like look, it's very likely they're "paint sick." This fall would be a good time to get rid of that old paint skin (see Figure 37). Plywood boats often show this type of problem, with minute "checks" or cracks all over the flat surface.

If your boat is paint sick, you've got only one choice: Remove the old paint completely and start from scratch. Removal of the old

Figure 37

paint may be done by burning (actually softening by heat) the surface with a torch, if your boatyard will allow, removal by chemical means, and sanding. Sanding is, of course, the very hardest way; it also can be the most rewarding if you're trying to get down to bare wood for varnishing or application of fiberglass. Burning paint off is a quick way, but it tends to leave hard-to-remove scorch marks; besides, most boatyards have regulations forbidding the use of torches. Chemical paint removal used to be an unpleasant chore and a not very productive one; now the newer paint removers flush away themselves and old paint with water and do an excellent job.

Figure 38

When the old paint's been removed, you will need to do a very complete sanding job. For large, flat surfaces, it would be well for you to rent or borrow a belt sander (if you don't have one of your own) rather than use a disk sander (see Figure 38). The disk will do a fine job, but using it can be a real problem, and it can leave semicircular gouges if you don't know the technique. Your boat's topsides are no place to practice. The belt sander will *create* a flat

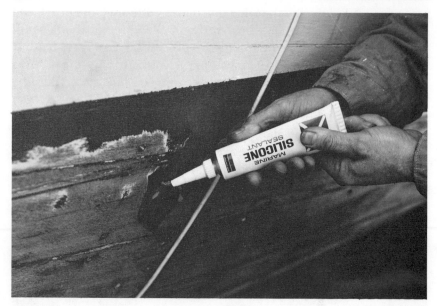

Figure 39

surface, just the thing you want it to do. As with all sanders, however, "keep it moving" is a good rule, even when you are concentrating on one rough spot. Work over and around the spot, rather than directly on it; you may well find it's the surrounding surface that needs to be sanded down to the rough spot anyway. For best results you will want to use an open-coat sandpaper if there is any tendency of the material being sanded to slough off and clog the pores of the abrasive. An open-coat sandpaper has the abrasive particles spaced more widely to prevent this type of clogging.

Whether or not you have removed all the paint from your wood boat, you may well want to protect the surface over the winter months with a fresh coat of paint. If you have gone down to the bare wood (this is known appropriately as "wooding"), you will have to use a filler on all the little nicks and dents you've uncovered (see Figure 39), then prime coat to prepare the surface for a finish coat and fill the wood pores.

If you've not had to wood your boat, don't hasten the day when you *will* have to by improper painting. Except on bottom surfaces, use a light prime coat. This is a matte-finish paint that holds later finish coats very well. When you uncover in the spring, you're going

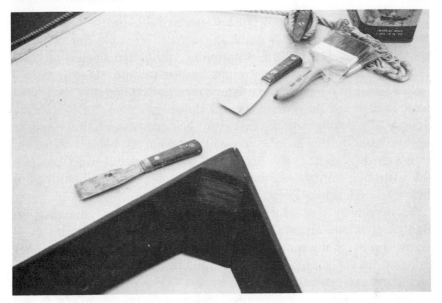

Figure 40

to find this prime coat pretty dirty. The advantage of it is that the surface chalks away extremely easily by washing and light sanding. There's nothing solid for dirt to cling to, and you'll be ready for spring finishing quickly—much more quickly than if you did no painting or used a finish coat in the fall.

There are wood boats, obviously, that have no seams to worry about: They are the plywood and the strip-planked ones. Nicks, bangs, and gouges on these hulls should be filled with a good compound that will take a smooth-sanding surface (see Figure 40). For hulls with seams to dry out—the clinker or lapstrake, and carvel ones—it's not only necessary to fill these but also important to have a look at the seams themselves. If the boat's been leaking, try to determine where right now, and take steps to remedy it before all the seams open up. While the boat's still swelled tight from having been in the water, there's little chance of your overcaulking the seams; possible leak spots should show up pretty readily.

For a planked-wood boat, it is important to keep the moisture content of the wood as high as possible to prevent drying out over the winter. You can do this in several ways. First, of course, put her back into the water as soon as possible in the spring: This is why fall working pays off. Next, put a protective skin on the bottom surfaces to slow air drying as much as possible. Most old-timers like to do this with a mixture of bottom paint and boiled linseed oil, in a fifty-fifty ratio. Others use straight linseed oil and claim it does a better job. I don't think the mixture matters too much as long as at least half of it's linseed oil. It will do an effective job of slowing your boat's drying out. If, however, you use one of the vinyl- or epoxy-based bottom paints, you will *not* want to make such a mixture (see Figure 41); the linseed oil and the paint aren't compatible. Instead, you should find that the paint itself will provide a heavy enough skin to keep the boat wet.

Varnishing is a touchy subject and not one to be sloughed off lightly. It is one chore you shouldn't tackle in the fall. You don't want to put on any more varnish than is absolutely necessary, so a fall coat isn't desirable. You don't want to leave the varnish unprotected, so early sanding isn't advisable. The varnish is its own best protection so you won't even need to wax your brightwork; wax and varnish aren't compatible either.

The Winter Frame

Once your boat's surfaces have been adequately protected by paint or wax from winter dirt, it's time to protect the whole boat from ice and snow. The only way to accomplish this is with a winter cover. The cover should be properly supported with a winter frame.

Many boatowners make this winter frame from scrap lumber each season and knock it apart in the spring. If you haven't space to store any lumber components, that may be the best way. It does, however, lead to procrastination in rebuilding a new winter frame each fall.

For a relatively small boat, you can make a very effective winter frame out of plywood formers and a ridgepole of some substantial timber. Some frames are elaborate structures that are numbered for exact fit and that bolt together. Somewhere between the scrap-lumber arrangement and the semihouse structure there may be a suitable compromise for you.

It is customary for the winter frame of a boat to rest on the boat itself and to be built with a substantial pitch to the "roof" so that

Figure 41

snow and ice will slide off. This obviates the need to make an overly sturdy structure, though some strength is absolutely essential to prevent the cover's sagging down into the boat. "Rafter" poles of some light wood should be spotted along each side of the ridgepole and follow the "roof" pitch angle down to the boat's deck level. Some installers like to extend the frame just a bit beyond the deck so the cover will stand out from the side of the boat and enhance ventilation. That also enhances the opportunity for the wind to get under the cover, as well; it's a matter of choice, I think.

At any rate, the best winter frame for you is whatever combines these qualities: It is easy for you to build and install; it provides the best possible support with at least a forty-five-degree roof pitch to shed ice and snow; it is protected by use of canvas pads or carpeting squares from marring the boat; it is padded so it won't tear the cover.

The Winter Cover

A winter cover serves only one purpose: to protect your boat from winter damage and the weather. Some boatowners, I feel, make a fetish out of creating an artistic winter "house" for their boats. The

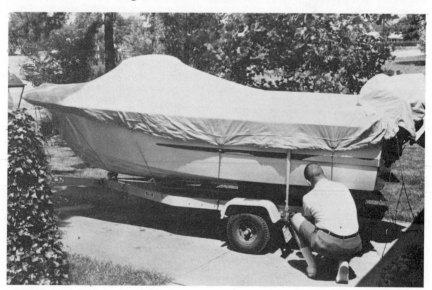

Figure 42

winter cover fits the boat better than the owner's suit does him! The amount of time, money, creativity, and energy you *could* put into a winter cover would probably be all out of proportion to its value. You might better put the same effort into improving your boat itself for its primary waterborne function: fun!

To begin with, the winter cover should be installed on a solid framework. You created such a framework with your boat when you securely placed that boat in its cradle or on its padding for the winter. You enhanced the framework by putting a solid but not fancy winter frame onto the boat itself. Don't get overly fancy by insisting now that the winter cover be fitted to a "T."

The winter cover should fit with two things in mind: first, it should be smooth enough to prevent trapping pockets of melted water or snow, which can turn into ice and drag the frame down; second, it should be smooth enough to shed wind and prevent the flapping that can work it and framework loose. This can be accomplished by securely lashing the cover under the entire boat and stretching it taut, as well as taping some of the bigger folds with a wide plastic tape that fliers in the South Pacific used to call "typhoon tape." It's nothing special, just a tape with a reasonably powerful adhesive; obviously, cellophane and masking tapes won't do the job.

A key to proper covering of any boat is ventilation. There should be a good flow of air under the cover from bow to stern. This means not taping the end openings shut but leaving them tautly ajar. A large cardboard tube such as is used to roll carpets will provide a very good air duct if it is securely laced into the cover and angled downward to prevent snow or rain from getting in. In addition to providing a means for air to get under the cover, you will certainly want to open your boat from bow to stern inside. If you have lockers, open them and leave them open; tape the doors open if there's a possibility they might blow or swing shut. If your boat has floorboards, pull them up; open the cabin and all portlights, too.

Winterizing Your Outboard Motor

As one firm of experts has put it, "the quiet approach of winter makes it necessary for the outboarder to take proper care of his motor or chance costly repairs come spring." That means *you.*

Any outboard will require some attention to prevent corrosion. These kinds of winterizing services can be provided for most boaters by the dealer for their appropriate make of outboard at a nominal fee. Often, winterizing and storage fees include tune-up and summerizing, as well as remounting the motor in the spring. The last time I was responsible for having this kind of thing done, the fee ran about forty dollars for an 85 hp, four-cylinder outboard; it was worth every penny.

The key, of course, is that phrase "remounting the motor." It implies, correctly, that the motor must be unmounted and stored inside during the winter. This is absolutely correct.

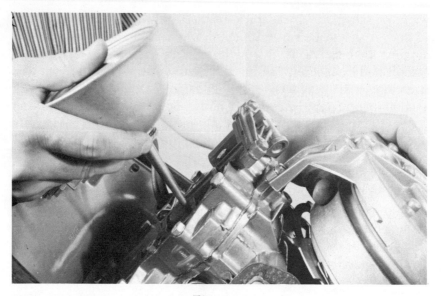

Figure 43

If you want to do your own work, here's how to go about it. With your rig still in the water, warm up the engine and remove the cowl or wrap-around. Disconnect the fuel line and, while the engine is idling, inject some sort of a storage sealing compound (see Figure 43)—available from your motor's dealer especially for your make— into the carburetor air intake. As the carburetors (the higher-horsepower models have more than one) start to run dry of gasoline, apply a last, extra-liberal dosage. This will effectively distribute the protective compound throughout the crankcase to prevent internal corrosion and also use up fuel in the carburetors to prevent varnish and gum formation.

Now remove the outboard from the transom, being careful to keep it upright and on its skeg. Sound easy? You bet, until you try to "rassle" one of those big fellas around. Better have plenty of help, even borrow one of the portable outboard hoists from your dealer if possible. There's a lifting ring on the motor under the cowl, by the way.

Figure 44

Make sure all water has been drained from the driveshaft housing. Then flush the cooling system with fresh water according to the manufacturer's instructions to clear out silt, sand, and mineral deposits. Operate the manual starter until the water pump has forced all water from the cooling system. Make sure that all water drain holes in the housing are open and free. Also be sure that the flushing plug is removed so that all water will drain out; this is vital. Trapped water may freeze if your motor's stored in a cold place; this can crack the gear housing or water pump housing.

Figure 45

Now remove the spark plugs and inject a small quantity of the storage sealer into each spark plug hole (see Figure 45). Reinstall the plugs hand-tight and operate the manual starter to distribute the storage seal throughout the combustion chamber. This extra dose will protect the piston rings and cylinder walls.

Next, remove the swivel pin if possible, or at least lubricate it thoroughly. Lube the steering tube, throttle linkage, and all other points as directed by your motor's owner-maintenance manual. For example, the Mercury Marine people recommend that their Quicksilver Anti-Corrosion Grease be applied to external bare metal parts to prevent corrosion.

The lower unit features importantly in this fall procedure too. Remove the air vent screw and grease filler plug with their accompanying washers from the lower unit. Insert a tube of the proper lubricant for your motor's gear case into the grease filler hole, and inject new grease until the old grease starts to flow out of the air vent hole (see Figure 44). That means the housing is completely filled with lubricant without space for water or condensed moisture. Replace the vent screw, filler, and washers.

The entire outboard motor should be washed or wiped down next, especially if there is an accumulation of grime or salt. Spray the entire powerhead with a coating of corrosion preventive to protect the finish of all parts inside the cowl. The exterior of the motor can either be sprayed with the corrosion preventive or coated with a thin film of clean, fresh engine oil. It will be important, too, to remove the propeller, clean the shaft with steel wool, and then apply an anticorrosion grease before reinstalling the prop.

Finally, store your motor in a clean, dry location. It should be covered, but there must be enough ventilation to prevent moisture build-up. The motor storage can be either cold or warm, as long as the temperature remains constant. Otherwise corrosion-causing condensation will occur.

Winterizing Your Inboard Motor

Unlike an outboard, your inboard engine can't be taken off your boat, winterized, then stored in a clean, dry location. Extra winter storage is one premium you pay for such inboard advantages as increased fuel economy.

The first thing to do is to run the engine sufficiently long to bring it up to normal operating temperature. Don't run it dry, however, or the water pump surely will be damaged. If you have a conventional inboard, and the boat's out of water, connect the water intake line to a garden hose with moderate pressure. If you have an inboard/outdrive, you can place a tank of water under the outdrive unit with a running hose to provide sufficient cooling water flow.

When the engine has warmed up sufficiently, shut it off and drain the crankcase completely, either by pumping or removing the oil drain plug from the oil pan. It is important that the engine be warmed before you do this, or foreign material might cling to the sides of the oil pan and not drain readily with the cold, slow-moving oil. Remove the oil filter cartridge and install a new one if your engine has such a filter.

The next step is to refill the crankcase with fresh SAE weight 20 oil and any manufacturer's oil additive that might be recommended by your owner's manual. Shut off the fuel line at the fuel tank.

Now restart your engine and operate it for a few minutes at fast idle, from 800 to 1200 rpm, to insure that the new oil is being well circulated and the new oil-filter cartridge is properly sealed. Now stop and recheck the oil level to be sure the oil's up to the "full" mark on the dip stick; add oil if necessary.

Remove the flame arrester and fog the internal surfaces of the carburetor and intake manifold by restarting the engine and running at the high idle speed while pouring in a cup of storage seal into the carburetor air intake. Stall the engine by pouring the last two ounces or so of seal rapidly into the carburetor.

Now it's time to winterize the engine systems. Remove the fuel filter and clean the sediment bowl. Release and inspect the alternator and water pump drive belts; replace each belt if necessary and reinstall it in a loose position for the winter. Remove the manifold and cylinder block drain plugs and allow all water to drain out. Be sure the front of the boat is higher than the transom, or all the water won't drain from the front of the block. Replace the drain plugs lightly, or better yet, put them in a bag and attach to the ignition key—this will prevent you from starting up in the spring without the plugs firmly in place. Put a drop of lube on the distributor cam surface and add a drop of light oil to the breaker lever pivot.

Remove the spark plugs and squirt an ounce of storage seal or SAE 40 oil into each cylinder. While the plugs are out, crank the engine for at least fifteen seconds with starter or hand crank to insure a good coating of oil on the cylinder walls. Be sure the high-tension lead is pulled out of the distributor and is grounded while you're cranking if you use an integral ignition-starter switch; it isn't necessary if you crank by hand. Replace the plugs hand-tight after you've oiled the threads.

You'll also want to clean the carburetor flame arrester and replace it, clean and reinstall the oil filter cap, and clean the outside of the engine. If your engine has overhead valves, remove the valve rocker arm covers and have a look at the valve train mechanism for signs of wear and damage; especially look for shiny metal where surfaces should be oil-coated, and any little flecks of metal. If condensation has occurred in the rocker arm cover, wipe away all traces of oil and water, then liberally coat the valve mechanism and the inside of the cover with storage seal.

Winterizing Your Stern Drive Unit

Ideally, most dealers prefer to remove outdrive units (see Figure 46) and store them inside. After all, this is the place inside of which all shifting and water pumping is done for your rig. Removal and inside storage, however, are matters for professional service and probably not for the casual mechanic. Here's what to do if you plan to leave the unit outside all winter.

Figure 46

Remove the flushing plug and allow all water to drain out. Trapped water will surely freeze and crack the gear and water pump housing. Be sure the water drain holes in the gear housing are open.

Check and refill the upper-gear chamber if appropriate and the lower-gear housing with the proper gear lubricant for the prevention of possible water leakage and damage.

Lubricate steering parts according to the manufacturer's instructions, using the recommended multipurpose lubricant. Lube the pivot and tilt pins according to the owner's manual. Remove the prop, apply a lubricant or waterproof grease to the shaft, and reinstall the prop. Clean the exterior of the unit and spray it with a rust preventive.

Winterizing Your Boat's Equipment

Clean thoroughly and store in a clean, dry location is the motto for almost all equipment you use on your boat (see Figure 47). Don't take a chance with freezing or vandalism. There are a few items that require some special care.

One example is the battery. The battery should be taken out of the boat for sure. Clean the top surface completely of grease, dirt, and any corrosion deposits on the terminal posts. An exterior corrosion preventive should be applied to the posts at this time; grease or petroleum jelly will do fine.

Also, check the electrolyte level and add water as necessary to bring the level up to the correct point. The battery should be charged until the specific gravity of the electrolyte reaches 1.260; you can purchase a very inexpensive hydrometer to check this, or borrow one from your friendly filling station. Every month and a half to two months, recheck the electrolyte level and take a specific-gravity reading. If the hydrometer reading drops below 1.230, apply a booster charge. At no time should the recharge rate exceed 6 amps, by the way. Checking specific gravity and electrolyte level is particularly important, since the battery can freeze if the "charge" gets too low in a cold place.

Any fuel remaining in your boat's fuel tank, outboard or inboard, should be used for some other purpose and not stored over the winter. Stored gasoline tends to break down and result in gum and

Figure 47

varnish deposits in the fuel system. There is a controversy over whether or not to store your boat with its integral (built-in) fuel tank full. The "pro" camp says that in case of fire, a full fuel tank will burn but not explode; this camp accedes you've got to discard all stored-in-tank fuel in the spring. For a boater left with thirty or forty gallons of gummy gas, this poses a major housekeeping problem.

The "con" camp says that this fuel-disposal problem mitigates against storing fuel over the winter, though it does admit that an empty fume-full tank will explode in a fire.

I happen to belong to the "con" group. Handling large amounts of fuel, draining them out of a fuel tank, is largely a suicidal proposition to me. Major concentrations of heavier-than-air fumes will gather in the bilges and could be set off by any random spark.

Moreover, any fireman will tell you (if he's fought a boatyard fire) that a burning fuel tank has to vent burned gases and is likely to open up anyway. This means that a full fuel tank may not explode, but will probably spill its entire fuel load into the boat, over the ground, and spread the fire all over the area. An empty fuel tank can only go "bang" once; there's nothing in it to burn or do damage after that happens. I store my boat's built-in fuel tank empty.

If you're a salt-water boater, take all covers, anchor lines, life preservers, and sails (if applicable) and give them a good fresh-water washdown to remove salt crystals (they cut). Your boat's radio and other electronic gear should be stored in a cool, very dry area.

If you put everything away dry and clean (see Figure 48), if you store your boat with the preliminary preparation done for next year, if you carefully log what you did this year (and how long it took), you're going to have an important jump on boating next season. Moreover, your service log will tell you what items should be repaired over the wintertime and, if they've needed repair or service before, will remind you how much time it took and what the costs were.

Fall Maintenance: Your Power Tools

For most of us, November signals the shutdown of our boating activities afloat. It means that our boats have been hauled, cradled, covered. It starts the time in which we do our most concentrated planning for next year's busy spring fitting-out period.

And, if we're wise, it also means we look at our inventory of the power tools we use so heavily—power drills, buffers, sanders, saws, and the like. If this equipment is old, outworn, or unsuitable to the tasks to which we put it, now's the time for replacement and/or refurbishing.

A representative of one major tool manufacturer, Rockwell Manufacturing Company of Pittsburgh, not long ago told me that his firm considers safety of primary importance to any boatowner in selecting power tools. The manager of the power tool product line at Rockwell cited the environment in which boatowner-employed

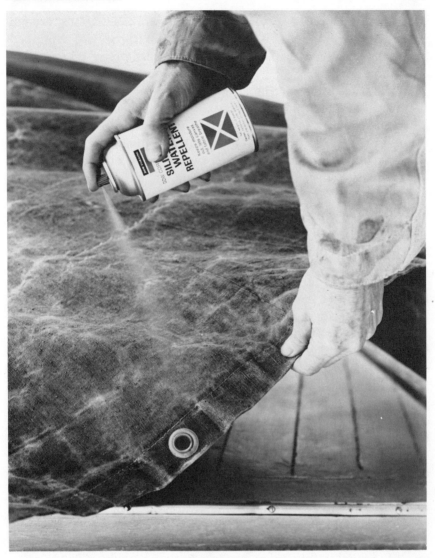

Figure 48

power tools are most often used—it's damp, cold, inclement, some-times downright dangerous when work is done from floating stages.

Shock, of course, is the No. 1 hazard. Most manufacturers have followed a Rockwell lead and are building lines of "double insu-lated" tools to minimize that danger. Unfortunately, good ground discipline is impossible to maintain in work situations around boatyards and marinas. Not all outlets are three-wire equipped (even though receptacles may accept the third-prong type of plug on your power tool).

Here's what I consider important in the selection of a safe power tool from the potential shock-hazard point of view. The difference between regularly insulated tools and the double-insulated variety is one in which the interior components are mounted. The double-insulated tools employ a clamshell outer casing of Lexan polycarbonate plastic. Because it's a nonconductor, and is strong enough to replace steel in some applications, the plastic shell eliminates any interior metal framing to support armature, gearing, or windings. It means that the Lexan-shelled tool is protected from the inside outward from electrical malfunction or accidental dampness-grounding inside. It, therefore, needs no third-prong ground.

Moreover, the all-insulated plastic-shrouded tool is protected from the outside inward as well. That means if the tool cord or line-wire is accidentally cut, or drilled into, the operator is protected against the hand-held portion of the unit's becoming hot or live with disastrous results. This doesn't mean that such tools will operate underwater, by the way; they definitely will not!

In addition, the double insulation has nothing to do with preventing the interior arcing of the brushes as they are swept by the commutator. That's a function you'll see in all normal tools. However, it should be pointed out that this is just one more reason that you should be wary of using tools where gasoline-laden bilge fumes could be present.

How do you buy a power tool that will do all the work you want it to? First of all, you should be aware that there are different grades of hand-held power tools—three grades, to be exact. *Consumer* grades are for intermittent use, about an hour's worth per week (or roughly fifty hours a year). *Building trade* grade tools are heavier duty and can be used for periods up to eight or ten hours per week (or about ten times that for the consumer grade). *Industrial* grade power tools are for extraheavy use up to twenty or thirty hours per week.

Though the better consumer grades are probably just fine for your use, remember that if you pick a tool in a too-low-duty grade, you may spend twice the extra amount the better tool would have cost, in repair and replacement. If you use an electric drill for heavy sanding on a big boat, you're probably better off buying a building trade grade tool, for example.

And that sort of brings up the business of buying the cheapie, on-sale tools featured at impossibly low prices in your discount house, supermarket, or even big drug chains. Though these tools may have brand-name identification, you should be aware that they don't represent outstanding bargains. Usually, they're specially designed and built to be sold for those low prices; you're getting just what you pay for: the lowest-grade consumer tool.

A good power drill, for example, for all-around heavy boating service use, might be a ⅜-inch, 1000rpm model that will take the larger bitts and has more torque power than the average ¼-incher.

A good bayonet, or saber saw, for you might be one of the variable-speed variety; at least you should consider a two-speed unit.

A good hand-held circular saw would be a 7-inch or larger variety. By sharpening a smaller saw-blade, you could reduce its diameter enough so it wouldn't cut through a 2-by-4 on a 45-degree angle.

Buyers often select on the basis of the price, as we discussed, and also on amp rating. Amp rating can be misleading, and price discounting goes hand in hand with it.

But you should be aware that there are some bargains in pricing on power tools from reputable manufacturers on top-quality equipment. They occur at certain specified times of the year. For example, most makers discount most during the spring on outside building trade types of tools, because that's the traditional season in which to do so. Buying in the spring might just save you some big money and make it worthwhile upgrading tool quality.

If you need to refurbish, rather than replace your power tools, now is the time to plan for a busy winter program. It's a good time to plan in-shop reconditioning.

The most important service help you have is the tool's service manual that you got when you bought your drill, saw, or whatever. I hope you filed the manual and parts list.

Tools should be inspected about every fifty hours of operation (see Figure 49). If you want to get very professional about this, you might make a use/maintenance chart and post it in your shop. Most people won't want to, so why don't you just plan a one-time-every-year session with your power tools? The first thing to do is to check the plug for tightness, the proper prongs, and good connection. If

Figure 49

the tool is of the grounded type, make absolutely sure that the third prong is still on it (and not removed by some borrowing neighbor at the yard or at home who was in a hurry and didn't have his three-prong adapter handy).

Check the cord for cuts and fraying (see Figure 50). The cord and its strain-relief next to the tool handle (or wherever the cord enters the body of the tool) are usually the first points of failure. Check for tightness of all housing screws, then check to insure that all external adjustments such as chucks and slides are free-working (see Figure 51). If they're rusty and stiff, clean them with a good rust remover and protect them with a silicone spray or lubricant.

The outside of the housing should be cleaned with acetone or paint thinner if it's metal, or *only* with hot water and soap if it's plastic (acetone will melt many plastics, so beware!).

On reassembly, use a stick lubricant on any sliding switches, plates, or adjustments.

All sanders are subject to lots of vibration and dust, so pad screws should be tightened and air-exhaust slots should be cleaned out. Belt sanders especially should be oiled only where indicated. Don't use one of the inexpensive household oils, which might have been cut with kerosene, which leeches other lubricants out of bearings and bushings.

Brushes should be checked for length. If the length is less than one-quarter inch, the brushes should be replaced. The commuta-

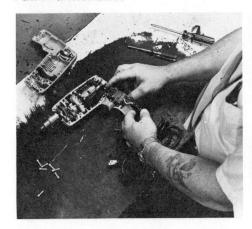

Figure 50   Figure 51

tor ring (on which the brushes ride) should be examined for excessive wear as indicated by grooving. If the commutator needs to be ground and undercut, have it done professionally.

If your tools have a gear chamber, you should clean and repack the gears with the proper lubricant in proper amounts as specified by the manufacturer. As a final parting shot, don't use just any type of water pump or similar grease, especially on the plastic-cased tools, because the lubricating and temperature, transmitting, and flow characteristics are bound to be all wrong.

8

A Repair Guide

Repairing your boat isn't like tinkering with a car. It's possible to run down to your local auto supply store for replacement car parts. It's not possible to get a replacement fender for your 1964 Chris-Craft, however.

This means that boat repairs are creative by nature. You may well decide to repair or replace one material with another. You can put a fiberglass patch on your aluminum canoe; you can cover your plywood deck with a vinyl decking material.

Any repair guide can be only that—a guide. It can give you the choices and the general procedures. Unfortunately, without knowing the specific job to be done and the individual skills involved, it would be wrong for me to imply any kind of guarantee of any process described. These things, however, have worked for me; they should for you.

Repairing Nicks and Gouges in Fiberglass

As one source for information, I was fortunate enough to have the counsel and guidance of the Ferro Corporation of Nashville, Tennessee. Ferro is a major fiberglass materials supplier for the boating industry and has prepared a number of excellent repair guides. Additional information came from Owens-Corning in Toledo, Ohio, and Pittsburgh Plate Glass.

Repairs to scratches, shallow nicks, gouges, and small holes that do not penetrate the hull are easy because the surface of the boat has been damaged but not the structure of the craft (see Figure 52). Such damage falls into two categories: damage to the gel coat

Figure 52

colored outer surface, and holes or gouges that are deep enough to penetrate the fiberglass-reinforced area of the boat. The repairs, however, are similar for both types of damage.

For damage to the gel coat surface, your repair kit will need to include a small can of gel coat, of the same color as your boat, and a small amount of catalyst. If your dealer can't help you get the gel coat resin you need, I suggest you write to the manufacturer of your boat directly. Tell him what model boat it is, what color it appears to be to you (remember, it may well have faded in use), and approximately what year you believe the boat was built. Builders do change resin suppliers from time to time, or do change their color pigmentation mixes. Be as complete as you can when you write, even to supplying the hull number if it is stamped into the boat somewhere (*not* the boat registration number, however).

For damage to the hull that consists of deeper holes or gouges of one-eighth inch or more, you are also going to need some short strands of fiberglass, which you can trim from fiberglass mat or purchase in the form of "milled fibers." They can be bought from most boat dealers.

A most important first chore is making sure the area around the damage is completely clean and dry. Since the repair substance will be feathered out beyond the hole, grease or moisture will prevent proper bonding and a permanent repair. If you have difficulty getting the job completely dry, wipe the surface with acetone or denatured alcohol. These have an affinity for water, will absorb and evaporate it. They also should help to remove any wax or oil from inside the hole or scratch.

Now get your power drill out; one of the little portable-electric tools will do the job, too. You will need a burr attachment to roughen the bottom and sides of the damaged area, as well as to feather out the edge surrounding the scratch or gouge. Be sure not to undercut the edge.

For damage that extends into the fiberglass reinforcement only, you will now need to mix a filler compound. Onto a jar lid or a flat piece of cardboard, pour a small amount of the gel coat resin. Use just enough to cover the area you've got to repair.

Mix an equal amount of the milled fibers with this gel coat, using a little flat stick like a tongue depressor. Now add two drops of catalyst—an eye dropper will help you make an accurate measurement, which is important to proper curing. For a half dollar-size pile of gel coat and milled fibers, this will give you fifteen to twenty minutes of working time before the mix begins to set. It's important to mix the catalyst into the repair compound thoroughly so that curing will be complete.

Work the mixture of gel coat, fibers, and catalyst into the damaged area, using the sharp point of your putty knife or any knife blade to press it into the bottom of the hole. You want to be sure to puncture any air bubble that might have formed, too. Fill the scratch or hole above the surrounding deck level about one-sixteenth inch.

Quickly lay a piece of cellophane or waxed paper over the repair to cut off the air and start the "curing" process. You will remember from the chapter on maintaining your fiberglass boat in the spring that gel coat resins are air-inhibited since they usually cure against the mold.

After about ten or fifteen minutes you'll find that the patch has partially cured. When it feels rubbery to the touch, lift off the cellophane and trim the patch material flush with the surface. A sharp, single-edge razor blade or X-Acto-type knife works best for trimming. Then replace your cellophane patch so the curing will start again. Let the patch cure completely; this will take a half hour or an hour. You will find that the patch has shrunk slightly below the surface as it cures.

Now break out your electric drill or porta-tool again. Use the burr to rough up the bottom again, as well as the edges of the hole. Make sure the hole has been completely feathered into the surrounding gel coat; again, do not undercut the hole.

For both damage to gel coat and completion of the deeper repair, now you're ready to create a new gel coat surface. Pour out a small amount of gel coat onto another clean jar lid or onto a cardboard. Add a drop or two of catalyst, and mix the resin and catalyst thoroughly. You should use a cutting motion rather than stirring, and you may well not know what that is—ask your wife how she folds ingredients into a cake mix. It's the same motion we call "cutting." Don't add any of the milled fibers.

Use either your fingertip or the tip of a putty knife to fill the hole to a raised one-sixteenth inch above the surrounding surface with the gel coat mixture you've just made.

Lay a piece of cellophane over the patch to start the curing process. After about fifteen minutes, peel off the cellophane and touch the patch with your fingertip. The patch should be rubbery. Carefully trim it with a sharp single-edge razor blade or razor knife flush with the surrounding gel coat surface.

As soon as you've done the trimming, place another small amount of gel coat on one edge of the patch area and cover it with cellophane. Then, using a rubber squeegee or the back of the razor blade, squeegee the patch level with the surrounding area. Leave the cellophane on the patch overnight if you can, for at least an hour or two at the least. Leave the cellophane on the patch for the length of time necessary for the full cure, in any case.

To complete the job, sand the patched area with 600-grit *wet* sandpaper. Finish up by rubbing or buffing with a fine rubbing compound. If you notice some slight color difference, allow the patch to weather shortly. Weathering should blend everything. If the color difference is too great, you may wish to paint.

A word about fiberglass filling compounds might be important here. There are some excellent ones on the market, though they usually come in white or gray and not in colors to match your gel coat. As well, they often take a very long time—five or six hours to twelve or twenty-four hours—to cure. For quick patches, emergency patching, or where the surface is going to be painted anyway, a commercially available product called Rez-Zin has always worked well for me; if your marine supply store doesn't carry Rez-Zin (mine doesn't either), try a regular paint store or even an auto supply outlet. I understand Rez-Zin was originally developed as an

Figure 53

auto body-lead compound for body and fender work. It is an epoxy resin that cures rapidly: Twenty minutes will give you a sanding cure in proper temperature conditions (see Figure 53). As well, Rez-Zin is thick enough to be good for vertical surfaces; it tends less to sag and run than some other fillers I have used. Color is light gray or green, so you'll have to paint. Marine-Tex is another excellent product, but it's extremely hard and tough to sand.

Repairing Crazing on a Gel Coat Surface

There are two schools of thought on repairing this type of damage of fiberglass. Which one you choose can depend on your understanding of how the damage occurred. A sharp rap or blow can cause the surface of the gel coat to fail locally; or, too-thick application of the wrong gel coat resin can create an unsupported surface structure that will fail all over the boat. Often the cracking or "checking" is found on the deck surfaces, where it is highly visible and unattractive in the extreme (see Figure 54).

Figure 54

Local crazing caused by a blow is the most serious kind; it is first necessary to make sure the blow hasn't caused some kind of failure of the basic structure, too. If it has not, and chances are it hasn't, the problem involves making a local repair.

So, according to school No. 1, remove all the crazed gel coat by sanding. Be very careful you don't create ridges or indentations you don't intend to cause with the sander. Then turn to the previous section on repairing nicks and gouges and follow the directions for making surface repairs to the area where you have, basically, removed the gel coat.

If the crazing has been caused by aging, you will have to make a decision: whether or not to resurface the entire boat. Crazing on the outside of the hull can be masked by using a glazing compound in the cracks, then by painting. You'll probably need to reglaze and repaint a number of times from year to year. It is still a relatively simple matter to keep this from showing on the outside of the hull.

The deck will be a different matter. It is often the first part of the boat an onlooker sees. It is the part directly exposed to sun, sand, and wear from feet. Paint tends to wear off rapidly. Glazing and painting may not be the answer for you.

Recently a kit has been developed for making this (and other types of repairs) to fiberglass boats. It involves a wood graining material laid under a clear fiberglass surface. The wood graining material is flexible enough to absorb further checking and shrinking of the undersurface while it hides the condition effectively. The new fiberglass layer protects the wood grain. The result in a test installation was curing the crazing condition and the creation of a handsome wood-grained deck on a fiberglass boat. Here's how it was done:

Steps in the job started with removal of all deck hardware. The old deck paint formerly used to hide the crazing was removed

Figure 55

with a regular paint and varnish remover, then the surface was thoroughly cleaned with a brushing thinner. Finally, the surface was completely sanded to remove all traces of paint. Cracks and indentations were glazed with Pettit's polyester mending compound, and the entire surface was resanded and cleaned with thinner again.

To make a bed for the wood-grain laminate cloth, Pettit Polyester Base Coat was applied to the surface (see Figure 55). It is a wax-free, air-inhibited resin that dries tacky and helps to hold the wood-grain film in place. To give a proper color base, a tan-colored pigment was added. The resin was allowed to set and become tacky.

A mahogany-grained wood-simulating laminate was applied

Figure 56   Figure 57

printed side up (see Figure 56). The tacky resin held the wood grain in place. At times, additional tack around corners and so on was necessary. This was achieved by careful wetting with acetone or styrene before the wood grain was applied. The material was trimmed to exact dimension with a razor knife, and holes for the deck hardware were punched (see Figure 57) to facilitate finding them at reinstallation time. The wood grain was allowed to follow

Figure 58   *Figure 59*

Figure 60

its natural "lie," since stretching creates wrinkles. Finally, a six-ounce fiberglass cloth was applied to the boat deck surface (see Figure 58) right over the wood grain. The fabric had a "water-white" polyester-compatible silane finish.

Finishing up the job involved the use of a low-viscosity, clear, light-stabilized polyester resin that was *not* air-inhibited (see Figure 59). It was allowed to set, and a second coat was applied.

Repairing Punctures, Breaks, and Holes in Fiberglass

I have a favorite philosophy concerning boat damage. If you hit *anything* hard enough, you can break it. On the other hand, if you work at making a repair hard enough, with fiberglass you can re-create the structure every bit as strong as it was before.

How much do you care about fixing your boat? Once I saw a forty-six-foot cruiser that had slammed into a projecting, unlighted bridge beam at night. The beam made a horizontal slice six feet back into the bow section of the boat about four feet below the deck level. Because the boat had been up on a plane, traveling at high speed, when the accident occurred, it came to rest *hanging* its whole weight from that tortured bow section. A huge crane was required to take the strain off the bow, back the boat loose, and swing it down into the water. It traveled several miles to the boat-yard under its own power and, when I saw the repair, the damage site was almost invisible. That's strength!

The materials you will need to fix a puncture, break, or hole include fiberglass mat and cloth, polyester resin and catalyst, some colored gel coat to match the surrounding boat surface, cellophane, and such back-up materials as cardboard or sheet aluminum. Specialized materials are available from your boat dealer. Sheet aluminum, which is ideal for this purpose, is often available at your newspaper or local printing office. Offset printing plates are made of thin, very workable aluminum sheet; when the printing job is done, the plates may then be salvaged or destroyed. Our local news-paper sells the aluminum-sheet plates for twenty cents apiece.

The place in which you should do your work is ideally one out of the direct sun (overmuch heat can speed curing of the resin) with room to stand and work comfortably. If possible, it also should be protected from any breeze, which could blow sand and dirt into the wet resin.

First, be sure that the area around the break or hole is clean and absolutely dry (see Figure 61). Use acetone or denatured alcohol to emulsify any dampness and evaporate it. Hull damage should be repaired as quickly as possible, since constant water penetration can weaken the hull around the break. Remove any dirt from the repair site.

Figure 61

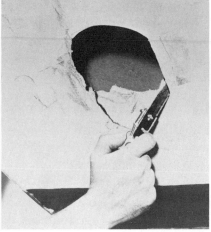

Figure 62

Figure 63

Figure 64

Now use a keyhole or electric saber saw to cut away the ragged edges of the damaged area (see Figure 62). Even if you must enlarge the hole, make sure you've cut well back to sound material.

Working inside the hull, rough-sand the hole and the area around it, using 80-grit dry sandpaper. Feather back for about two inches all around the hole (see Figure 63). This roughens the surface so the patch will be able to make a strong bond with the hull. If you cannot reach the hole inside the boat, turn to the later section on repairing "blind" holes from the outside only.

To prepare a former, cover a piece of cardboard with cellophane. It is only necessary to tape it in place to the outside of the hull (see Figure 64). Make sure the former covers the hole completely. The cellophane should face through the hole toward the inside of the hull. If the break is on a sharp contour, you will probably find that sheet aluminum will work best (see Figure 65). Form it first over a similar, undamaged contour. Of course, the aluminum also should be cellophane-covered.

After you've placed the former, prepare a patch of fiberglass mat and cloth. Cut it about two inches larger than the hole (see Figure 66). Mix a small amount of your resin and catalyst in a ratio of about ten parts of resin to a single part of catalyst. You'd better mix it only in small quantities as you need them for each set, since the resin has a short "pot life": It will cure in thirty minutes to an hour.

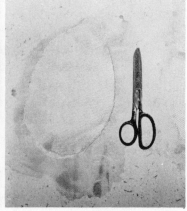

Figure 65   Figure 66

Thoroughly wet out the mat and cloth with the catalyzed resin. Daub the resin onto the mat first and then onto the cloth. The mat should be applied to the hull surface from the inside with the cloth on top. That will mean, in the finished repair, that the smoother cloth will be toward the outside of the hull, while the thicker mat will be inside. It may be easiest to wet out both pieces on a chunk of cellophane, then apply them to the patch area as a sandwich.

With the patch applied to the hull from the inside, cover the inner surface of the patch with cellophane. Squeegee from the center to the edges to remove all air bubbles and assure the best adhesion around the edge of the hole. Bubbles will show up as white spots in the patch, and they should all be worked out to the edge. Allow the patch to cure thoroughly; this will take an hour or two.

Now take the cardboard from outside the hole and rough-sand the patch and the edge of the hole. Again, feather the edge of the hole with your sander to about two or three inches over the surrounding undamaged area.

To prevent extra clean-up when the job is over, mask the area about four or five inches away from the hole and the surrounding hull with tape and newspaper.

Now cut a piece of fiberglass mat about an inch larger than the hole, along with one or two pieces of cloth two to three inches larger than the hole. Brush catalyzed resin over the hole, then lay the mat over the hole, and do a thorough job of wetting out with catalyzed resin. Use a daubing action with your brush.

Apply the additional layer or layers of fiberglass cloth to build the patch up slightly above the surface of the boat. Wet out each layer with resin as you did the layer of mat.

With a rubber squeegee or a broad knife, work all air bubbles out of the patch, going from the center toward the edges and pressing the patch firmly against the hull. Allow the patch to cure for fifteen to twenty minutes.

Now the patch will begin to set up. While it's still rubbery, take a razor blade, razor knife, or very sharp penknife and cut away any extra cloth and mat, outside the edge of the feathering. Strip the cut edges off the hull. If you do this before the cure is complete, you will save considerable grinding and sanding. Allow the patch to cure overnight now.

With 80-grit dry sandpaper on your power sander, smooth the patch and blend it into the surrounding surface (see Figure 67).

Figure 67

If air pockets show up while sanding, puncture them with a sharp instrument and fill them with catalyzed resin. They should be allowed to cure and then be resanded. A syringe used for giving shots makes an ideal tool for puncturing and filling these bubbles if you can talk your doctor into giving you one that has been used and is of the disposable variety. He may be legally prevented from doing so, so don't feel insulted if he refuses.

Finally, mix a small amount of gel coat and catalyst. Spread it over the patch with your fingers, working the material into any crevices or holes. Cover the gel coat with cellophane immediately and squeegee it smooth. Allow it to cure completely before you remove the cellophane. For large areas, you will want to spray the gel coat. The proper spray mixture should be approximately gel coat and acetone, mixed half-and-half by liquid measure, with 5cc of catalyst for each pint of the finished mix. Complete finishing involves sanding with various grades of wet sandpaper, starting with 220 grit and finishing with 600 grit on a sanding block. Buff with polishing compound for the final finish, and protect with wax.

Repairing Blind Holes in Fiberglass

When a damage site is found below the level of a boat's floorboards or inside a flotation tank, the work must often be done completely from the outside. It is harder, but no less satisfactory.

First, you must cut away the edges of the hole at least enough to allow you to reach inside the damaged area with your hand. Sand the inside with rough paper on a sanding block, feathering the hole two to three inches away from the edge.

Now you must prepare a blind patch. Here's how:

Cut a piece of corrugated cardboard slightly larger than the patch. Don't cover the cardboard with cellophane, but instead prepare a patch of a layer of fiberglass mat, then a layer of cloth on the cardboard surface directly. Wet out the patch with catalyzed resin. Make sure the mat is on top to bond to the hull.

To hold the patch in place, prepare several long strips of wood and U-shaped pieces of wire. The wood must be long enough to bridge the hole, and the wires should be inserted through the patch and cardboard backer with the ends outside as close to the edge of the hole as possible.

Now push the patch into the hole, and pull it back against the inside edge with the wires. Tighten the wires around the sticks to pull the patch into complete contact with the inside of the hull. Allow the patch to cure completely before you go any farther.

Now cut the wires at the surface of the patch, and go forward with the repairs just as you would under normal conditions (see the previous section on working from both sides). The cardboard backing will remain in place but will be bonded inside to the patch.

Making Unit Replacement in Fiberglass

Not too long ago, I saw a nineteen-foot sailboat on which the entire bow section had been destroyed. It was at first considered a complete loss, since the difficulties of creating formers out of cardboard and aluminum to remold the bow shape were insurmountable.

Ultimately the boat was repaired simply by having the original manufacturer mold a five-foot bow section complete, including deck, at his factory in the molds. The damaged section of the boat was completely cut loose and the new bow grafted on using a method similar to that described in making standard fiberglass repairs.

Repairing Dents in Aluminum

The Marine Aluminum Committee of the Aluminum Association has provided a number of important tips toward the repair and maintenance of aluminum boats. It seems certain that this should not be a process that will frighten or be too difficult for the average "handy" boatowner.

Figure 68

Ordinary dents, for example, can easily be knocked out with a rubber mallet or automotive body tools. Stretching may well have taken place in the dent, however, and must be provided for. One way, in very small dents, is to drill a small hole in the very center of the dent. This will allow the metal to be pushed back to its former shape without wrinkling. The dent should then be caulked to seal the hole.

By far the more sophisticated way to handle stretched aluminum is by heating. This isn't, however, an easy matter when there is paint to be considered. On all natural aluminum, temperature can, however, be a useful tool. It should be maintained at about 500° F using the "Tempilstik" crayons; these melt at predetermined temperatures. The heating torch should be played around the outside of the dent and the metal worked back to its original contour with progressive tapping. The metal can be cooled with water when the job is completed.

Repairing Structural Damage in Aluminum

Damage to a metal hull may include bent or broken reinforcing members as well as skin distortion or destruction. Usually the rivets are loosened around this damaged area.

If the damage isn't too great, you can repair the original part by reshaping it with a mallet. Use wooden blocks to distribute the impact of the hammering, however, and prevent further distortion and stretching. On a minor repair job, you may find that it is possible to retighten the loose rivets by putting a heavy bar on the head side and peening the bucktail.

When the reinforcing members have been broken or bent beyond repair or straightening, you will have to get a new part of the proper marine alloy from the boat's manufacturer. When you send in your order, be sure to give the maker the serial and model numbers of the boat if possible, as well as a sketch or photo of the damaged portion.

To prepare for a unit replacement like this, you often have to remove some of the original rivets. Completely drilling out the rivet will usually distort the hole and can complicate reriveting as well as making the boat difficult to make watertight.

Figure 69   Figure 70

The Marine Aluminum Committee recommends this procedure:

Center-punch the exact center of the rivet's manufactured head, then drill out the rivet to the depth of that head, using one of these drill sizes: ⅛ rivet, use No. 30 drill; ⁵⁄₃₂ rivet, use No. 21 drill; ³⁄₁₆ rivet, use No. 11 drill; ¼ rivet, use Catetory F drill; ⁵⁄₁₆ rivet, use Category P drill; ⅜ rivet, use Category W drill. The head of the rivet will then be held only by a thin ring of metal.

Now snap the drilled head off, using a punch and light hammer taps. The punch should be carefully held parallel to the skin surface. Finally, hold a bucking bar against the skin adjacent to the rivet and drive out the rivet body with a punch and hammer. Use a round shank drift punch the next size under the rivet size.

Riveting Aluminum

The best results for home riveting will be gained by using simple tools. Hold a heavy bar or the heavier of two hammers against the head of the rivet (make sure it's an aluminum rivet, by the way!). Hammer the bucktail end of the rivet with increasing force until it has expanded to the same size as the similar rivets in the boat. Of course, this will create a deformation in the rivet head, which may not look very sightly. A tool called a "head set" held between the head of the rivet and the bucking bar or hammer will create the popular and neat, round look. Your boat dealer may have a head set you can borrow or rent.

Repairing Punctures and Skin Fractures in Aluminum

Emergency repairs can, contrary to popular belief, be quite easily accomplished in the field. The first job, of course, is to pound the ruptured portion back to its original contour without creating a lot of stretch dimples by hammering. Use a mallet and some wood blocks to distribute the blow force. The simplest way to complete the repair is to back it with another sheet of aluminum riveted in place. Some caulking compound will prevent leaking.

Before applying the patch, drill at each end of any crack or fracture with a small (No. 30 or No. 50) bit. This is called stop-drilling and will prevent the crack from extending itself.

Now center the patch over the damaged area and draw a pencil line around it. Remove the patch, and drill a hole in each corner of the patch piece. Again place the patch against the hull and drill through the hull at one corner, using the patch hole as a guide. Secure this corner temporarily with a small bolt, then proceed with each corner hole temporary fastening. Lay out a hole pattern, drilling on a line one-half inch in from the edge of the patch, on half-inch centers. If the patch is a very large one, you'll want to lay out a second row of holes another inch or so in. Stagger these with the outside row.

Now drill all the holes and take the patch off again. Remove all burrs and shavings from the boat and patch, then apply a thin layer of caulking over the entire patch. Refasten the patch to the boat using the temporary corner fasteners again. Rivet the patch progressively around the exterior, then remove the temporary corner bolts and rivet there, too. The crack itself can be filled smooth from outside with a fiberglass patching compound, sanded, and finally painted to match the rest of the boat.

Welding repairs are difficult to make for amateur handymen. A sophisticated Heliarc, Metal-Inert-Gas (MIG), or Tungsten-Inert-Gas (TIG) process is involved. They should be made by a competent dealer.

Repairing Ribs and Frames in Wooden Boats

Not all types of wooden boats have structural frame members. For example, a strip-planked boat is built over molds that are then removed. A few major bulkheads serve quite adequately to stiffen the hull. The same is true of a molded plywood boat. A boat built up of sheet plywood is constructed over a series of bulkheads that become formers to insure the proper shape of the boat; it is the skin structure in any of these types of construction, however, that insures strength.

Carvel-planked and lapstrake wood boats need either frames or ribs. The difference between the structural members is that frames are somewhat heavier and placed farther apart on centers. Ribs are lighter and placed more closely together. Size and spacing depend on the boat.

There are several ways to replace ribs and frames when they become cracked or broken. And they do fail. My own thirty-two-year-old wooden sailboat has eighty-six ribs; somewhere during her career some owner detected that more than half of them were broken and had the framework of the boat strengthened with sister ribs.

"Sistering" ribs involves the strengthening of your boat's framework by placing solid ribs *next to* broken ribs. The rationale is based on the fact that it is all but impossible sometimes to get old fastenings out. Moreover, where the rib is only broken in one spot, it serves a useful function over the rest of its length in both directions from the break. A sister rib duplicates the size and shape of the original rib and is seated right against its broken sibling.

Sister ribs—or replacement ones, for that matter, if you elect to remove the old ribs completely—can be steam bent to the proper shape, or they can be laminated. Fastenings can be of the conventional flat-head wooden screw type, or they can be small bolts, nuts, and washers.

To prepare steam bent ribs, you will want to start with seasoned oak stock sawn to the proper dimension. Since the wood is tough and springy (or you wouldn't use it for ribs), it won't bend to the shape of the hull readily. It needs to be softened. Steaming is the best way, though bending can be accomplished by simply soaking the wood in water.

A steam jenny can be readily obtained from most tool rental outlets or, if that's impossible, made on the spot. Basically, the jenny is nothing more than a large stovepipe made closed and watertight on one end by use of a cap. The pipe is propped up at about a forty-five-degree angle, with the closed end down and the open end up. The length of the pipe depends on how long are the ribs you need to bend into place.

The low end of your jenny pipe should be high enough off the ground so a burner or flame can be located under it. With a gallon or two (make sure you keep an eye on the level, or you'll burn out your jenny) of water in the low end of the pipe and the flame burning brightly, the rest of the pipe will be bathed in steam. Lay ribs in place inside the jenny pipe, one at a time, and let them steam. How long depends on the density of the wood and the sharpest necessary bend; the sharper the bend and denser the wood, the longer the steaming. Do a little experimentation, and you will soon be able to develop a staggered schedule for steaming the wood long enough, while giving yourself enough time to set the previously bent rib in place.

The steamed ribs can be prebent on a jig if you wish, but this seems to me to be the hard way. Instead, by setting up a series of braces and using some clamps inside the hull, you should be able to lay the steamed, unbent rib into place, then force it down to the hull's contour without too much difficulty. Brace it into place, and proceed with the fastening. Use the same type of fastenings that were originally used (don't mix copper or brass, brass and bronze with iron or steel); predrill pilot holes for the screws, and set the heads about a third of the plank depth. Fill the screw-head holes with wooden plugs made of dowels, and set in a waterproof glue. The plugs can be set in a bit long to facilitate handling, then cut off and sanded flush when the glue has dried.

If you don't have access to the proper weight stock, if the ribs or frames you need to make are too thick for you to handle, or if internal bracing would be difficult in your boat, it is possible to laminate ribs. Laminating eliminates the need for steam bending if the sections of the laminate are thin enough.

Obviously, you will need to cut the number of plys to the proper dimension. Laminating should be done with a really first-rate waterproof glue. Bending and gluing can be done to preprepared templates and forms outside the boat, but to my mind they can more easily be done in place.

When the entire thickness of laminated rib has been built up, bracing each layer in place as you go, the whole should be fastened in the conventional manner with screws or bolts.

Recaulking a Carvel-Planked Wooden Boat

From time to time in the life of every boat, especially when she has been refastened, it becomes necessary to do a recaulking job. The old caulking often has dried out or fallen away in chunks. Touch-up caulking becomes a thankless and impossible chore (see Figure 71).

Figure 71

In recaulking, the most necessary chore is to remove all vestiges of old caulking right back to the clean-wood edges of the seams. Leaving ridges or bumps of hardened caulking prevents the seams from closing properly against the fresh caulking and could make the boat leak even worse than before. A good uncaulking tool can be made by bending the rat-tail end of a file into a hook. Even better, a small, portable-circular handsaw set to cut about half the depth of the planking's thickness should remove the old caulking

Figure 72

cleanly (see Figure 72). In many cases, it will not be necessary to pull out the old caulking cotton, but only the hardened compound on top.

Replacement of caulking starts with priming the seams (see Figure 73). If you are using one of the linseed-oil-based compounds, prime the seams with white lead or thick white paint to seal the

Figure 73

Figure 74

pores of the wood. If you are using one of the silicone rubber compounds, be sure to prime with the proper stuff as recommended by the manufacturer.

Whether laid in the seam with a caulking (putty) knife or forced in with a caulking gun, penetration is the byword (see Figure 74). The outer surface of the new caulking should be grooved with your caulking knife, because the plank will otherwise squeeze out a ridge of caulking. If you haven't any idea how much to groove the caulking, then fill the seam, and later in the season, when the boat has completely swelled tight, beach her long enough to take a sharp knife and cut away the ridges of caulking compound.

The thing to be particularly guarded against is overcaulking. It is always possible to add caulking if the boat continues to leak slightly. If you put in too much caulking, there will be no place for the plank to swell. It will be pushed outward by the caulking. This will cause the fastenings to be pulled out by the very swelling of the boat. The planking will buckle at the edges like a washboard, the boat will begin to leak in a worse way than before, and you will have a major refastening chore on your hands.

Refastening a Carvel-Planked Wooden Boat

Refastening will be necessary if your boat has been overcaulked or if the old fastenings have failed due to electrolysis or age. You can be sure an older planked wooden boat is suffering from "fastening sickness" if, for example, rust spots begin to bleed through her hull paint like measles. It's time to refasten.

You can refasten either by removing the old fastenings and using the same holes, or by drilling new holes. The reason for the former is that drilling more holes in planks and ribs weakens them. It may not be possible, because it often is impossible to remove corroded fastenings from their holes, at least in one piece, and you'll make a mess if you try to drill them out. In any case, replace fastenings with ones of identical material or another that is compatible—bronze and brass are compatible, for example, with Monel and Everdur, as is *passivated* stainless steel with any ferrous metal. Don't mix ferrous and nonferrous, however, or you are creating a giant battery that will destroy any ferrous metal in the boat in very short order.

Replacement of Planking in a Carvel-Planked Wooden Boat

Sometimes you may find that leaking is caused by a rotten plank or by a split in a plank. That plank should be replaced.

When you remove the old plank, make very sure that you don't do irreparable damage to the ribs by violent wrenching out of the old fastenings. If you can take the old plank out in one piece, you will have a very valuable pattern for cutting the new one.

It will be necessary to shape your new plank very carefully—to do a process known to old-time boatbuilders as "spiling." Here's how:

Consider the way your boat is built. There are the same *number* of planks at the bow and stern as there are in the middle of the boat. This means that the planks at the ends of the boat are much narrower than they are in the middle to accommodate that number, because the boat is much fuller in the middle than it is in the ends. If that isn't clear to you, go back over it while you look at your boat; it's essential that you understand it because it is the basic reason for spiling.

When the plank has been removed, measure the distance between rib centers and count the number of ribs involved—then number the ribs from bow to stern "1," "2," "3," etc. Then take your service log notebook and a tape measure and begin your calculations. Let's suppose that, at the stem (the bowmost frame member), the plank is 2 inches wide with some allowance for the seam width about ¼ inch on either side). Six inches to the back of the boat (at the No. 1 rib), the plank has expanded to 2¼ inches wide. Six inches farther back (at the No. 2 rib), it is now 2½ inches wide. Continue your spiling measurements from bow to stern, noting the widest needed width. The piece of wood you use should be a bit wider than that maximum. Now lay out the measurements on the plank itself.

Start by marking the center line on the plank, the full length. If you're using an 8-inch-wide plank, for example, mark the 4-inch center with a heavy line. On that line, mark the distances between ribs, and number them like the ribs themselves. Draw crosswise lines at each rib interval.

To create the spiling line on which you will do your cutting, take the measurements from your notebook. At rib line No. 1, for example, you would mark off half the plank width on either side of the center line. According to our hypothetical case cited two paragraphs above, at the stem end you'd make a mark one inch on either side of the center line. At frame No. 1 line, you'd mark off 1⅛ inches; at rib No. 2 line, you'd mark off 1¼ inches on either side of the center line. Do this the whole length of the line, marking half the measured plank width on the frame line either side of center. When you're done, connect these lines on either side of the center line and you have created a line on which to cut the plank to fit. In other words, you have spiled a plank. The cut plank will be a strange, wavy-looking thing, especially if you've always thought of planking as a straight run of board. Don't worry—if you've done your measuring carefully, it will fit properly.

If you want to do the job really well, you will have cut your plank slightly oversize—just the amount oversize, in fact, to allow the plank to swell (perhaps, for example, ¼ inch over on each side) tight. Then, with a block plane, bevel the plank back to your measured line. This will bevel the seams—the larger dimension should be placed toward the rear of the seam—so that water pressure cannot easily force the caulking out of the seam. This is the most workmanlike way to do the job.

A word about whether or not to run the planks full length could be important. The best boats were always made with full-length planking. Having to join planks in the length of the run can lead to problems. However, it is much better to join planks than to use one length of planking that is less than perfect. Knots and splits in the planking can lead to worse problems. If you have to join planks, do it in the middle of the "cove" or space between ribs; don't try to make the joint over a rib. Back the joint with a butt block or piece of wood the same size as the planking and fastened to the back of the plank ends with screws. Remember, the planks will not swell in a lengthwise dimension, so caulk the end seams tight and fasten them as close together as possible. The butt block should be covered with caulking before fastening, too.

When you are replacing a section of planking only, it is possible to "scarf" in a section of new wood. This involves cutting out the old section on a forty-five-degree diagonal at each end, as well as with a similar bevel at each end. The bevel should be opposite on both ends with the small dimension inside, spreading wider toward the outside. A butt-block inside will complete the join and make it watertight.

Repair by Replacement of Plywood Sections

Like most boatbuilding materials, marine plywood is a strong material when properly used. It offers a number of outstanding advantages, however: Marine plywood is resilient, resistant to rot, won't swell or warp, and has no seams. If you hit it hard, though, you'll poke a hole in it. The holed section should probably be replaced.

Plywood is like other laminates in that a sharp blow can cause delamination. Repairing plywood should be done in a manner similar to repairing fiberglass. In fact, plywood lends itself uniquely to fiberglassing.

First, I would recommend that you cut back to solid wood all around the break, even if it means enlarging the hole significantly. Make sure all lamination is sound. If you find a void (you shouldn't in marine-grade plywood; exterior-grade plywood may have some voids), you should fill it with a waterproof, hard, filler compound. You may then refer to the section on making major repairs to fiberglass in which the process of installing a back-up form, creating an overlapping patch, and smooth finishing are described. Obviously, you won't use a final gel coat finish but will paint your patch instead.

To create a plywood patch, it will be necessary to remove damaged wood in a predetermined pattern carefully with a keyhole or electric saber saw. The section removed is then used as a pattern to trace and fit an exact duplicate out of sound marine plywood. The new patch should be of plywood the same thickness as the hull, obviously. The raw edges of both hull and patch should be carefully sealed and any voids filled.

To back up the patch, you may wish to use simple cleats of wood that will overlap both patch and hull about two inches on either side of the joint. The cleats should be screwed on from the outside of the hull through the cleat with flat-head, countersunk wood screws of the same metal originally used to fasten the boat. Don't ever mix ferrous and nonferrous fastenings. Drill the hole pattern with screws about two inches apart on centers. Fill the seam with a good waterproof caulking compound and the screw holes with a filler. Prime-coat the new plywood, then sand and finish-coat.

Occasionally, sheet-plywood-built boats will offer some problems with leaking seams. When plywood seams are made, they feature a soft material (often linen strips) and glue to retain waterproofness and flexibility. The panacea often suggested is fiberglass taping the seams. It's not a bad idea, but fiberglass is not a substitute in the plywood construction for good fastenings. What has happened is that the fastenings have pulled loose.

Therefore, I would recommend that you first remove the fastenings from the leaking seam, open the seam up, and remove any hardened caulking or rotten linen strips. Replace with a good silicone rubber caulking compound that will not harden in use, then redrive the screw fastenings. *Then* apply fiberglass if you wish.

Taping seams with fiberglass is not dissimilar to applying fiberglass to the whole boat and will be discussed in a somewhat later section.

Repair by Replacement of Strip Planking

A strip-planked boat is tremendously strong and flexible at the same time. It is created of thin, narrow planks that are glued to each other and edge-fastened over a set of molds. When the glue has cured, the skin of the boat (the strips of planking) has formed a light, whippy, prestressed type of monocoque construction that has the advantage of being seamless and leakless. Usually, the molds—or those that are not used as interior bulkheading—are removed from the finished hull. This means, when there is a break in the structure, that a mold must be recreated to re-establish the boat's shape for reconstruction.

That, then, will be the first job. A mold can be a template of plywood or other wood, a bent strap of metal, anything strong enough to have the new planking strips bent around it and still remain in place. This obviously requires some pretty thorough bracing.

Replanking and edge-fastening (usually done with ridged boat nails) will be somewhat of a problem because of the closing hole. You may well find that a plywood panel or a fiberglass patch (see previous sections in this chapter) will be easier and more practical to create. One expert in the area of strip-planked construction in this country is Mr. E. Farnham Butler of the Mount Desert Yacht Yard, Mount Desert, Maine. If you write to Mr. Butler, be courteous enough to remember that this is how he makes his living;

don't expect a lot of free information, which Mr. Butler may not be too pleased (but will be too gracious to refuse) to give.

Removing Old Paint (Wooding Down)

Wooding down a boat may be necessary for a number of reasons. A fiberglass boat may have a too-great build-up of paint to be attractive; so may a wood boat. You may need to remove paint from the area surrounding a repair site. When recaulking or refastening wood-planked boats it is almost always a good idea to remove the paint, too, so you have the best possible view of the job at hand.

In any case, there are three time-honored methods of paint removal: by chemical means and scraping; by heat and scraping; and by sanding.

Paint removal by chemical means is probably the most satisfactory all-around because it is safest. It may well require several coats of remover to do the job thoroughly, and working under a boat with paint remover can be a messy proposition. In any case, pick your paint remover carefully and follow the manufacturers' directions for its use and the proper precautions to protect your eyes and skin.

Paint removal by heat can be done quickly but is prohibited by many boatyards and marinas. It is most commonly done with a torch, though there are electrical heating pads that do the job safely without danger of fire. These often are not banned, though they're not popular because of the amount of electrical current they use.

Paint removal by sanding is a tedious and difficult business and and is often messy, too, with paint dust and perspiration making a terrible combination on a hot sticky day. The best mechanical paint-removing devices are also those that can do the most damage to undersurfaces. The disk sander, for example, cuts beautifully but can leave semicircular gouges in the surface in the hands of an unskilled worker. A belt sander with ultracourse, open-coat production belts will do a marvelous job.

Since torching is obviously dangerous, suffice it to say this should be used for the toughest, roughest jobs where no one else's boat can be endangered. Torching also leaves scorch marks, which can only be removed with difficulty, so it is perhaps not the best, easiest means after all. It should never be used on plywood (interior glues are embrittled), fiberglass, aluminum, canvas decks, or where fiberglass is later to be applied. The same general rules apply for the heating pads, too. Heating paint for removal is best on a heavily planked wood boat that will be repainted.

Chemical paint removers, especially those that are water-washable, are an obvious choice for almost all kinds of boats—plywood, aluminum, fiberglass, etc. However, this method should probably not be used on a canvas deck.

Sanding, too, can be used on all types of boats, providing it is done with care to avoid damage to the undersurface. It is definitely the way to remove paint from a canvas deck, but it must be done with finesse. A little prepractice will pay big dividends in control and the subsequent quality of the job.

Repair of Wood Boats by Application of Fiberglass

Generally, the procedures to be followed in application of fiberglass are found in an earlier section of this chapter on preparing a fiberglass patch for a fiberglass boat. The chemistry of preparing resins and wetting out fiberglass cloth are identical and need not be covered again.

Several words of caution may be useful here. Fiberglass is, again, not a panacea for all the things that ail wood boats. Applied heavily enough, it does indeed create a new hull outside the old one. That new hull does indeed have a monumental structural strength of its own, which it applies to the old structure, too.

Especially for plywood hulls, decks, and/or deckhouses, application of fiberglass is an excellent cure for failing surface, some leaking, bad fastenings, etc. Of course, plywood is stable like the fiberglass (neither swell nor shrink or warp with moisture), so both constructions complement each other.

The first step is complete removal of old paint, by sanding, from any plywood surface to have application of fiberglass. For best results, you should never heat plywood; chemical paint removers may prevent the fiberglass from bonding adequately. Also, you should sand down any rough spots, raised areas, or bumps, and fill

Figure 75

all nicks and gouges with a plasterlike trowel cement before application of fiberglass.

The wood should be completely dry and clean when you start the glassing procedure. If you have doubts about dampness, wipe the wood down well with acetone to "pull" all moisture and evaporate it.

I recommend that you use a Dynel cloth that can be stapled into place first and need not be laid in a prime coat of wet resin; it may, however, be necessary to apply a resin prime coat and allow it to cure before placing the Dynel to prevent overmuch soaking of the first resin, which is intended to seal the cloth to the plywood. The Dynel has an open weave, which permits dry placement in any case, and allows the cloth to be carefully "tailored" and stapled firmly down for the best finished results.

A polyester resin will, for all practical purposes, suit you best. It is not as thick as an epoxy, can be easily brushed, shows air bubbles readily in time to do something about them, and causes the Dynel and itself to go absolutely clear. This is quite a decorative effect and a very practical way to finish a transom bright, for example, without the need for revarnishing every year. Curing and sanding needs, in terms of time and temperature, are clearly spelled out by resin makers. I recommend that you follow these directions explicitly. The finished surface may be sprayed with gel coat (more trouble than it's worth, I think) or painted; see the section in the material on spring maintenance on painting fiberglass for suggestions.

There will be people who will now take exception to what I am going to say. Let the chips fall as they may, but I personally have never known of an application of fiberglass that was successful on any but a strip-planked wood boat. I cannot in good conscience recommend it for your planked carvel or lapstrake boat. I don't think it will work in the long run, and you will have wasted time and money.

I can recommend that you take an aged and failing wood boat and use it as a male mold from which to create a new fiberglass hull. This means, of course, reinstalling all interior fittings, engines, decks, fittings, hardware, etc. I don't recommend leaving the old hull inside the new one as a "hanger" for all these things; that just adds to weight and decreases efficiency. If your wood-planked boat has failed, its fastenings are bad, its ribs are broken, it would be better and more profitable to rebuild it by replacing fastenings, planking, and ribs than to cover the hull with a new skin.

The new skin will not be nearly as flexible as the old hull was. The skin won't be able to swell and shrink with the planks. And swell and shrink those planks will, from the moisture present in the marine environment. They will cause the new fiberglass skin to buckle, ridge, and delaminate; then, when they move again, they will cause splitting.

Repairing Dry Rot in Wooden Boats

Dry rot is a fungus that occurs when a boat is stored with a damp, closed-air pockets inside it (see Figure 76). The fungus grows in damp, still places. Fresh-rain or condensation-water accumulations in poorly ventilated areas, or under bad canvas decks, will help nurture the dry rot fungus.

In appearance the fungus makes the wood punky and soft. It is possible to poke a penknife or ice pick right through a rotted plank without effort. The fungus destroys the structural integrity of the

Figure 76

Figure 77

wood. It is also possible to detect the dry rot spots by thumping the hull with a wood or rubber mallet. Sound structure has a good, solid ring to it; rotted structure sounds "dead."

The real cure for dry rot is complete removal and replacement of the rotten structure. Therefore, this is to be most completely recommended. It's also expensive and difficult.

Several manufacturers do make a rot-repair substance. Flo-Paint, for example, markets Git-Rot, which is a two-part plastic compound (see Figure 77). Predrilling of a series of holes or placement in the wood's end grain insures soak-up of the plastic, which then penetrates all through the rotted area. Its purpose is to replace the rot with plastic, or a least reinforce the wood fiber; it does the job well.

Redecking a Wooden Boat with Vinyl Decking Material

You go down to your boat one summer morning. Everything beneath the canvas-covered deck is soaking wet from last night's rain. You look at the deck; it's worn out and leaking badly. Do you replace the canvas or apply fiberglass to it?

A third alternative is replacement with a vinyl-surfaced decking material especially designed to provide a long-wearing, predecorated surface (see Figure 78).

Figure 78 *Figure 79*

Figure 80

Figure 81

Figure 82

Figure 83

Two years ago I replaced the canvas deck of my own boat with a new Burlington vinyl fabric one. I started by carefully removing the old material with a razor knife in one piece to facilitate its use as a pattern for cutting the new vinyl accurately (see Figure 79).

Though I found the vinyl was heavy, it was easy to handle and cut readily with scissors (see Figure 80). I thoroughly sanded the old plywood underdeck and washed it with acetone to remove dirt, grease, and moisture.

The loose new vinyl was then rolled up toward the center from each end, after having been checked dry for a perfect fit. A line of staples was loosely driven across the middle to prevent any "working."

Application of two heavy coats of the specially provided cement was essential; (see Figure 81); one assured closing the pores of the plywood; the other assured an adequate wet bed for the vinyl. Both coats were applied a section at a time, one right after the other. Section by section, the vinyl was smoothed into the wet glue (see Figure 82) and stapled at the edges to prevent creeping (see Figure 83). A final trim-strip was added all round the edge to insure seal and mechanical fastening (see Figure 84).

Figure 84

Service Products Directory

Abrasives

Carborundum Co., Merchandising Sales, Box 477, Niagara Falls, N.Y. 14302

Carter Products Co., P.O. Box 1924, Columbus, O. 43216

Raybestos-Manhattan, Inc., 205 Middle St., Bridgeport, Conn. 06603

Abrasives, coated

Coastal Abrasive and Tool Co., Inc., P.O. Box 337, Merritt Industrial Park, Trumbull, Conn. 06611

Falcon Safety Products, Inc., 1137 Rt. 22, Mountainside, N.J. 07092

Jonard Industries Corp., 3047 Tibbett Ave., Bronx, N.Y. 10463

Additives, cooling-system

Bardahl Mfg. Corp., 1400 N.W. 52nd St., Seattle, Wash. 98107

Malco Products, Inc., 361 Fairview Ave., P.O. Box 892, Barberton, O. 44203

Oil Center Research, 211 Rayburn, Lafayette, La. 70501

Sudbury Laboratory, Dutton Rd., Sudbury, Mass. 01776

Additives, gasoline and oil

Bardahl Mfg. Cor., 1400 N.W. 52nd St., Seattle, Wash. 98107

Castoleum Corp., 31 Fullerton Ave., Yonkers, N.Y. 10704

Dew Coated Lubricants, P.O. Box 5755, Chicago, Ill. 60680

Fuel Activator Chemical Corp., 23–25 E. 26th St., New York, N.Y. 10010

Gumout Div., Pennsylvania Refining Co., 2686 Lisbon Road, Cleveland, O. 44104

Intercontinental Lubricants Corp., 19 Michael St., East Haven, Conn. 06512

Mercury Marine, Fond du Lac, Wis. 54935

Livingston Co., 8609 N.W. Plaza Dr., Dallas, Tex. 75225

Malco Products, Inc., 361 Fairview Ave., P.O. Box 892, Barberton, O. 44203

Micro-Lube, Inc., 8505 Directors Row, Dallas, Tex. 75247

Oil Center Research, 211 Rayburn, Lafayette, La. 70501

Pryoil Co., Inc., 20 Copeland Avenue, La Crosse, Wis. 54601

R S A Products Co., 3450 Lovett, Detroit, Mich. 48210

Adhesives, liquid-rubber

Allied Resin Products Corp., Weymouth Industrial Park, Pleasant St., East Weymouth, Mass. 02189

Carboline Co., 328 Hanley Ind. Ct., St. Louis, Mo. 63144

DAP, Inc., 5300 Huberville Rd., Dayton, O. 45431

Dennis Chemical Co., 2701 Papin St., St. Louis, Mo. 63103

Dolphin Paint and Chemical Co., 922 Locust St., Box 1927 Central Station, Toledo, O. 43603

Gates Engineering, Div. SCM Corp., 100 S. West Street, Wilmington, Del. 19899

General Electric Co., Silicone Products Dep't., Waterford, N.Y. 12188

General Electric Co., Wiring Device Dept., 95 Hathaway St., Providence, R.I. 02904

Intercoastal Corp., Dundalk P.O. Baltimore, Md. 21222

International Paint Co., Inc., 21 West St., New York, N.Y. 10006

H. B. Fred Kuhls, 49 Sumner St., Milford, Mass. 01757

Magic American Chemical Corp., 14215 Caine Ave., Cleveland, O. 44128

3M Co., 3M Center, St. Paul, Minn. 55101

National Casein of New Jersey, P.O. Box 151, Riverton, N.J. 08077

Sav-Cote Chemical Laboratories, 20 S. Dove St., P.O. Box 2128 Potomac Station, Alexandria, Va. 22301

Schwartz Chemical Co., Inc., 50–01 2nd St., Long Island City, N.Y. 11101

Smooth-On, Inc., 1000 Valley Rd., Stirling, N.J. 07933

Stay-Tite Products Co., Inc., 2889 E. 83rd St., P.O. Box 20130, Cleveland, O. 44120

Thiokol Chemical Corp., 780 N. Clinton Ave., Trenton, N.J. 08607

Unival Corp., 157 Summerfield St., Scarsdale, N.Y. 10583

Woodhill Chemical Sales Corp., 18731 Cranwood Pkwy., Cleveland, O. 44128

Adhesives, vinyl

Chrysler Corp., Chemical Div., 5437 W. Jefferson, Trenton, Mich. 48183

Dolphin Paint and Chemical Co., 922 Locust St., P.O. Box 1927 Central Station, Toledo, O. 43603

Pettit Paint Co., Inc., 507 Main St., Rockaway, N.J. 07866

Unival Corp., 157 Summerfield St., Scarsdale, N.Y. 10583

Adhesives, waterproof

American Cyanamid Co., Plastic Div., South Cherry St., Wallingford, Conn. 06492

BoatLIFE Div., Flo-Paint, Inc., 5–45 49th Ave., Long Island City, N.Y. 11101

Borden Chemical Div., Borden, Inc., 350 Madison Ave., New York, N.Y. 10017

Samuel Cabot, Inc., 246 Sumner St., Boston, Mass. 02128

H. A. Calahan, Inc., 859 Mamaroneck Ave., Mamaroneck, N.Y. 10543

Chrysler Corp., Chemical Div., 5437 W. Jefferson, Trenton, Mich. 48183

Commodore Nautical Supplies, 396 Broadway, New York, N.Y. 10013

DAP, Inc., 5300 Huberville Rd., Dayton, O. 45431

Darworth, Inc., Chemical Products Div., Simsbury, Conn. 06070

Dennis Chemical Co., 2701 Papin St., St. Louis, Mo. 63103

Dolphin Paint and Chemical Co., 922 Locust St., P.O. Box 1927 Central Station, Toledo, O. 43603

Dow Corning Corp., Consumer Products Div., P.O. Box 592, Midland, Mich. 48640

General Electric Co., Silicone Products Dept., Waterford, N.Y. 12188

General Tire and Rubber Co., Chemical/Plastics Div., P.O. Box 875, Toledo, O. 43601

Gloucester Co., Inc., 235 Cottage, Franklin, Mass. 02038

Intercoastal Corp., Dundalk P.O., Baltimore, Md. 21222

Kristal Kraft, Inc., 900 4th St., Palmetto, Fla. 33561

H. B. Fred Kuhls, 49 Sumner St., Milford, Mass. 01757

3M Co., 3M Center, St. Paul, Minn. 55101

Miracle Adhesives Corp., 250 Pettit Ave., Bellmore, N.Y. 11710

National Casein of New Jersey, P.O. Box 151, Riverton, N.J. 08077

PPG Industries, Inc., Adhesive Products, 225 Belleville Ave., Bloomfield, N.J. 07003

Raybestos-Manhattan, Inc., 205 Middle St., Bridgeport, Conn. 06603

W. J. Ruscoe Co., 483 Kenmore Blvd., Akron, O. 44301

Schwartz Chemical Co., Inc., 50–01 2nd St., Long Island City, N.Y. 11101

U. S. Plywood Div., U. S. Plywood-Champion Paper, Inc., 777 Third Ave., New York, N.Y. 10017

Unival Corp., 157 Summerfield St., Scarsdale, N.Y. 10583

Wilhold Glues, Inc., 8707 Millergrove Dr., Santa Fe Springs, Calif. 90670

Antiskid Surfacing Material

Coated Abrasives and Tape Divs., Norton Co., Dept. 695, Troy, N.Y. 12181

Bowman-Winter, Inc., 222 Wisconsin Ave., Lake Forest, Ill. 60045

Bristol Products, Inc., P.O. Box 30, 20 Stran Rd., Milford, Conn. 06460

Carborundum Co., Merchandising Sales, Box 477, Niagara Falls, N.Y. 14302

Garelick Mfg. Co., 644 2nd St., St. Paul Park, Minn. 55071

Goodyear Tire and Rubber Co., Industrial Products Div., 1144 E. Main St., Akron, O. 44316

Landy Associates, 349 Fifth Ave., New York, N.Y. 10016

Link Marine and Plyfoam, Inc., Vanderbilt Industrial Pkwy., Hauppauge, N.Y. 11787

Minnesota Mining and Mfg., Co., 3M Center, St. Paul, Minn. 55101

Ren Plastics, Inc., 5656 S. Cedar St., Lansing, Mich. 48909

W. J. Ruscoe Co., 483 Kenmore Blvd., Akron, O. 44301

Tri-State Ind., Inc., 10 S. Main, Dubuque, Ia. 52001

United Flotation Systems, 2400 Fairwood Ave., Columbus, O. 43207

Wooster Products, Inc., Spruce St., Wooster, O. 44691

Bitts, drill

Coastal Abrasive and Tool Co., Inc., P.O. Box 337, Merritt Industrial Park, Trumbull, Conn. 06611

W. L. Fuller, Inc., 1163 Warwick Ave., Warwick, R.I. 02888

Millers Falls Co., 57 Wells St., Greenfield, Mass. 01301

Moody Machine Products Co., Inc., 42–46 Dudley St., Providence, R.I. 02905

Stanley Tools, 600 Myrtle St., New Britain, Conn. 06050

Bleach, wood

Jasco Chemical Corp., P.O. Drawer "J," Mountain View, Calif. 94111

Boat wiring kits and harnesses

Allan Marine, 91 Industry Ct., Deer Park, N.Y. 11729

Bowman Products Div., Associated Spring Corp., 850 E. 72nd St., Cleveland, O. 44103

Cole-Hersee Co., 20 Old Colony Ave., Boston, Mass. 02127

Olson Industries, Inc., P.O. Box 2520, Sarasota, Fla. 33578

Preferred Electric and Wire Corp., 68 33rd St., Brooklyn, N.Y. 11232

Protect-A-Systems, Inc., 73 Ruth Ann Terr., Milford, Conn. 06460

N. A. Taylor Co., Inc., Gloversville, N.Y. 12078

Teleflex, Inc., Electrical Systems, Box 180, Tallevast, Fla. 33588

Waber Electronics, Inc., 2000 N. 2nd St., Philadelphia, Pa. 19122

Brushes, cleaning and scrubbing

Fuller Brush Co., Marine Div., East Hartford, Conn. 06108

Jonard Industries Corp., 3047 Tibbett Ave., Bronx, N.Y. 10463

Wright-Bernet, Inc., 1524 Bender Ave., Hamilton, O. 45011

Brushes, electric motor and generator

Coastal Abrasive and Tool Co., Inc., P.O. Box 337, Merritt Industrial Park, Trumbull, Conn. 06611

Preferred Electric and Wire Corp., 68 33rd St., Brooklyn, N.Y. 11232

United Motors Service, Div. General Motors, 3044 West Grand Blvd., Detroit, Mich. 48202

Brushes, paint and varnish

Allan Marine, 91 Industry Ct., Deer Park, N.Y. 11729

Chilton Paint Co., 109–09 15th Ave., College Point, N.Y. 11356

Glass Plastics/Valspar Corp., Marine Div., 200 Sayre St., Rockford, Ill. 61101

International Paint Co., Inc., 21 West St., New York, N.Y. 10006

Pettit Paint Co., Inc., 507 Main St., Rockaway, N.J. 07866

Phillips Hardware Co., 490 N.W. S. River Dr., Corner N.W. 9th Ave. and 5th St., Miami, Fla. 33128

Wooster Brush Co., 604 Madison Ave., Wooster, O. 44691

Brushes, wire

Coastal Abrasive and Tool Co., Inc., P.O. Box 337, Merritt Industrial Park, Trumbull, Conn. 06611

Phillips Hardware Co., 490 N.W. S. River Dr., Corner N.W. 9th Ave. and 5th St., Miami, Fla. 33128

Wright-Bernet, Inc., 1524 Bender Ave., Hamilton, O. 45011

Carburetor repair kits

Bendix Corp., Automotive Service Div., 1217 S. Walnut St., South Bend, Ind. 46620

Guaranteed Parts Co., Inc., R.D. 1, Seneca Falls, N.Y. 13148

Preferred Electric and Wire Corp., 68 33rd St., Brooklyn, N.Y. 11232

Sierra Supply Co., P.O. Box 596, McHenry, Ill. 60050

Standard Motor Products, Inc., 3718 Northern Blvd., Long Island City N.Y. 11101

United Motors Service Div., General Motors Corp., 3044 West Grand Blvd., Detroit, Mich. 48202

Cement, canvas

John Boyle and Co., Inc., 112–14 Duane St., New York, N.Y. 10007

Dolphin Paint and Chemical Co., 922 Locust St., P.O. Box 1927 Central Station, Toledo, O. 43603

Dow Canvas Products, Inc., 2705 Calumet Ave., Manitowoc, Wis. 54220

Gloucester Co., Inc., 235 Cottage St., Franklin, Mass. 02038

International Paint Co., Inc., 21 West St., New York, N.Y. 10006

H. B. Fred Kuhls, 49 Sumner St., Milford, Mass. 01757

Magic American Chemical Corp., 14215 Caine Ave., Cleveland, O. 44218

Miracle Adhesives Corp., 250 Pettit Ave., Bellmore, N.Y. 11710

Phillips Hardware Co., 490 N.W. S. River Dr., Corner N.W. 9th Ave. and 5th St., Miami, Fla. 33128

W. J. Ruscoe Co., 483 Kenmore Blvd., Akron, O. 44301

Schwartz Chemical Co., Inc., 50–01 2nd St., Long Island City N.Y. 11101

Smooth-On, Inc., 1000 Valley Rd., Stirling, N.J. 07933

Cement, epoxy

Allan Marine, 91 Industry Ct., Deer Park, N.Y. 11729

Baltimore Copper Paint Co., 501 Key Hwy., Baltimore, Md. 21230

Borden Chemical Div., Borden, Inc., 350 Madison Ave., New York, N.Y. 10017

Chrysler Corp., Chemical Div., 5437 W. Jefferson, Trenton, Mich. 48183

Dolphin Paint and Chemical Co., 922 Locust St., P.O. Box 1927 Central Station, Toledo, O. 43603

Engelhard Minerals and Chemicals Corp., Instruments and Systems Dep't., 850 Passaic Ave., East Newark, N.J. 07029

G. C. Electronics Co., 400 S. Wyman St., Rockford, Ill. 61101

Glass Plastics/Valspar Corp., Marine Div., 200 Sayre St., Rockford, Ill. 61101

Hysol Div., Dexter Corp., 1100 Seneca Ave., Olean, N.Y. 14760

Magic American Chemical Corp., 14215 Caine Ave., Cleveland, O. 44218

Marblette Corp., 37–31 30th St., Long Island City, N.Y. 11106

Metalcrete Mfg., Co., 2446 W. 25th St., Cleveland, O. 44113

Miracle Adhesives Corp., 250 Pettit Ave., Bellmore, N.Y. 11710

Pettit Paint Co., Inc., 507 Main St., Rockaway, N.J. 07866

Phillips Hardware Co., 490 N.W. S. River Dr., Corner N.W. 9th Ave. and 5th St., Miami, Fla. 33128

Plastic Sales and Mfg. Co., Inc., 3030 McGee Trafficway, Kansas City, Mo. 64129

Ram Chemicals, 219 E. Alronda Blvd., Gardena, Calif. 90247

Ren Plastics, Inc., 5656 S. Cedar, Lansing, Mich. 48909

W. J. Ruscoe Co., 483 Kenmore Blvd., Akron, O. 44301

Schwartz Chemical Co., Inc., 50–01 Second St., Long Island City, N.Y. 11101

Smooth-On, Inc., 1000 Valley Rd., Stirling, N.J. 07933

Tra-Con, Inc., Resin Systems Div., 55 North St., Medford, Mass. 02155

Cement, gasket

Chrysler Corp., Chemical Div., 5437 W. Jefferson, Trenton, Mich. 48183

H. B. Fred Kuhls, 49 Sumner St., Milford, Mass. 01757

Permatex Co., Inc., P.O. Box 1350, West Palm Beach, Fla. 33402

Phillips Hardware Co., 490 N.W. S. River Dr., Corner N.W. 9th Ave. and 5th St., Miami, Fla. 33128

J. C. Whitlam Mfg., Co., Box 71, Wadsworth, O. 44281

Woodhill Chemical Sales Corp., 18731 Cranwood Pkwy., Cleveland, O. 44128

Cement, linoleum

International Paint Co., Inc., 21 West St., New York, N.Y. 10006

H. B. Fred Kuhls, 49 Sumner St., Milford, Mass. 01757

Cement, plastic

Allan Marine, 91 Industry Ct., Deer Park, N.Y. 11729

Borden Chemical Div., Borden, Inc., 350 Madison Ave., New York, N.Y. 10017

H. B. Fred Kuhls, 49 Sumner St., Milford, Mass. 01757

Magic American Chemical Corp., 14215 Caine Ave., Cleveland, O. 44128

PPG Industries, Inc., Adhesive Products, 225 Belleville Ave., Bloomfield, N.J. 07003

Plastimayd Corp., 2204 S.E. 7th Ave., Portland, Ore. 97214

Smooth-On, Inc., 1000 Valley Rd., Stirling, N.J. 07933

Cement, rubber

Chrysler Corp., Chemical Div., 5437 W. Jefferson, Trenton, Mich. 48183

Dolphin Paint and Chemical Co., 922 Locust St., P.O. Box 1927 Central Station, Toledo, O. 43603

General Electric Co., Silicone Products Dept., Waterford, N.Y. 12188

Glass Plastics/Valspar Corp., Marine Div., 200 Sayre St., Rockford, Ill. 61101

Groenydk Mfg. Co., Inc., P.O. Box 278, Buchanan, Va. 24066

Hecht Rubber Corp., 482–84 Riverside Ave., Jacksonville, Fla. 32207

Intercoastal Corp., Dundalk P.O., Baltimore, Md. 21222

International Paint Co., Inc., 21 West St., New York, N.Y. 10006

H. B. Fred Kuhls, 49 Sumner St., Milford, Mass. 01757

Magic American Chemical Corp., 14215 Caine Ave., Cleveland, O. 44128

Permatex Co., Inc., P. O. Box 1350, West Palm Beach, Fla. 33402

Phillips Hardware Co., 490 N.W. S. River Dr., Corner N.W. 9th Ave. and 5th St., Miami, Fla. 33128

Schwartz Chemical Co., Inc., 50–01 Second St., Long Island City, 11101

Smooth-On, Inc., 1000 Valley Rd., Stirling, N.J. 07933

Stay-Tite Products Co., Inc., 2889 E. 83rd St., P.O. Box 20130, Cleveland, O. 44120

Wilhold Glues, Inc., 8707 Millergrove Dr., Santa Fe Springs, Calif. 90670

Chamois

American Sponge and Chamois Co., Inc., 47–00 34th St., Long Island City, N.Y. 11101

Garelick Mfg., Co., 644 2nd St., St. Paul Park, Minn. 55071

Gulf and West Indies Co., Inc., 141 Front St., New York, N.Y. 10005

Hoyt and Worthen Tanning Corp., Railroad St., Haverhill, Mass. 01830

Clamps, hose

Admiral Marine Products, 2003 W. 8-Mile Rd., Detroit, Mich. 48203

Aqua-Marine, Inc., 2445 Michigan Ave., Detroit, Mich. 48216

Corbin Cabinet Lock Div., Emhart Corp. 225 Episcopal Rd., Berlin, Conn. 06037

Hecht Rubber Corp., 482–84 Riverside Ave., Jacksonville, Fla. 32207

Kainer-Wesco Corp., 301 W. Alice St., Wheeling, Ill. 60090

Mirax Chemical Products Corp., Marine Products Div., 4999 Fyler Ave., St. Louis, Mo. 63139

Murray Corp., Schilling Circle, Cockeysville, Md. 21030

Oetiker, Inc., 71 Okner Pkwy., Livingston, N.J. 07039

Perkins Marine Lamp and Hdwe. Corp., 16490 N.W. 13th Ave., P.O. Box D, Miami, Fla. 33164

Phillips Hardware Co., 490 N.W. S. River Dr., Corner N.W. 9th Ave. and 5th St., Miami, Fla. 33128

Preferred Electric and Wire Corp., 68 33rd St., Brooklyn, N.Y. 11232

Richo Plastic Co., 5825 N. Tripp Ave., Chicago, Ill. 60646

Rule Industries, Inc., Cape Ann Industrial Park, Gloucester, Mass. 01930

Wilcox-Crittenden Div., Gulf and Western Co., Dept. 8, Middletown, Conn. 06457

Wittek Mfg. Co., 4326 W. 24th Pl., Chicago, Ill. 60623

Clamps, hose, quick-release

Breeze Corporations, Inc., 700 Liberty Ave., Union, N.J. 07083

Ideal Corp., 435 Liberty Ave., Brooklyn N.Y. 11207

Murray Corp., Schilling Circle, Cockeysville, Md. 21030

Cleaners, bilge

Allan Marine, 91 Industry Ct., Deer Park, N.Y. 11729

Beck Equipment and Chemical Co., 3350 W. 137th St., Cleveland, O. 44111

H. A. Calahan, Inc., 859 Mamaroneck Ave., Mamaroneck, N.Y. 10543

Captain Babbit's Locker, Inc., 110 W. 40th St., New York, N.Y. 10018

Custom Crest, Syracuse, Ind. 46567

Dakoline Chemical Co., Inc., 916 Pacific St., Brooklyn, N.Y. 11238

Fine Organics, Inc., 205 Main St., Lodi, N.J. 07644

Fuller Brush Co., Marine Div., East Hartford, Conn. 06108

Insco Chemical Corp., P.O. Drawer "J," Mountain View, Calif. 94111

International Paint Co., Inc., 21 West St., New York, N.Y. 10006

H. B. Fred Kuhls, 49 Sumner St., Milford, Mass. 01757

Lee Polish Mfg. Co., Inc., Lee Bldg., Brooklyn, N.Y. 11203

Lure Products, 2191 N.W. 26th Ave., Miami, Fla. 33142

Pad, Inc., 375 Park Ave., New York, N.Y. 10022

Pettit Paint Co., Inc., 507 Main St., Rockaway, N.J. 07866

Schaefer Chemical Products Co., 3000 Carrollton Rd., Saginaw, Mich. 48604

Solvit Marine Products Co., Div. Solvit Chemical Co., Inc., 7001 Raywood Rd., Madison, Wis. 53713

SPC, Inc., 2213 15th Ave. West, Seattle, Wash. 98119

Stay-Tite Products Co., Inc., 2889 E. 83rd St., P.O. Box 20130, Cleveland, O. 44120

Sudbury Laboratory, Dutton Rd., Sudbury, Mass. 01776

Travaco Laboratories, 345 Eastern Ave., Chelsea, Mass. 02150

Unival Corp., 157 Summerfield St., Scarsdale, N.Y. 10583

Woolsey Marine Industries, Inc., 201 E. 42nd St., New York, N.Y. 10017

Cleaners, bottom

H. A. Calahan, Inc., 859 Mamaroneck Ave., Mamaroneck, N.Y. 10543

H. B. Fred Kuhls, 49 Sumner St., Milford, Mass. 01757

Lan-O-Sheen, 1 W. Water St., St. Paul, Minn. 55107

Schaefer Chemical Products Co., 3000 Carrollton Rd., Saginaw, Mich. 48604

Solvit Marine Products Co., Div., Solvit Chemical Co., Inc., 7001 Raywood Rd., Madison, Wis. 53713

SPC, Inc., 2213 15th Ave. West, Seattle, Wash. 98119

Woolsey Marine Industries, Inc., 201 E. 42nd St., New York, N.Y. 10017

Cleaners, brush

Beck Equipment and Chemical Co., 3350 W. 137th St., Cleveland, O. 44111

Chemical Products Co., Inc., P.O. Box 111, Aberdeen, Md. 21001

International Paint Co., Inc., 21 West St., New York, N.Y. 10006

Jonard Industries Corp., 3047 Tibbett Ave., Bronx, N.Y. 10463

Pettit Paint Co., Inc., 507 Main St., Rockaway, N.J. 07866

Savogran Co., P.O. Box 130, Norwood, Mass. 02062

Sta-Lube, Inc., 3039 Ana St., Compton, Calif. 90221

Sterling Quality Products, Inc., 184 Commercial St., Malden, Mass. 02148

Cleaners, carburetor

Bardahl Mfg. Corp., 1400 N.W. 52nd St., Seattle, Wash. 98107

Bendix Automotive Service Div., 1217 S. Walnut St., South Bend, Ind. 46620

Bray Oil Co., 1925 N. Marianna St., Los Angeles, Calif. 90032

CRC Chemicals Div., C. J. Webb, Inc., Limekiln Pike, Dresher, Pa. 19025

Crosbie-Bamert, Inc., 1717 4th St., Berkeley, Calif. 94710

Dew-Coated Lubricants, P.O. Box 5755, Chicago, Ill. 60680

Gale Products Div., Outboard Marine Corp., Galesburg, Ill. 61401

Gumout Div., Pennsylvania Refining Co., 2686 Lisbon Rd., Cleveland, O. 44104

Kleer-Flo Co., Div. Practical Mfg. Co., 250 W. 57th St., New York, N.Y. 10019

Malco Products, Inc., 361 Fairview Ave., P.O. Box 892, Barberton, O. 44203

Micro-Lube, Inc., 8505 Directors Row, Dallas, Tex. 75247

R S A Products Co., 3450 Lovett St., Detroit, Mich. 48210

United Motors Service Div., General Motors Corp., 3044 West Grand Blvd., Detroit, Mich. 48202

Unival Corp., 157 Summerfield St., Scarsdale, N.Y. 10583

Cleaners, fabric

John Boyle and Co., Inc., 112–14 Duane St., New York, N.Y. 10007

Custom Crest, Syracuse, Ind. 46567

SPC, Inc., 2213 15th Ave. West, Seattle, Wash. 98119

Unival Corp., 157 Summerfield St., Scarsdale, N.Y. 10583

Cleaners, metal

Bendix Automative Service Div., 1217 S. Walnut St., South Bend, Ind. 46620

H. A. Calahan, Inc., 859 Mamaroneck Ave., Mamaroneck, N.Y. 10543

Chem-Plastics, Inc., 321 Boston Post Rd., Weston, Mass. 02193

Clayton Mfg. Co., 4213 N. Temple City Blvd., El Monte, Calif. 91731

CRC Chemicals Div., C. J. Webb, Inc., Limekiln Pike, Dresher, Pa. 19025

Crosbie-Bamert, Inc., 1717 4th St., Berkeley, Calif. 94710

Ditzler Automotive Finishes, PPG Industries, 8000 W. Chicago, Detroit, Mich. 48204

Kleer-Flo Co., Div., Practical Mfg. Co., 250 W. 57th St., New York, N.Y. 10019

Lee Polish Mfg. Co., Inc., Lee Bldg., Brooklyn, N.Y. 11203

Magnus Div., Economics Laboratory, Inc., Osborn Bldg., St. Paul, Minn. 55102

Metalcrete Mfg. Co., 2446 W. 25th., Cleveland, O. 44113

Nu Steel Co., 1714 S. Ashland Ave., Chicago, Ill. 60608

Phillips Mfg. Co., 7334 N. Clark St., Chicago, Ill. 60626

Polishes Imported, Ltd., 41 Elm Pl., P.O. Box 35, Rye, N.Y. 10580

Schaefer Chemical Products Co., 3000 Carrollton Rd., Saginaw, Mich. 48604

SPC, Inc., 2213 15th Ave. West, Seattle, Wash. 98119

Unival Corp., 157 Summerfield St., Scarsdale, N.Y. 10583

Woolsey Marine Industries, Inc., 201 E. 42nd St., New York, N.Y. 10017

Cleaners, paint and varnish

International Paint Co., Inc., 21 West St., New York, N.Y. 10006

Lan-O-Sheen, 1 W. Water St., St. Paul, Minn. 55107

Lee Polish Mfg. Co., Inc., Lee Bldg., Brooklyn, N.Y. 11203

Lure Products, 2191 N.W. 26th Ave., Miami, Fla. 33142

Metalcrete Mfg. Co., 2446 W. 25th St., Cleveland, O. 44113

Savogran Co., P.O. Box 30 Norwood, Mass. 02062

Schaefer Chemical Products Co., 3000 Carrollton Rd., Saginaw, Mich. 48604

SPC, Inc., 2213 15th Ave. West, Seattle, Wash. 98119

Texize Chemicals, Inc., P.O. Box 368, Greenville, S.C. 29601

Woolsey Marine Industries Inc., 201 E. 42nd St., New York, N.Y. 10017

Cleaners, teak

Byrne Plywood Co., 2400 Cole St., Birmingham, Mich. 48008

International Paint Co., 21 West St., New York, N.Y. 10006

H. B. Fred Kuhls, 49 Sumner St., Milford, Mass. 01757

Lan-O-Sheen, 1 W. Water St., St. Paul, Minn. 55107

Lure Products, 2191 N.W. 26th Ave., Miami, Fla. 33142

Nautical Mfg. and Sales Co., Box 292, Bay Head, N.J. 08742

Ransberger's, 406 W. Madison St., South Bend, Ind. 46601

Woolsey Marine Industries, Inc., 201 E. 42nd St., New York, N.Y. 10017

Cleaners and polishes, chromium

Custom Crest, Syracuse, Ind. 46567

Fuller Brush Co., Marine Div., East Hartford, Conn. 06108

Malco Products, Inc., 361 Fairview Ave., P.O. Box 892, Barberton, O. 44203

Nu Steel Co., 1714 S. Ashland Ave., Chicago, Ill. 60608

Schwartz Chemical Co., Inc., 50–01 Second St., Long Island City, N.Y. 11101

SPC, Inc., 2213 15th Ave. West, Seattle, Wash. 98119

Woodhill Chemical Sales Corp., 18731 Cranwood Pkwy., Cleveland, O. 44128

Cleaners and polishes, fiberglass

Captain Babbit's Locker, Inc., 110 W. 40th St., New York, N.Y. 10018

Custom Crest, Syracuse, Ind. 46567

Fuller Brush Co., Marine Div., East Hartford, Conn. 06108

Johnson Wax, 1525 Howe St., Racine, Wis. 53403

Kristal Kraft, Inc., 900 4th Ave., Palmetto, Fla. 33561

Lan-O-Sheen, 1 W. Water St., St. Paul, Minn. 55107

Lee Polish Mfg. Co., Inc., Lee Bldg., Brooklyn, N.Y. 11203

Livingston Co., 8609 N.W. Plaza Dr., Dallas, Tex. 75225

Micro-Lube, Inc., 8505 Directors Row, Dallas, Tex. 75247

Ram Chemicals, 210 E. Alronda Blvd., Gardena, Calif. 90247

RSA Products Co., 3450 Lovett St., Detroit, Mich. 48210

SPC, Inc., 2213 15th Ave. West, Seattle, Wash. 98119

N. A. Taylor Co., Inc., Gloversville, N.Y. 12078

Woolsey Marine Industries, Inc., 201 E. 42nd St., New York, N.Y. 10017

Cleaners and polishes, metal

Byrne Plywood Co., 2400 Cole St., Birmingham, Mich. 48008

Custom Crest, Syracuse, Ind. 46567

Fuller Brush Co., Marine Div., East Hartford, Conn. 06108

Garelick Mfg. Co., 644 2nd St., St. Paul Park, Minn. 55071

Johnson Wax, Service Products Div., 1525 Howe St., Racine, Wis. 53403

Lee Polish Mfg. Co., Inc., Lee Bldg., Brooklyn, N.Y. 11203

Malco Products, Inc., 361 Fairview Ave., P.O. Box 892, Barberton, O. 44203

Marine Development and Research Corp., 381 Park Ave. S., New York, N.Y. 10016

Nu Steel Co., 1714 S. Ashland Ave., Chicago, Ill. 60608

RSA Products Co., 3450 Lovett St., Detroit, Mich. 48210

SPC, Inc., 2213 15th Ave. West, Seattle, Wash. 98119

Cleaners and polishes, plastic

Dakoline Chemical Co., Inc., 916 Pacific St., Brooklyn, N.Y. 11238

Johnson Wax, Service Products Div., 1525 Howe St., Racine, Wis. 53403

Lee Polish Mfg. Co., Inc., Lee Bldg., Brooklyn, N.Y. 11203

Malco Products, Inc., 361 Fairview Ave., P.O. Box 892, Barberton, O. 44203

SPC, Inc., 2213 15th Ave. West, Seattle, Wash. 98119

N. A. Taylor Co., Inc., Gloversville, N.Y. 12078

Cleaners and polishes, vinyl

Johnson Wax, Service Products Div., 1525 Howe St., Racine, Wis. 53403

H. B. Fred Kuhls, 49 Sumner St., Milford, Mass. 01757

Lee Polish Mfg. Co., Inc., Lee Bldg., Brooklyn, N.Y. 11203

SPC, Inc., 2213 15th Ave. West, Seattle, Wash. 98119

N. A. Taylor, Co., Inc., Gloversville, N.Y. 12078

Woolsey Marine Industries, Inc., 201 E. 42nd St., New York, N.Y. 10017

Cleaners and polishes, windshield

Fuller Brush Co., Marine Div., East Hartford, Conn. 06108

Johnson Wax, Service Products Div., 1525 Howe St., Racine, Wis. 53403

Lee Polish Mfg. Co., Inc., Lee Bldg., Brooklyn, N.Y. 11203

Malco Products, Inc., 361 Fairview Ave., P.O. Box 892, Barberton, O. 44203

Schwartz Chemical Co., Inc., 50–01 2nd St., Long Island City, N.Y. 11101

N. A. Taylor Co., Inc., Gloversville, N.Y. 12078

Woolsey Marine Industries, 201 E. 42nd St., New York, N.Y. 10017

Coatings, corrosion-resistant

American Petrochemical Corp., 3134 California St. N.W., Minneapolis, Minn. 55418

BoatLIFE Div., Flo-Paint, Inc., 5–45 49th Ave., Long Island City, N.Y. 11101

Andrew Brown Co., 5431 District Blvd., P.O. Box 22066, Los Angeles, Calif. 90022

Samuel Cabot, Inc., 246 Sumner St., Boston, Mass. 02128

H. A. Calahan, Inc., 859 Mamaroneck Ave., Mamaroneck, N.Y. 10543

Philip Carey Corp., 320 W. Wayne St., Cincinnati, O. 45215

Coopers Creek Chemical Corp., 28 River Ave., West Conshohocken, Pa. 19428

Coricone Corp., 3605 Long Beach Blvd., Long Beach, Calif. 90807

CRC Chemicals Div., C. J. Webb, Inc., Limekiln Pike, Dresher, Pa. 19025

Dolphin Paint and Chemical Co., 922 Locust St., P.O. Box 1927 Central Station, Toledo, O. 43803

General Electric Co., Silicone Products Dept., Waterford, N.Y. 12188

Hecht Rubber Corp., 482–84 Riverside Ave., Jacksonville, Fla. 32207

Mercury Marine, Fond du Lac, Wis. 54935

LPS Research Labs, Inc., 2050 Cotner Ave., W. Los Angeles, Calif. 90025

M and T Chemicals, Inc., Rahway, N.J. 07065

Maas and Waldstein Co., 2121 McCarter Hwy., Newark, N.J. 07104

Marblette Corp., 37–31 30th St., Long Island City, N.Y. 11106

Metalcrete Mfg. Co., 2446 W. 25th St., Cleveland, O. 44113

Pettit Paint Co., Inc., 507 Main St., Rockaway, N.J. 07866

Presto Chemical, Inc., 9346 Glenoaks Blvd., Sun Valley, Calif. 91352

Profile Plastic Coatings, Inc., 3024 Rosslyn St., Los Angeles, Calif. 90065

SPC, Inc., 2213 15th Ave. West, Seattle, Wash. 98119

Travaco Laboratories, 345 Eastern Ave., Chelsea, Mass. 02150

Unival Corp., 157 Summerfield St., Scarsdale, N.Y. 10583

West Chester Chemical Co., 439 S. Belmar St., West Chester, Pa. 19380

Wisconsin Protective Coating Corp., Box 3396, Green Bay, Wis. 54303

Woolsey Marine Industries, Inc., 201 E. 42nd St., New York, N.Y. 10017

Coatings, fire retardant

Champion Products, Inc., 4939 S. Austin Ave., Chicago, Ill. 60638

Maas and Waldstein Co., 2121 McCarter Hwy., Newark, N.J. 07104

Benjamin Moore and Co., 548 Fifth Ave., New York, N.Y. 10036

Tenneco Advanced Materials, Inc., 300 Needham St., Newton, Mass. 02164

Coatings, plastic

Aero Marine Div., Aeroceanic Corp., 6737 E. Washington Blvd., El Monte, Calif. 91731

Atlas Minerals and Chemicals Div., ESB, Inc., Mertztown, Pa. 19539

Carlon Prods. Co., 1 New Haven Ave., Derby, Conn. 06418

Corlon Products, Mfg., 1711 Floradale St., El Monte, Calif. 91733

Craft Plastics Corp., P.O. Box 33, Parcel Post Station, Worcester, Mass. 01604

Falcon Safety Products, Inc., 1137 Rt. 22, Mountainside, N.J. 07092

Goodall Vinyl Fabrics Div., Burlington, Inc., 846-H Merchandise Mart, Chicago, Ill. 60654

Hastings Plastics, Inc., 1704 Colorado Ave., Santa Monica, Calif. 90404

Herculite Protective Fabrics Corp., 1107 Broadway, New York, N.Y. 10010

Interplastics Corp., Commercial Resins Div., 2015 N.W. Broadway, Minneapolis, Minn. 55413

Kristal Kraft, Inc., 900 4th St., Palmetto, Fla. 33561

Maas and Waldstein Co., 2121 McCarter Hwy., Newark, N.J. 07104

Marblette Corp., 37–31 30th St., Long Island City, N.Y. 11106

Marine Development and Research Corp., 381 Park Ave. South, New York, N.Y. 10016

Plastic Sales and Mfg. Co., Inc., 3030 McGee Trafficway, Kansas City, Mo. 64129

Presto Chemicals, Inc., 9346 Glenoaks Blvd., Sun Valley, Calif. 91352

Profile Plastic Coatings, Inc., 3024 Rosslyn St., Los Angeles, Calif. 90065

Resin Coatings Corp., 3595 N.W. 74th St., Miami, Fla. 33147

Schwartz Chemical Co., Inc., 50–01 2nd St., Long Island City, N.Y. 11101

SPC Inc., 2213 15th Ave. West, Seattle, Wash. 98119

Sav-Cote Chemical Laboratories, 20 S. Dove St., P.O. Box 2128 Potomac Station, Alexandria, Va. 22301

W. S. Shamban and Co., 11543 West Olympic Blvd., Los Angeles, Calif. 90064

Tenneco Advanced Materials, Inc., 300 Needham St., Newton, Mass. 02164

Wisconsin Protective Metal Coating Corp., Box 3396, Green Bay, Wis. 54303

Woolsey Marine Industries, Inc., 201 E. 42nd St., New York, N.Y. 10017

Coating, protective, metal

Allube Div., Far-Best Corp., 928 Allen Ave., Glendale, Calif. 91201

American Petrochemical Corp., 3134 Caliornia St., N.E., Minneapolis, Minn. 55418

Bray Oil Co., 1925 N. Marianna St., Los Angeles, Calif. 90032

Andrew Brown Co., 5431 District Blvd. P.O. Box 22066, Los Angeles, Calif. 90022

Samuel Cabot, Inc., 246 Sumner St., Boston, Mass. 02128

H. A. Calahan, Inc., 859 Mamaroneck Ave., Mamaroneck, N.Y. 10543

Canadian Pittsburgh Industries, Ltd., 3730 Lakeshore Blvd. West, Long Branch, Ont., Canada

Chrysler Corp., Chemical Div., 5437 W. Jefferson, Trenton, Mich. 48143

Coopers Creek Chemical Corp., 28 River Ave., West Conshohocken, Pa. 19428

Coricone Corp., 3605 Long Beach Blvd., Long Beach, Calif. 90807

CRC Chemicals Div., C. J. Webb, Inc., Limekiln Pike, Dresher, Pa. 19025

Dolphin Paint and Chemical Co., 922 Locust St., P.O. Box 1927 Central Station, Toledo, O. 43603

General Electric Co., Silicone Products Dept., Waterford, N.Y. 12188

Glass Plastics/Valspar Corp., Marine Div., 200 Sayre St., Rockford, Ill. 61101

Johnson Wax, Service Products Div., 1525 Howe St., Racine, Wis. 53403

Kristal Kraft Inc., 900 4th St., Palmetto, Fla. 33561

LPS Research Labs, Inc., 2050 Cotner Ave., West Los Angeles, Calif. 90025

Maas and Waldstein Co., 2121 McCarter Hwy., Newark, N.J. 07104

Marine Development and Research Corp., 381 Park Ave. South, New York, N.Y. 10016

Minnesota Mining and Mfg. Co., 3M
Center, St. Paul, Minn. 55101

Benjamin Moore and Co., 548 Fifth
Ave., New York, N.Y. 10036

Pettit Paint Co., Inc., 507 Main St.,
Rockaway, N.J. 07866

Phillips Mfg. Co., 7334 N. Clark St.,
Chicago, Ill. 60626

Presto Chemicals, Inc., 9346 Glenoaks
Blvd., Sun Valley, Calif. 91352

Profile Plastic Coatings, Inc., 3024
Rosslyn St., Los Angeles, Calif.
90065

SPC, Inc., 2213 15th Ave. West, Seattle, Wash. 98119

Speco, Inc., 7308 Associate Ave.,
Cleveland, O. 44109

Structural Concepts, 15120 Keswick
St., Van Nuys, Calif. 91405

Travaco Laboratories, 345 Eastern
Ave., Chelsea, Mass. 02150

Unival Corp., 157 Summerfield St.,
Scarsdale, N.Y. 10583

Valvoline Oil Co. Div., Ashland Oil
and Refining Co., 1409 Winchester
Ave., Ashland, Ky. 41101

White and Bagley Co., P.O. Box 1171,
100 Foster St., Worchester, Mass.
01601

Woolsey Marine Industries, Inc., 201
E. 42nd St., New York, N.Y. 10017

Coatings, protective, wood

Allan Marine, 91 Industry Ct., Deer
Park, N.Y. 11729

BoatLIFE Div., Flo-Paint, Inc., 5–45
49th Ave., Long Island City, N.Y.
11101

Andrew Brown Co., 5431 District
Blvd., P.O. Box 22066, Los Angeles, Calif. 90022

H. A. Calahan, Inc., 859 Mamaroneck,
Ave., Mamaroneck, N.Y. 10543

Canadian Pittsburgh Industries, Ltd.,
3730 Lakeshore Blvd. West, Long
Branch, Ont., Canada

Chemiseal Co., 353 N. Western Ave.,
Chicago, Ill. 60612

Dolphin Paint and Chemical Co., 922
Locust St., P.O. Box 1927 Central
Station, Toledo, O. 43603

Glass Plastics/Valspar Corp., Marine
Div., 200 Sayre St., Rockford, Ill.
61101

International Paint Co., Inc., 21 West
St., New York, N.Y. 10006

Interplastics Corp., Commercial
Resins Div., 2015 N.E. Broadway,
Minneapolis, Minn. 55413

Kristal Kraft, Inc., 900 4th Ave., Palmetto, Fla. 33561

M and T Chemicals, Inc., Rahway,
N.J. 07065

Marblette Corp., 37–31 30th St.,
Long Island City, N.Y. 11106

Benjamin Moore and Co., 548 Fifth
Ave., New York, N.Y. 10036

Pettit Paint Co., Inc., 507 Main St.,
Rockaway, N.J. 07866

Presto Chemicals, Inc., 9346 Glenoaks
Blvd., Sun Valley, Calif. 91352

SPC, Inc., 2213 15th Ave. West, Seattle, Wash. 98119

Structural Concepts, 15120 Keswick
St., Van Nuys, Calif. 91405

Travaco Laboratories, 345 Eastern
Ave., Chelsea, Mass. 02150

Watco Dennis Corp., 1756 22nd St.,
Santa Monica, Calif. 90404

Woolsey Marine Industries, Inc., 201
E. 42nd St., New York, N.Y. 10017

Coils, ignition

Bendix Automative Service Div., 1217
S. Walnut St., South Bend, Ind.
46620

Guaranteed Parts Co., Inc., Auburn
Rd., Seneca Falls, N.Y. 13148

Marine Electric Supply Co., Inc., Box 206, West Branch, Mich. 48661

C. E. Niehoff and Co., 4925 Lawrence Ave., Chicago, Ill. 60630

R. E. Phelon Co., Inc., 70 Maple St., East Longmeadow, Mass. 01028

Prestolite Co., 511 Hamilton St., Toledo, O. 43601

Sierra Supply Co., P.O. Box 596, McHenry, Ill. 60050

Tungsten Contact Mfg. Co., Inc., 7311 Cottage Ave., North Bergen, N.J. 07040

Coils, ignition-resistor

Bendix Automotive Service Div., 1217 S. Walnut St., South Bend, Ind. 46620

Cole-Hersee Co., 20 Old Colony Ave., Boston, Mass. 02127

Preferred Electric and Wire Corp., 68 33rd St., Brooklyn, N.Y. 11232

Coils, ignition, waterproof

Standard Motor Products, Inc., 37–18 Northern Blvd., Long Island City, N.Y. 11101

Tungsten Contact Mfg. Co., Inc., 7311 Cottage Ave., North Bergen, N.J. 07040

Collars, electrolysis

Bunker Hill Co., Pacific Div., 2700 16th Ave., S.W., Seattle, Wash. 98134

Perkins Marine Lamp and Hardware Corp., 16490 N.W. 13th Ave., P.O. Box D, Miami, Fla. 33164

Wilcox-Crittenden Div., Gulf and Western Co., Dept. 8, Middletown, Conn. 06457

Compass correctors

Aqua Meter Instrument Corp. Div., Ketcham and McDougall, Inc., 465 Eagle Rock Ave., Roseland, N.J. 07068

Davis Instruments Corp., 857 Thornton St., San Leandro, Calif. 94677

H. G. Dietz Products Co., 14–26 28th Ave., Long Island City, N.Y. 11102

Shang's, 223 Walter Ct., Box 504, Elgin, Ill. 60120

Compounds, antifouling

BoatLIFE Div., Flo-Paint, Inc., 5–45 49th Ave., Long Island City, N.Y. 11101

Dolphin Paint and Chemical Co., 922 Locust St., P.O. Box 1927 Central Station, Toledo, O. 43603

International Paint Co., Inc., 21 West St., New York, N.Y. 10006

M and T Chemicals, Inc., Rahway, N.J. 07065

Pettit Paint Co., Inc., 507 Main St., Rockaway, N.J. 07866

Woolsey Marine Industries, Inc., 201 E. 42nd St., New York, N.Y. 10017

Compounds, bedding

Baltimore Copper Paint Co., 501 Key Hwy., Baltimore, Md. 21230

Dolphin Paint and Chemical Co., 922 Locust St., P.O. Box 1927 Central Station, Toledo, O. 43603

General Electric Co., Wiring Device Dept., 95 Hathaway St., Providence, R.I. 02904

Gloucester Co., Inc., 235 Cottage St., Franklin, Mass. 02038

Intercoastal Corp., Dundalk P.O., Baltimore, Md. 21222

International Paint Co., Inc., 21 West St., New York, N.Y. 10006

Miracle Adhesives Corp., 250 Pettit Ave., Bellmore, N.Y. 11710

Pettit Paint Co., Inc., 507 Main St., Rockaway, N.J. 07866

Thiokol Chemical Corp., 780 N. Clinton Ave., Trenton, N.J. 08607

Valspar Corp., Marine Div., 200 Sayre St., Rockford, Ill. 61101

Woolsey Marine Industries, Inc., 201 E. 42nd St., New York, N.Y. 10017

Compounds, cleaning

Clayton Mfg. Co., 4213 N. Temple City Blvd., El Monte, Calif. 91731

CRC Chemicals Div., C. J. Webb, Inc., Limekiln Pike, Dresher, Pa. 19025

Fine Organics, Inc., 205 Main St., Lodi, N.J. 07644

Kleer-Flo Co., Div., Practical Mfg. Co., 250 W. 57th St., New York, N.Y. 10019

Magnus Div., Economics Laboratory, Inc., Osborn Bldg., St. Paul, Minn. 55102

Malco Products, Inc., 361 Fairview Ave., P.O. Box 892, Barberton, O. 44203

Micro-Lube, Inc., 8505 Directors Row, Dallas, Tex. 75247

Savogran Co., P.O. Box 58, Norwood, Mass. 02062

Solvit Marine Products Co., Div., Solvit Chemical Co., Inc., 7001 Raywood Rd., Madison, Wis. 53713

SPC, Inc., 2213 15th Ave. West, Seattle, Wash. 98119

Texize Chemicals, Inc., P.O. Box 368, Greenville, S.C. 29601

Unival Corp., 157 Summerfield St., Scarsdale, N.Y. 10583

Valspar Corp., Marine Div., 200 Sayre St., Rockford, Ill. 61101

Weaver Div., Walter Kidde and Co., Inc., 2171 S. 9th St., Springfield, Ill. 62703

Woolsey Marine Industries, Inc., 201 E. 42nd St., New York, N.Y. 10017

Compounds, cooling system, flushing

Bardahl Mfg. Corp., 1400 N.W. 52nd St., Seattle, Wash. 98103

Malco Products, Inc., 361 Fairview Ave., P.O. Box 892, Barberton, O. 44203

Oil Center Research, 211 Rayburn, Lafayette, La. 70501

Compounds, deck and seam-filling

Baltimore Copper Paint Co., 501 Key Hwy., Baltimore, Md. 21230

BoatLIFE Div., Flo-Paint, Inc., 5–45 49th Ave., Long Island City, N.Y. 11101

H. A. Calahan, Inc., 859 Mamaroneck Ave., Mamaroneck, N.Y. 10543

Darworth, Inc., Chemical Products Div., Simsbury, Conn. 06070

Dolphin Paint and Chemical Co., 922 Locust St., Box 1927 Central Station, Toledo, O. 43603

Gloucester Co., Inc., 235 Cottage St., Franklin, Mass. 02038

Intercoastal Corp., Dundalk P.O., Baltimore, Md. 21222

International Paint Co., Inc., 21 West St., New York, N.Y. 10006

Miracle Adhesives Corp., 250 Pettit Ave., Bellmore, N.Y. 11710

Mutual Hardware Corp., 5–45 49th Ave., Long Island City, N.Y. 11101

Pettit Paint Co., Inc., 507 Main St., Rockaway, N.J. 07866

Phillips Hardware Co., 490 N.W. S. River Dr., Corner N.W. 9th Ave. and 5th St., Miami, Fla. 33128

Thiokol Chemical Corp., 780 N. Clinton Ave., Trenton, N.J. 08607

U. S. Yacht Paint Co., Box 525, Roseland, N.J. 07068

Valspar Corp., Marine Div., 200 Sayre St., Rockford, Ill. 61101

Woolsey Marine Industries, Inc., 201 E. 42nd St., New York, N.Y. 10017

Phillips Mfg. Co., 7334 N. Clark St., Chicago, Ill. 60626

RSA Products Co., 3450 Lovett St., Detroit, Mich. 48210

Texize Chemicals, Inc., P.O. Box 368, Greenville, S.C. 29601

Unival Corp., 157 Summerfield St., Scarsdale, N.Y. 10583

Woodhill Chemical Sales Corp., 18731 Cranwood Pkwy., Cleveland, O. 44128

Compounds, degreasing

Beck Equipment and Chemical Co., 3340 W. 137th St., Cleveland, O. 44111

Bendix Corp., Automotive Service Div., 1217 S. Walnut St., South Bend, Ind. 46620

Clayton Mfg. Co., 4213 N. Temple City Blvd., El Monte, Calif. 91731

CRC Chemicals Div., C. J. Webb, Inc., Limekiln Pike, Dresher, Pa. 19025

Crosbie-Bamert, Inc., 1717 4th St., Berkeley, Calif. 94710

Fine Organics, Inc., 205 Main St., Lodi, N.J. 07644

Gumout Div., Pennsylvania Refining Co., 2686 Lisbon Rd., Cleveland, O. 44104

Kleer-Flo Co., Div. Practical Mfg. Co., 250 W. 57th St., New York, N.Y. 10019

Lee Polish Mfg. Co., Lee Bldg., Brooklyn, N.Y. 11203

Magnus Div., Economics Laboratory, Inc., Osborn Bldg., St. Paul, Minn. 55102

Malco Products, Inc., 361 Fairview Ave., P.O. Box 892, Barberton, O. 44203

Micro-Lube, Inc., 8505 Directors Row, Dallas, Tex. 75247

Compounds, disinfecting and deodorizing

John Clarke and Company, Inc., 420 Lexington Ave., New York, N.Y. 10017

Fine Organics, Inc., 205 Main St., Lodi, N.J. 07644

Lan-O-Sheen, Inc., 1 W. Water St., St. Paul, Minn. 55107

Landy Associates, 349 Fifth Ave., New York, N.Y. 10016

Oh Dear Laboratories, Inc., 661 Western Ave. N., St. Paul, Minn. 55103

Sea-Lawn Products Co., 365 E. Park Ave., Long Beach, N.Y. 11561

Compounds, double-planking

Dolphin Paint and Chemical Co., 922 Locust St., Box 1927 Central Station, Toledo, O. 43603

Gloucester Co., Inc., 235 Cottage St., Franklin, Mass. 02038

Intercoastal Corp., Dundalk P.O., Baltimore, Md. 21222

International Paint Co., Inc., 21 West St., New York, N.Y. 10006

Minnesota Mining and Mfg. Co., 3M Center, St. Paul, Minn. 55101

Mutual Hardware Corp., 5–45 49th Ave., Long Island City, N.Y. 11101

Thiokol Chemical Corp., 780 N. Clinton Ave., Trenton, N.J. 08607

Compounds, engine, flushing

Bardahl Mfg. Corp., 1400 N.W. 52nd St., Seattle, Wash. 98107

Compounds, epoxy

BoatLIFE Div., Flo-Paint, Inc., 5–45 49th Ave., Long Island City, N.Y. 11101

Chrysler Corp., Chemical Div., 5437 W. Jefferson, Trenton, Mich. 48143

Conap, Inc., 184 E. Union St., Allegany, N.Y. 14706

Craft Plastics Corp., P.O. Box 33, Parcel Post Station, Worcester, Mass. 01604

Dolphin Paint and Chemical Co., 922 Locust St., P.O. Box 1927 Central Station, Toledo, O. 43603

Kristal Kraft, Inc., 900 4th St., Palmetto, Fla. 33561

Link Marine and Plyfoam, Inc., Vanderbilt Industrial Pkwy., Hauppauge, N.Y. 11787

Metalcrete Mfg. Co., 2446 W. 25th St., Cleveland, O. 44113

Minnesota Mining and Mfg. Co., 3M Center, St. Paul, Minn. 55101

Pettit Paint Co., Inc., 507 Main St., Rockaway, N.J. 07866

Ren Plastics, Inc., 5656 S. Cedar, Lansing, Mich. 48909

Smooth-On, Inc., 100 Valley Rd., Stirling, N.J. 07933

Valspar Corp., Marine Div., 200 Sayre St., Rockford, Ill. 61101

Woodhill Chemical Sales Corp., 18731 Cranwood Pkwy., Cleveland, O. 44128

X-Pando Corp., 43–15 36th St., Long Island City, N.Y. 11100

White and Bagley Co., P.O. Box 1171, 100 Foster St., Worcester, Mass. 01601

Compounds, grinding

White and Bagley Co., P.O. Box 1171, 100 Foster St., Worcester, Mass. 01601

Compounds, lapping

Mistic Metal Mover, Inc., 19 E. Peru, Princeton, Ill. 61356

Thiokol Chemical Corp., 780 N. Clinton Ave., Trenton, N.J. 08607

Compounds, mildew-proofing

Andrew Brown Co., 5431 District Blvd., P.O. Box 22066, Los Angeles, Calif. 90022

John Clarke and Co., Inc., 420 Lexington Ave., New York, N.Y. 10017

International Paint Co., Inc., 21 West St., New York, N.Y. 10006

Lan-O-Sheen, Inc., 1 W. Water St., St. Paul, Minn. 55107

M and T Chemicals, Inc., Rahway, N.J. 07065

Marine Development and Research Corp., 381 Park Ave. South, New York, N.Y. 10016

Pettit Paint Co., Inc., 507 Main St., Rockaway, N.J. 07866

Compounds, nonskid

Dolphin Paint and Chemical Co., 922 Locust St., P.O. Box 1927 Central Station, Toledo, O. 43603

International Paint Co., Inc., 21 West St., New York, N.Y. 10006

Miracle Adhesives Corp., 250 Pettit Ave., Bellmore, N.Y. 11710

Pettit Paint Co., Inc., 507 Main St., Rockaway, N.J. 07866

Valspar Corp., Marine Div., 200 Sayre St., Rockford, Ill. 61101

Woolsey Marine Industries, 201 E. 42nd St., New York, N.Y. 10017

Wooster Products Inc., Spruce St., Wooster, O. 44691

Compounds, plastic putty

Beverly Mfg. Co., 9118 S. Main St., Los Angeles, Calif. 90003

Clausen Co., 1055 King George Rd., Fords, N.J. 08863

Craft Plastics Corp., P.O. Box 33, Parcel Post St., Worcester, Mass. 01604

DAP, Inc., 5300 Huberville Ave., Dayton, O. 45431

Dolphin Paint and Chemical Co., 922 Locust St., P.O. Box 1927 Central Station, Toledo, O. 43603

Harbor Sales Co., Inc., 1401 Russell St., Baltimore, Md. 21230

Hysol Div., Dexter Corp., 1100 Seneca Ave., Olean, N.Y. 14760

International Paint Co., Inc., 21 West St., New York, N.Y. 10006

Kristal Kraft, Inc., 900 Fourth Ave., Palmetto, Fla. 33561

Marblette Corp., 37–31 30th St., Long Island City, N.Y. 11106

D. J. Peterson Company, Inc., P.O. Box 955, Sheboygan, Wis. 53081

Pettit Paint Co., Inc., 507 Main St., Rockaway, N.J. 07866

Ren Plastics, Inc., 5656 S. Cedar, Lansing, Mich. 48909

Valspar Corp., Marine Div., 200 Sayre St., Rockford, Ill. 61101

Unican Plastics Co., 915 Hartford Pike, Shrewsbury, Mass. 01545

Wacanda Marine, Inc., Box 122, Colrille, Wash. 99114

Compounds, plastic-surfacing

DAP, Inc., 5300 Huberville Ave., Dayton, O. 45431

Marblette Corp., 37–31 30th St., Long Island City, N.Y. 11106

Pettit Paint Co., Inc., 507 Main St., Rockaway, N.J. 07866

Ren Plastics, Inc., 5656 S. Cedar, Lansing, Mich. 48909

Structural Concepts, 15120 Keswick St., Van Nuys, Calif. 91405

Valspar Corp., Marine Div., 200 Sayre St., Rockford, Ill. 61101

Wacanda Marine, Inc., Box 122, Colrille, Wash. 99114

Ward International, Inc., P.O. Box 1377, Studio City, Calif. 91604

Compounds, polyester

Clausen Co., 1055 King George Rd., Fords, N.J. 08863

Craft Plastics Corp., P.O. Box 33, Parcel Post Station, Worcester, Mass. 01604

DAP, Inc., 5300 Huberville Ave., Dayton, O. 45431

Glas-Mate Div., Ransburg Electro-Coating Corp., 2959 N.W. 12th Terrace, Fort Lauderdale, Fla. 33307

Interplastics Corp., Commercial Resins Div., 2015 N.W. Broadway, Minneapolis, Minn. 55413

Kristal Kraft, Inc., 900 4th St., Palmetto, Fla. 33561

Link Marine and Plyfoam, Inc., Vanderbilt Industrial Pkwy., Hauppauge, N.Y. 11787

Magic American Chemical Corp.,
14215 Caine Ave., Cleveland, O.
44128

Plastic Sales and Mfg. Co., Inc., 3030
McGee Trafficway, Kansas City,
Mo. 64129

PPG Industries, Inc., Plastic Sales,
Bldg. 1, Gateway Center, Pittsburgh, Pa. 15222

Presto Chemicals, Inc., 9346 Glenoaks
Blvd., Sun Valley, Calif. 91352

Ram Chemicals, 210 E. Alronda
Blvd., Gardena, Calif. 90247

Structural Concepts, 15120 Keswick
St., Van Nuys, Calif. 91405

Unican Plastics Co., 915 Hartford
Pike Shrewsbury, Mass. 01545

Valspar Corp., Marine Div., 200
Sayre St., Rockford, Ill. 61101

Wacanda Marine, Inc., Box 122,
Colrille, Wash. 99114

Woodhill Chemical Sales Corp., 18731
Cranwood Pkwy., Cleveland, O.
44128

Compounds, polyurethane

BoatLIFE Div., Flo-Paint, Inc., 5–45
49th Ave., Long Island City, N.Y.
11101

Freeman Chemical Corp., 222 Main
St., Port Washington, Wis. 53074

Interplastics Corp., Commercial
Resins Div., 2015 N.W. Broadway,
Minneapolis, Minn. 55413

Mutual Hardware Corp., 5–45 49th
Ave., Long Island City, N.Y. 11101

PPG Industries, Inc., Plastic Sales,
Bldg. 1, Gateway Center, Pittsburgh, Pa. 15222

Valspar Corp., Marine Div., 200
Sayre St., Rockford, Ill. 61101

Compounds, rustproofing

Samuel Cabot, Inc., 246 Sumner St.,
Boston, Mass. 02128

CRC Chemicals Div., C. J. Webb,
Inc., Limekiln Pike, Dresher, Pa.
19025

Dolphin Paint and Chemical Co., 922
Locust St., P.O. Box 1927 Central
Station, Toledo, O. 43603

Dow Corning Corp., Consumer Products Div., P.O. Box 592, Midland,
Mich. 48640

Gumout Div., Pennsylvania Refining
Co., 2686 Lisbon Rd., Cleveland,
O. 44104

Johnson Wax, Service Products Div.,
1525 Howe St., Racine, Wis. 53403

H. B. Fred Kuhls, 49 Sumner St.,
Milford, Mass. 01757

LPS Research Laboratories, Inc.,
2050 Cotner Ave., West Los Angeles, Calif. 90025

Magnus Div., Economics Laboratory,
Inc., Osborn Bldg., St. Paul, Minn.
55102

Oil Center Research, 211 Rayburn,
Lafayette, La. 70501

Rust Lick Inc., 755 Boylston St., Boston, Mass. 02116

Rusticide Products Co., 3125 Perkins
Ave., Cleveland, O. 44114

Shell Oil Co., 50 W. 50th St., New
York, N.Y. 10020

SPC, Inc., 2213 15th Ave. West, Seattle, Wash. 98119

Unival Corp., 157 Summerfield St.,
Scarsdale, N.Y. 10583

Valvoline Oil Co. Div., Ashland Oil
and Refining Co., 1409 Winchester
Ave., Ashland, Ky. 41101

X-I-M Products, Inc., 1169 Bassett
Rd., Westlake, O. 44145

Compounds, rust-removing

Beck Equipment and Chemical Co.,
3350 W. 137th St., Cleveland, O.
44111

Andrew Brown Co., 5431 District Blvd., P.O. Box 22066, Los Angeles, Calif. 90022

CRC Chemicals Div., C. J. Webb, Inc., Limekiln Pike, Dresher, Pa. 19025

Fine Organics, Inc., 205 Main St., Lodi, N.J. 07644

LPS Research Labs, Inc., 2050 Cotner Ave., West Los Angeles, Calif. 90025

Magnus Div., Economics Laboratory, Inc., Osborn Bldg., St. Paul, Minn. 55102

Oil Center Research, 211 Rayburn, Lafayette, La. 70501

Phillips Mfg. Co., 7334 N. Clark St., Chicago, Ill. 60626

Rust Lick, Inc., 755 Boylston St., Boston, Mass. 02116

Rusticide Products Co., 3125 Perkins Ave., Cleveland, O. 44114

SPC, Inc., 2213 15th Ave. West, Seattle, Wash. 98119

Unival Corp., 157 Summerfield St., Scarsdale, N.Y. 10583

Woodhill Chemical Sales Corp., 18731 Cranwood Pkwy., Cleveland, O. 44128

Woolsey Marine Industries, Inc., 201 E. 42nd St., New York, N.Y. 10017

Compounds, sealing and caulking

Allied Resin Products Corp., Weymouth Industrial Park, Pleasant St., East Weymouth, Mass. 02189

BoatLIFE Div., Flo-Paint, Inc., 5–45 49th Ave., Long Island City, N.Y. 11101

Dakoline Chemical Co., Inc., 916 Pacific St., Brooklyn, N.Y. 11238

DAP, Inc., 5300 Huberville Ave., Dayton, O. 45431

Darworth, Inc., Chemical Products Div., Simsbury, Conn. 06070

Dolphin Paint and Chemical Co., 922 Locust St., P.O. Box 1927 Central Station, Toledo, O. 43603

Dow Corning Corp., Midland, Mich. 48640

General Electric Co., Silicone Products Dept., Waterford, N.Y. 12188

General Electric Co., Wiring Device Dept., 95 Hathaway St., Providence, R.I. 02904

Gloucester Co., Inc., 235 Cottage St., Franklin, Mass. 02038

Intercoastal Corp., Dundalk P.O., Baltimore, Md. 21222

International Paint Co., Inc., 21 West St., New York, N.Y. 10006

Macklanburg-Duncan Co., P.O. Box 25188, Oklahoma City, Okla. 73125

Marblette Corp., 37–31 30th St., Long Island City, N.Y. 11106

Marine Industries, Inc., 1000 Northwest Hwy., Barrington, Ill. 60010

Minnesota Mining and Mfg. Co., 2501 Hudson Rd., St. Paul, Minn. 55119

Miracle Adhesives Corp., 250 Pettit Ave., Bellmore, N.Y. 11710

Mutual Hardware Corp., 5–45 49th Ave., Long Island City, N.Y. 11101

Pettit Paint Co., Inc., 507 Main St., Rockaway, N.J. 07866

W. J. Ruscoe Co., 483 Kenmore Blvd., Akron, O. 44301

Smooth-On, Inc., 1000 Valley Rd., Stirling, N.J. 07933

Stay-Tite Products Co., Inc., 2889 E. 83rd St., P.O. Box 20130, Cleveland, O. 44120

Travaco Laboratories, 345 Eastern Ave., Chelsea, Mass. 02150

U. S. Yacht Paint Co., Box 525, Roseland, N.J. 07068

Valspar Corp., Marine Div., 200 Sayre St., Rockford, Ill. 61101

Woodhill Chemical Sales Corp., 18731 Cranwood Pkwy., Cleveland, O. 44128

Woolsey Marine Industries, Inc., 201
E. 42nd St., New York, N.Y. 10017
X-Pando Corp., 43–15 36th St., Long
Island City, N.Y. 11100

Compounds, waterproofing

Allube Div., Far-Best Corp., 928
Allen Ave., Glendale, Calif. 91201
BoatLIFE Div., Flo-Paint, Inc., 5–45
49th Ave., Long Island City, N.Y.
11101
Samuel Cabot, Inc., 246 Sumner St.,
Boston, Mass. 02128
Champion Products, Inc., 4939 S.
Austin Avenue, Chicago, Ill. 60638
Coopers Creek Chemical Corp., 28
River Ave., West Conshohocken,
Pa. 19428
Dolphin Paint and Chemical Co., 922
Locust St., P.O. Box 1927 Central
Station, Toledo, O. 43603
Dow Corning Corp., Midland,
Mich. 48640
Fumol Corp., 49–65 Van Dam St.,
Long Island City, N.Y. 11101
General Electric Co., Silicone Prod-
ucts Dept., Waterford, N.Y. 12188
Lan-O-Sheen, 1 W. Water St., St.
Paul, Minn. 55107
Macklanburg-Duncan Co., P.O. Box
25188, Oklahoma City, Okla. 73125
Mutual Hardware Corp., 5–45 49th
Ave., Long Island City, N.Y. 11101
Pettit Paint Co., Inc., 507 Main St.,
Rockaway, N.J. 07866
SPC, Inc., 2213 15th Ave. West, Se-
attle, Wash. 98119
Thiokol Chemical Corp., 780 N. Clin-
ton Ave., Trenton, N.J. 08607
Travaco Laboratories, 345 Eastern
Ave., Chelsea, Mass. 02150
X-Pando Corp., 43–15 36th St., Long
Island City, N.Y. 11100

Compounds, winterizing

CRC Chemicals Div., C. J. Webb,
Inc., Limekiln Pike, Dresher, Pa.
19025
Marine Development and Research
Corp., 381 Park Ave. South, New
York, N.Y. 10016

Compounds, wood-filling

DAP, Inc., 5300 Huberville Ave.,
Dayton, O. 45431
Dolphin Paint and Chemical Co., 922
Locust St., P.O. Box 1927 Central
Station, Toledo, O. 43603
International Paint Co., Inc., 21
West St., New York, N.Y. 10006
Magic American Chemical Corp.,
14215 Caine Ave., Cleveland, O.
44128
Marine Industries, Inc., 1000 North-
west Hwy., Barrington, Ill. 60010
Pettit Paint Co., Inc., 507 Main St.,
Rockaway, N.J. 07866
Travaco Laboratories, 345 Eastern
Ave., Chelsea, Mass. 02150
U. S. Yacht Paint Co., Box 525,
Roseland, N.J. 07068
Valspar Corp., Marine Div., 200
Sayre St., Rockford, Ill. 61101
Woodhill Chemical Sales Corp.,
18731 Cranwood Pkwy., Cleveland,
O. 44128

Compression testers

Schauer Mfg. Corp., 4538 Alpine
Ave., Cincinnati, O. 45242
Simpson Electric Co., Automotive
Div., 5200 W. Kinzie St., Chicago,
Ill. 60644

Cotton caulking

Wm. E. Hooper and Sons Co., P.O. Box 416, Staten Island, N.Y. 10308

Massasoit Co., Marine Products Div., 3500 Parkdale Ave., Baltimore, Md. 21211

Phillips Hardware Co., 490 N.W. S. River Dr., Corner N.W. 9th Ave. and 5th St., Miami, Fla. 33128

Countersinks and counterbores

W. L. Fuller, Inc., 1163 Warwick Ave., Warwick, R.I. 02888

Phillips Hardware Co., 490 N.W. S. River Dr., Corner N.W. 9th Ave. and 5th St., Miami, Fla. 33128

Stanley Tools, 600 Myrtle St., New Britain, Conn. 06050

Deck coverings

Act Lite Step Co., 1516 S. Wabash Ave., Chicago, Ill. 60605

Dade Trading Corp., 2401 N.W. 33rd Ave., Miami, Fla. 33142

Falcon Safety Products, Inc., 1137 Rt. 22, Mountainside, N.J. 07092

General Tire and Rubber Co., Chemical/Plastics Div., P.O. Box 875, Toledo, O. 43601

Goodall Vinyl Fabrics Div., Burlington, Ind., 846–H Merchandise Mart, Chicago, Ill. 60654

Herculite Protective Fabrics Corp., 1107 Broadway, New York, N.Y. 10010

Ren Plastics, Inc., 5656 S. Cedar St., Lansing, Mich. 48909

Valspar Corp., Marine Div., 200 Sayre St., Rockford, Ill. 61101

Weymouth Art Leather Co., Inc., 180 Pearl St., South Braintree, Mass. 02185

Distributor parts

C. E. Niehoff and Co., 4925 Lawrence Ave., Chicago, Ill. 60630

Preferred Electric Wire Corp., 68 33rd St., Brooklyn, N.Y. 11232

Drills, power portable

Millers Falls Co., 57 Wells St., Greenfield, Mass. 01301

Milwaukee Electric Tool Corp., 13135 W. Lisbon Rd., Brookfield, Wis. 53005

Rockwell Tools, The Thomas Flynn Highway, Pittsburgh, Pa.

Skil Corp., 5033 Elston Ave., Chicago, Ill. 60603

Snap-On Tools Corp., 8029 28th Ave., Kenosha, Wis. 53140

Superior Pneumatic and Mfg., Inc., P.O. Box 9667, Cleveland, O. 44140

Thor Power Tool Co., 175 N. State St., Aurora, Ill. 60507

Elbows, exhaust

Aero Marine Div., Aeroceanic Corp., 6737 E. Washington Blvd., El Monte, Calif. 91731

Allcraft Mfg. Co., 27 Heyward St., Cambridge, Mass. 02142

Alloy Marine, Inc., 4618 Point Tremble Rd., Algonac, Mich. 48001

Gray/Star Marine Engine Works, 2920 Seventh St., Berkeley, Calif. 94700

Mercury Boat Co., 3986 E. Telegraph Rd., Piru, Calif. 93040

Exhaust silencers

Aero Marine Div., Aeroceanic Corp., 6737 E. Washington Blvd., El Monte, Calif. 91731

Allcraft Mfg. Co., Inc., 27 Hayward St., Cambridge, Mass. 02142

AMF Beaird, Inc., Sub. American Machine and Foundry, Inc., P.O. Box 1115, Shreveport, La. 71102

Apex Equipment, Inc., 4001 21st Ave W., Seattle, Wash. 98199

Aquadynamic, Inc., 6940 Farmdale Ave., No. Hollywood, Calif. 91605

Griffith Rubber Mills, 2439 N.W. 22nd Ave., Portland, Ore. 97210

Marine Mufflers, Inc., 302 N.E. 45th Ct., Pompano Beach, Fla. 33064

D. L. Parker Co., Box 176, Brighton, Mich. 48116

Phillips Hardware Co., 490 N.W. S. River Dr., Corner N.W. 9th Ave. and 5th St., Miami, Fla. 33128

Salisbury Rubber Products, W. H. Salisbury & Co., 410 N. Morgan St., Chicago, Ill. 60600

Submarine Research Laboratories, Inc., Hingham Shipyard, Hingham, Mass. 02043

Vernay Products, Inc., S. College St., Yellow Springs, O. 45387

Wilcox-Crittenden Div., Gulf and Western Co., Dept. 8, Middletown, Conn. 06457

Zurn Industries, Inc., Marine Div., 1801 Pittsburgh Ave., Erie, Pa. 16512

Exhaust systems, pipes and manifolds

Aero Marine Div., Aeroceanic Corp., 6737 E. Washington Blvd., El Monte, Calif. 91731

Babbitt Missile Co., Circuit St., West Hanover, Mass. 02380

Barr Marine Products Co., 2700 E. Castor Ave., Philadelphia, Pa. 19134

Gray/Star Marine Engine Works, 2920 Seventh St., Berkeley, Calif. 94700

Marine Mufflers, Inc., 302 N.E. 45th Ct., Pompano Beach, Fla. 33064

Nicson Engineering Co., 11850 Burke St., Santa Fe Springs, Calif. 90670

Osco, Motors Corp., Souderton, Pa. 18964

Vernay Products, Inc., S. College St., Yellow Springs, O. 45387

Fabric, dynel

Defender Industries, Inc., 384 Broadway, New York, N.Y. 10013

Landy Associates, 349 Fifth Ave., New York, N.Y. 10016

Fabric, fluorescent

John Boyle and Co., Inc., 112 Duane St., New York, N.Y. 10007

Werlin Safety Products, 1506 Elmwood Ave., Folcroft, Pa. 19032

Fabric, polypropylene

Allied Resin Products Corp., Weymouth Industrial Park, Pleasant St., E. Weymouth, Mass. 02189

Astrup Co., 2937 W. 25th St., Cleveland, O. 44113

Defender Industries, Inc., 384 Broadway, New York, N.Y. 10013

Fabric vents

John Boyle and Co., Inc., 112–14 Duane St., New York, N.Y. 10007

Fabric, vinyl-coated

Also see Upholstery material.

Arno Adhesive Tapes, Inc., U. S. 20 at Ohio St., Michigan City, Ind. 46360

Astrup Co., 2937 W. 25th St., Cleveland, O. 44113

John Boyle and Co., Inc., 112-14 Duane St., New York, N.Y. 10007

Converse-Hodgman, 392 Pearl St., Malden, Mass. 02148

Douglass Fabrics, Marine Div., 186 N. Main St., Pleasantville, N.J. 08232

General Tire and Rubber Co., Chemical/Plastics Div., P.O. Box 875, Toledo, O. 43601

Goodall Vinyl Fabrics Corp., Burlington, Ind., 846-H Merchandise Mart, Chicago, Ill. 60654

Haartz Auto Fabric Co., Hayward Rd., P.O. Box 286, Acton, Mass. 01720

M and B Sales Co., Inc., 2615 Love Field Dr., Dallas, Tex. 75235

Masland Duraleather Co., Amber and Willard Sts., Philadelphia, Pa. 19134

Pipestone-Mariner Corp., Box 311, S. Highway 75, Pipestone, Minn. 56164

Reeves Bros., Inc., 1071 Avenue of the Americas, New York, N.Y. 10018

Sportmen's Industries, Inc., 7878 N. W. 103rd St., Hialeah, Fla. 33016

Van Brode Sales Co., 20 Cameron St., Clinton, Mass. 01510

Weblon, Inc., 220 Ferris Ave., White Plains, N.Y. 10603

Werlin Safety Products, 1506 Elmwood Ave., Folcroft, Pa. 19032

Weymouth Art Leather Co., Inc., 180 Pearl St., South Braintree, Mass. 02185

Fasteners, hull

Aero Marine Div., Aeroceanic Corp., 6737 E. Washington Blvd., El Monte, Calif. 91731

Allan Marine, 91 Industry Ct., Deer Park, N.Y. 11729

Aluminum Co. of America, 1501 Alcoa Bldg., Pittsburgh, Pa. 15219

Handy-Man Fasteners Div., Industrial Bolt and Nut Co., 191 Fabyan Place, Newark, N.J. 17112

Heli-Coil Corp., Insert Products Div., Shelter Rock Lane, Danbury, Conn. 06810

Hillwood Mfg. Co., 21700 St. Claire Ave., Cleveland, O. 44117

Independent Nail, Inc., 106 Hale St., Bridgewater, Mass. 02324

Market Forge Co., 35 Garvey St., Everett, Mass. 02149

Pan American Screw Corp., P.O. Box 816, Jacksonville, Fla. 32201

Reed and Prince Mfg. Co., 1 Duncan Ave., Worcester, Mass. 01601

Sealand Sport Co., P.O. Box 2842, Kalamazoo, Mich. 49001

Star Stainless Screw Co., 655 Union Blvd., Totowa, N.J. 07511

Fasteners, nonferrous

Bowman Products Div., Associated Spring Corp., 850 E. 72nd St., Cleveland, O. 44103

Handy-Man Fasteners Div., Industrial Bolt and Nut Co., 191 Fabyan Place, Newark, N.J. 17112

Independent Nail, Inc., 106 Hale St., Bridgewater, Mass. 02324

Pan American Screw Co., P.O. Box 816, Jacksonville, Fla. 32201

Star Stainless Screw Co., 655 Union Blvd., Totowa, N.J. 07511

Fasteners, top and curtain

Astrup Co., 2937 W. 25th St., Cleveland, O. 44113

Baltimore Canvas Products, Inc., 2861 W. Franklin St., Baltimore Md. 21223

Bilt-Rite Sailmakers, Inc., 1342 W. 11th St., Long Beach, Calif. 90813

Handy-Man Fasteners Div., Industrial Bolt and Nut Co., 191 Fabyan Place, Newark, N.J. 17112

Kainer Hy Styles Corp., 301 W. Alice St., Wheeling, Ill. 60090

Manart Textile Co., 116 Franklin St., New York, N.Y. 10013

Perkins Marine Lamp and Hardware Corp., 16490 N.W. 13th Ave., P.O. Box D, Miami, Fla. 33164

Sportmen's Industries, Inc., 7878 N.W. 103rd St., Hialeah, Fla. 33016

N. A. Taylor Co., Inc., Gloversville, N.Y. 12078

Fastenings

Al-Sail, Inc., 14 North St., Hingham, Mass. 02043

John Boyle and Co., Inc., 112–14 Duane St., New York, N.Y. 10007

H. M. Harper Co., 8200 Lehigh Ave., Morton Grove, Ill. 60053

Heli-Coil Corp., Shelter Rock Lane, Danbury, Conn. 06810

Kainer Hy Styles Corp., 301 W. Alice St., Wheeling, Ill. 60090

Independent Nail, Inc., 106 Hale St., Bridgewater, Mass. 02324

Phillips Hardware Co., 490 N.W. S. River Dr., Corner N.W. 9th Ave. and 5th St., Miami, Fla. 33128

Seaboard Marine Supply Co., Inc., 214 Montauk Hwy., Islip, N.Y. 11751

Fiberglass board

Johns-Manville Fiber Glass Textile Sales, 22 E. 40th St., New York, N.Y. 10016

Owens-Corning Fiberglas Corp., 717 Fifth Ave., New York, N.Y. 10022

Pittsburgh Plate Glass Co., Fiber Glass Div., 1 Gateway Center, Pittsburgh, Pa. 1522

Zurn Industries, Inc., Marine Div., 1801 Pittsburgh Ave., Erie, Pa. 16512

Fiberglass cloth

Allied Resin Products Corp., Weymouth Industrial Park, Pleasant St., East Weymouth, Mass. 02189

Atlas Asbestos Co., 492 Walnut St., North Wales, Pa. 19454

Berton Plastics, Inc., 170 Wesley St., South Hackensack, N.J. 07606

Burlington Glass Fabrics Co., 1450 Broadway, New York, N.Y. 10018

Cadillac Plastic Co., 1511 2nd Ave., Detroit, Mich. 48203

Clark-Schwebel Fiber Glass Corp., 245 Park Ave., New York, N.Y. 10017

Coast Mfg. Div., Hexcel Corp., 11711 Dublin Blvd., Dublin, Calif. 94566

Craft Plastic Corp., P.O. Box 33, Parcel Post Station, Worcester, Mass. 01604

Defender Industries, Inc., 384 Broadway, New York, N.Y. 10013

Ferro Corporation, 4150 E. 56th St., Cleveland, O. 44105

Fiber Glass Industries, Inc., Homestead Place, Amsterdam, N.Y. 12010

Hysol Div., Dexter Corp., 1100 Seneca Ave., Olean, N.Y. 14760

International Paint Co., Inc., 21 West
St., New York, N.Y. 10006

Kristal Kraft, Inc., 900 4th St., Palmetto, Fla. 33561

Owens-Corning Fiberglas Corp., 717
Fifth Ave., New York, N.Y. 10022

Pettit Paint Co., Inc., 507 Main St.,
Rockaway, N.J. 07866

Plastic Sales and Mfg. Co., Inc., 3030
McGee Trafficway, Kansas City,
Mo. 64129

Resin Coatings Corp., 3595 N.W. 74th
St., Miami, Fla. 33147

J. P. Stevens and Co., Inc., 1460
Broadway, New York, N.Y. 10036

Uniglass, Inc., Glasscoat Div., 150
N.W. 176th St., Miami, Fla. 33169

Valspar Corp., Marine Div., 200
Sayre St., Rockford, Ill. 61101

Werlin Safety Products, 1506 Elmwood Ave., Folcroft, Pa. 19032

Fiberglass covering kits

Algonquin Mfg., Ltd., 6 Bartlett
Ave., Toronto, Ont., Canada

Apex Fibre-Glass Products, Washington and Elm Sts., Cleveland O.
44138

Defender Industries, Inc., 384 Broadway, New York, N.Y. 10013

Glass Plastics/Valspar Corp., Marine
Div., 200 Sayre St., Rockford, Ill.
61101

Pettit Paint Co., Inc., 507 Main St.,
Rockaway, N.J. 07866

Plastic Sales and Mfg. Co., Inc., 3030
McGee Trafficway, Kansas City,
Mo. 64129

Tra-Con, Inc., Resin Systems Div., 55
North St., Medford, Mass. 02155

I. J. Turner Co., Ltd., 280 George
St., Peterborough, Ont., Canada

Valspar Corp., Marine Div., 200 Sayre
St., Rockford, Ill. 61101

Fiberglass layup equipment

DeVilbiss Co., P.O. Box 913, 300
Phillips Ave., Toledo, O. 43601

Glas-Mate Div., Ransburg Electro-
Coating Corp., 2959 N.E. 12th Terrace, Fort Lauderdale, Fla. 33307

Plastic Engineering and Chemical Co.,
3501 N.W. 9th Ave., Fort Lauderdale, Fla. 33309

Structural Concepts, 15120 Keswick
St., Van Nuys, Calif. 91405

Fiberglass mat

Allied Resin Products Corp., Weymouth Industrial Park, Pleasant St.,
East Weymouth, Mass. 02189

Berton Plastics, Inc., 170 Wesley St.,
South Hackensack, N.J. 07606

Cadillac Plastic Co., 15111 2nd Ave.,
Detroit, Mich. 48203

Craft Plastics Corp., P.O. Box 33,
Parcel Post Station, Worcester,
Mass. 01604

Ferro Corp., Fiber Glass Div., Fiber
Glass Road, Nashville, Tenn. 37211

Johns-Manville Fiber Glass Textile
Sales, 22 E. 40th St., New York,
N.Y. 10016

Owens-Corning Fiberglas Corp., Box
901, Toledo, O. 43601

Pettit Paint Co., Inc., 507 Main St.,
Rockaway, N.J. 07866

Pipestone-Mariner Corp., Box 311, S.
Highway 75, Pipestone, Minn.
56164

Pittsburgh Plate Glass Co., Fiber
Glass Div., 1 Gateway Center, Pittsburgh, Pa. 15222

Plastic Sales and Mfg. Co., Inc., 3030
McGee Trafficway, Kansas City,
Mo. 64116

Uniglass Industries, Glascoat Div.,
150 N.W. 176th St., Miami, Fla.
33169

Valspar Corp., Marine Div., 200
Sayre St., Rockford, Ill. 61101

Fiberglass reinforcement

Berton Plastics, Inc., 170 Wesley St.,
South Hackensack, N.J. 07606
Burlington Glass Fabrics Co., Div.
Burlington Inds., 345 Ave. of the
Americas, New York, N.Y. 10011
Cadillac Plastic Co., 15111 2nd Ave.,
Detroit, Mich. 48203
Clark-Schwebel Fiber Glass Corp.,
245 Park Ave., New York, N.Y.
10017
Ferro Corp., Fiber Glass Div., Fiber
Glass Road, Nashville, Tenn. 37211
Fiber Glass Industries, Inc., Home-
stead Place, Amsterdam, N.Y.
12010
Flightex Fabrics Div., Belding Cor-
ticelli Fiberglass Fabrics, Inc., 10
E. 32nd St., New York, N.Y. 10036
Hastings Plastics, 1704 Colorado
Ave., Santa Monica, Calif. 90404
Johns-Manville, Fiber Glass Textile
Sales, 22 E. 40th St., New York,
N.Y. 10016
Kristal Kraft, Inc., 900 4th St., Pal-
metto, Fla. 33561
H. B. Fred Kuhls, 49 Sumner St.,
Milford, Mass. 01757
Link Marine and Plyfoam, Inc., Van-
derbilt Industrial Pkwy., Haup-
pauge, N.Y. 11787
Marine Industries, Inc., 1000 North-
west Hwy., Barrington, Ill. 60010
Owens-Corning Fiberglas Corp., Box
901, Toledo, O. 43601
Pittsburgh Plate Glass Co., Fiber
Glass Div., 1 Gateway Center, Pitts-
burgh, Pa. 15222
Structural Concepts, 15120 Keswick
St., Van Nuys, Calif. 91405

Uniglass Industries, Glascoat Div.,
150 N.W. 176th St., Miami, Fla.
33169
Valspar Corp., Marine Div., 200
Sayre St., Rockford, Ill. 61101

Fiberglass roving

Allied Resin Products Corp.,
Weymouth Industrial Park, Pleas-
ant St., East Weymouth, Mass.
02189
Cadillac Plastic Co., 15111 2nd Ave.,
Detroit, Mich. 48203
Clark-Schwebel Fiber Glass Corp.,
245 Park Ave., New York, N.Y.
10017
Coast Mfg. Div., Hexcel Corp. 11711
Dublin Blvd., Dublin, Calif. 94566
Ferro Corporation, 4150 E. 56th St.,
Cleveland, O. 44105
Glass Plastics/Valspar Corp., Marine
Div., 200 Sayre St., Rockford, Ill.
61101
Johns-Manville Fiber Glass Textile
Sales, 22 E. 40th St., New York,
N.Y. 10016
Owens-Corning Fiberglas Corp., Box
901, Toledo, O. 43601
Pettit Paint Co., Inc., 507 Main St.,
Rockaway, N.J. 07866
Pittsburgh Plate Glass Co., Fiber
Glass Div., 1 Gateway Center, Pitts-
burgh, Pa. 15222
J. P. Stevens and Co., Inc., 1460
Broadway, New York, N.Y. 10036

Fiberglass tape

Allied Resin Products Corp., Weymouth Industrial Park, Pleasant St.,
East Weymouth, Mass. 02189

Berton Plastics, Inc., 170 Wesley St., South Hackensack, N.J. 07606

Burlington Glass Fabrics Co., Div., Burlington Inds., 345 Ave. of the Americas, New York, N.Y. 10011

Cadillac Plastic Co., 15111 2nd Ave., Detroit, Mich. 48203

Clark-Schwebel Fiber Glass Corp., 245 Park Ave., New York, N.Y. 10017

Coast Mfg. Div., Hexcel Corp. 11711 Dublin Blvd., Dublin, Calif. 94566

Craft Plastics Corp., P.O. Box 33, Parcel Post Station, Worcester, Mass. 01604

Defender Industries, Inc., 384 Broadway, New York, N.Y. 10013

Fiber Glass Industries, Inc., Homestead Place, Amsterdam, N.Y. 12010

International Paint Co., Inc., 21 West St., New York, N.Y. 10006

Kristal Kraft, Inc., 900 4th St., Palmetto, Fla. 33561

Owens-Corning Fiberglas Corp., 717 Fifth Ave., New York, N.Y. 10022

Pettit Paint Co., Inc., 507 Main St., Rockaway, N.J. 07866

Ren Plastics, Inc., 5656 S. Cedar, Lansing, Mich. 48909

J. P. Stevens and Co., Inc., 1460 Broadway, New York, N.Y. 10036

Uniglass Industries, Glascoat Div., 150 N.W. 176th St., Miami, Fla. 33169

Valspar Corp., Marine Div., 200 Sayre St., Rockford, Ill. 61101

Filters, air

AC Spark Plug Div., General Motors Corp., 1300 N. Dort Hwy., Flint, Mich. 48556

Bendix Filter Div., 434 W. 12-Mile Rd., Madison Heights, Mich. 48071

Fleetguard Div., Cummins Engine Co., Inc., Box 750, Cookeville, Tenn. 38501

Hilliard Corp., 100 W. 4th St., Elmira, N.Y. 14901

Liberty Industries, Inc., 651 Lexington Ave., Brooklyn, N.Y. 11221

North American Rockwell Corp., Industrial and Marine Prods. Div., 5th Ave. and Wood St., Pittsburgh, Pa. 15222

Preferred Electric and Wire Corp., 68 33rd St., Brooklyn, N.Y. 11232

Superior Pneumatic and Mfg., Inc., P.O. Box 9667, Cleveland, O. 44140

Tillotson Mfg. Co., 761–69 Berdan Ave., Toledo, O. 43612

Watts Regulator Co., 10 Embarkment Rd., Lawrence, Mass. 01841

Westinghouse Air Brake Co., 1953 Mercer Rd., Lexington, Ky. 40505

Wix Corporation, P.O. Box 1967, Gastonia, N.C. 28052

Filters, diesel-fuel

AC Spark Plug Div., General Motors Corp., 1300 N. Dort Hwy., Flint, Mich. 48556

AMBAC Industries, Inc., American Bosch Div., 3664 Main St., Springfield, Mass. 01107

Bendix Automotive Service Div., 1217 S. Walnut St., South Bend, Ind. 46620

Bendix Filter Div., 434 W. 12-Mile Rd., Madison Heights, Mich. 48071

D. A. Comstock and Co., Inc., 85 Washington St., South Norwalk, Conn. 06854

Fleetguard Div., Cummins Engine Co., Inc., Box 750, Cookeville, Tenn. 38501

Fram Corp., 105 Pawtucket Ave., Providence, R.I. 02916

Hilliard Corp., 100 W. 4th St.,
Elmira, N.Y. 14901

Kraissl Co., Inc., 148 Old Hoboken
Rd., Hackensack, N.J. 07606

North American Rockwell Corp., Industrial and Marine Prods. Div.,
5th Ave. and Wood St., Pittsburgh,
Pa. 15222

Wix Corporation, P.O. Box 1967, Gastonia, N.C. 28052

Filters, gasoline

AC Spark Plug Div., General
Motors Corp., 1300 N. Dort Hwy.,
Flint, Mich. 48556

Alondra, Inc., 826 W. Hyde Park
Blvd., Inglewood, Calif. 90302

Bendix Automative Service Div., 1217
S. Walnut St., South Bend., Ind.
46620

Bendix Corp., Automotive Service
Div., 1217 S. Walnut St., South
Bend, Ind. 46620

Bendix Filter Div., 434 W. 12-Mile
Rd., Madison Heights, Mich.
48071

D. A. Comstock and Co., Inc., 85
Washington St., South Norwalk,
Conn. 06854

Fleetguard Div., Cummins Engine
Co., Inc., Box 750, Cookeville,
Tenn. 38501

Fram Corp., 105 Pawtucket Ave.,
Providence, R.I. 02916

Hilliard Corp., 100 W. 4th St.,
Elmira, N.Y. 14901

Kraissl Co., Inc., 148 Old Hoboken
Rd., Hackensack, N.J. 07606

Liberty Industries, Inc., 651 Lexington Ave., Brooklyn, N.Y. 11221

Lunkenheimer Co., Beekman St. at
Waverly Pl., Cincinnati, O. 45214

North American Rockwell Corp., Industrial and Marine Prods. Div.,
5th Ave. and Wood St., Pittsburgh,
Pa. 15222

Perkins Marine Lamp and Hardware
Corp., 16490 N.W. 13th Ave., P.O.
Box D, Miami, Fla. 33164

Phillips Hardware Co., N.W. South
River Dr., Corner N.W. 9th Ave.
and 5th St., Miami, Fla. 33128

Preferred Electric and Wire Corp.,
68 33rd St., Brooklyn, N.Y. 11232

Wilcox-Crittenden Div., Gulf and
Western Co., Dept 8, Middletown,
Conn. 06457

Wix Corporation, P.O. Box 1967, Gastonia, N.C. 28052

Zenith Carburetor Div., Bendix Corp.,
696 Hart Ave., Detroit, Mich.
48214

Filters, oil

AC Spark Plug Div., General
Motors Corp., 1300 N. Dort Hwy.,
Flint, Mich. 48556

Auto-Matic Products Co., 1918 S.
Michigan Ave., Chicago, Ill. 60616

Bendix Filter Div., 434 W. 12-Mile
Rd., Madison Heights, Mich.
48071

Fleetguard Div., Cummins Engine
Co., Inc., Box 750 Cookeville, Tenn.
38501

Fram Corp., 105 Pawtucket Ave.,
Providence, R.I. 02916

Hilliard Corp., 100 W. 4th
St., Elmira, N.Y. 14901

Kraissl Co., Inc., 148 Old Hoboken
Rd., Hackensack, N.J. 07606

Liberty Industries, Inc., 651 Lexington Ave., Brooklyn, N.Y. 11221

Lunkenheimer Co., Beekman St. at
Waverly Pl., Cincinnati, O. 45214

Preferred Electric and Wire Corp.,
68 33rd St., Brooklyn, N.Y. 11232

WH Distributing Co., 11 W. Main
St., Mooresville, Ind. 46158

Wix Corporation, P.O. Box 1967, Gastonia, N.C. 28053

Filters, water

AMF Cuno Div., American Machine and Foundry Co., 80 S. Vine St., Meriden, Conn. 06450

D. A. Comstock and Co., Inc., 85 Washington St., South Norwalk, Conn. 06854

Dakoline Chemical Co., Inc., 916 Pacific St., Brooklyn, N.Y. 11238

Fram Corp., 105 Pawtucket Ave., Providence, R.I. 02916

Hilliard Corp., 100 W. 4th St., Elmira, N.Y. 14901

Perkins Marine Lamp and Hardware Corp., 16490 N.W. 13th Ave., P.O. Box D, Miami, Fla. 33164

Phillips Hardware Co., 490 N.W. S. River Dr., Corner N.W. 9th Ave. and 5th St., Miami, Fla. 33128

Raritan Engineering Co., 1025 N. High St., Millville, N.J. 08332

Sen-Dure Products, Inc., 25 Moffitt Blvd., Bay Shore, N.Y. 11706

Flotation material, bulk

Balsa Ecuador Lumber Corp., 500 Fifth Ave., New York, N.Y. 10036

Balsa Products, Inc., 3354 N.W. 38th St., Miami, Fla. 33142

C. M. Buethe Co., 833 Bancroft Way, Berkeley, Calif. 94710

Danco Div., Nicholson File Co., Danco Rd., Putnam, Conn. 06260

Diamond Shamrock Chemical Co., Flexible Foam Dept., Lesinous Prods. Div., Plainfield, N.J. 07601

Ero Mfg. Co., 714 Monroe St., Chicago, L6, Ill. 60603

Floatco Corp., Market St., Wappinger Falls, N.Y. 12590

Formex Corp., 505 Belvedere Rd., Elkhart, Ind. 46514

Goodhue Enterprises, 190 Central St. (Rt. No. 2), Leominster, Mass. 01453

Iowa Fibre Products, Inc., 2425 Dean Ave., Des Moines, Ia. 50317

Johns-Manville, Fiberglass Textile Sales, 22 E. 40th St., New York, N.Y. 10016

Jones and Yandell, P.O. Box 208, Canton, Miss. 39046

Link Marine and Plyfoam, Inc., Vanderbilt Industrial Pkwy., Hauppauge, N.Y. 11787

Lorraine, Textile Specialties, Inc., 1750 Plaza Ave., New Hyde Park, N.Y. 11040

MEECO Marinas, Inc., Box 518, McAlester, Okla. 74401

William T. Morris, 2200 Jackson Ave., Seaford, N.Y. 11783

Pettit Paint Co., Inc., 507 Main St., Rockaway, N.J. 07866

Polyfoam, Inc., Lester Prairie, Minn. 55354

United Flotation Systems, 2400 Fairwood Ave., Columbus, O. 43207

Upjohn Co., CPR Div., 565 Alaska Ave., Torrance, Calif. 90503

Fuel Injectors, diesel

Bendix Corp., Electrical Components Div., Delaware Ave., Sidney, N.Y. 13838

Robert Bosch Corp., 2800 S. 25th Ave., Broadview, Ill. 60153

Research Enterprises, Inc., P.O. Box 232, Nutley, N.J. 07110

Gasket material

Auburn Mfg. Co., 200 Stack St., Middletown, Conn. 06457

Belko Corp., Kingsville, Md. 21087

General Electric Co., Silicone Products Dept., Waterford, N.Y. 12188

Raybestos-Manhattan, Inc., 205 Middle St., Bridgeport, Conn. 06603

W. S. Shamban and Co., 11543 West Olympic Blvd., Los Angeles, Calif. 90064

Gaskets, engine and motor

Auburn Mfg. Co., 200 Stack St., Middletown, Conn. 06457

Billy Boy Products, Inc., 35 E. Chicago St., Quincy, Mich. 49082

Hecht Rubber Corp., 482–84 Riverside Ave., Jacksonville, Fla. 32207

Sierra Supply Co., P.O. Box 596, McHenry, Ill. 60050

Gaskets, water

Auburn Mfg. Co., 200 Stack St., Middletown, Conn. 06457

Glues, marine

Borden Chemical Div., Borden, Inc., 350 Madison Ave., New York, N.Y. 10017

Darworth, Inc., Chemical Products Div., Simsbury, Conn. 06070

Harbor Sales Co., Inc., 1401 Russell St., Baltimore, Md. 21230

International Paint Co., Inc., 21 West St., New York, N.Y. 10006

Macklanburg-Duncan Co., P.O. Box 25188, Oklahoma City, Okla. 73125

Phillips Hardware Co., 490 N.W. S. River Dr., Corner N.W. 9th Ave. and 5th St., Miami, Fla. 33128

Stay-Tite Products Co., Inc., 2889 E. 83rd St., P.O. Box 20130, Cleveland, O. 44120

Valspar Corp., Marine Div., 200 Sayre St., Rockford, Ill. 61101

Wilhold Glues, Inc., 8707 Millergrove Dr., Santa Fe Springs, Calif. 90670

Glues, plywood

Gloucester Co., Inc., 235 Cottage St., Franklin, Mass. 11710

Harbor Sales Co., Inc., 1401 Russell St., Bellmore, N.Y. 21230

Schwartz Chemical Co., Inc., 50–01 Second St., Long Island City, New York 11101

Stay-Tite Products Co., Inc., 2889 E. 83rd St., P.O. Box 20130, Cleveland, O. 44120

Glues, vinyl

Sealand Sport Co., P.O. Box 2842, Kalamazoo, Mich. 49001

Grease

Bardahl Mfg. Corp., 1400 N.W. 52nd St., Seattle, Wash. 98107

Chevron Oil Co., 1200 State St., Perth Amboy, N.J. 08861

Gale Products Div., Outboard Marine Corp., Galesburg, Ill. 60601

Intercontinental Lubricants Corp., 19 Michael St., East Haven, Conn. 06512

Kendall Refining Co., 77 N. Kendall Ave., Bradford, Pa. 16701

Mercury Marine, Fond du Lac, Wis. 54935

Lubriplate Div., Fisk Bros. Refining Co., 129 Lockwood St., Newark, N.J. 07105

Mobil Oil Co., Inc., Marine Retail Dept., 150 E. 42nd St., New York, N.Y. 10017

Motor State Oil and Grease Co., 155 Hobart St., Jackson, Mich. 49202

Phillips Petroleum Co., Bartlesville, Okla. 74003

Quaker State Oil Refining Corp., P.O. Box 989, Oil City, Pa. 16301

Shell Oil Co., 50 W. 50th St., New York, N.Y. 10020

Sta-Lube, Inc., 3039 Ana St., Compton, Calif. 90221

Unival Corp., 157 Summerfield St., Scarsdale, N.Y. 10583

Valvoline Oil Co., Div., Ashland Oil and Refining Co., 1409 Winchester Ave., Ashland, Ky. 41101

White and Bagley Co., P.O. Box 1171, 100 Foster St., Worcester, Mass. 01601

Grease, waterproof

Allube Div., Far-Best Corp., 928 Allen Ave., Glendale, Calif. 91201

Almasol Corp., 1628 Rogers Rd., P.O. Box 11396, Fort Worth, Tex. 76107

Bray Oil Co., 1925 N. Marianna St., Los Angeles, Calif. 90032

Humble Oil and Refining Co., P.O. Box 2180, Houston, Tex. 77001

Kendall Refining Co., 77 N. Kendall Ave., Bradford, Pa. 16701

Lubriplate Div., Fiske Bros. Refining Co., 129 Lockwood St., Newark, N.J. 07105

Motor State Oil and Grease Co., 155 Hobart St., Jackson, Mich. 49202

Quaker State Oil Refining Corp., P.O. Box 989, Oil City, Pa. 16301

Shell Oil Co., 50 W. 50th St., New York, N.Y. 10020

Sta-Lube, Inc., 3039 Ana St., Compton, Calif. 90221

Grease guns

Chevron Oil Co., 1200 State St., Perth Amboy, N.J. 08861

Graco, Inc., 60 11th Ave., N.E., Minneapolis, Minn. 55413

Mercury Marine, Fond du Lac, Wis. 54935

Landy Associates, 349 Fifth Ave., New York, N.Y. 10016

Unival Corp., 157 Summerfield St., Scarsdale, N.Y. 10583

Universal Lubricating Systems, Inc., 743 Allegheny Ave., Oakmont, Pa. 15139

Grommets and grommet irons

Astrup Co., 2937 W. 25th St., Cleveland, O. 44113

John Boyle and Co., Inc., 112–14 Duane St., New York, N.Y. 10007

M and B Sales Co., Inc., 2615 Love Field Dr., Dallas, Tex. 75235

Russell Industries, Inc., 96 Station Plaza, Lynbrook, N.Y. 11563

Gunwale guards

Belko Corp., Kingsville, Md. 21087

Griffith Rubber Mills, 2439 N.W. 22nd Ave., Portland, Ore. 97210

Industrial Plastics Corp., 816 W. Beardsley Ave., Elkhart, Ind. 46514

J and B Plastics Co., Inc., W. Stone Ave., Fairfield, Ia. 52556

Lake Rubber, Inc., Box 547, Willoughby, O. 44094

Marine Rubber Prod. Co., Box 547, Willoughby, O. 44094

Phillips Hardware Co., 490 N. W. S. River Dr., Corner N.W. 9th Ave. and 5th St., Miami, Fla. 33128

Salisbury Rubber Products, W. H. Salisbury and Co., 410 N. Morgan St., Chicago, Ill. 60600

Standard Products Co., Inc., 2130 W. 110th St., Cleveland. O. 44102

Zurn Industries, Inc., Marine Div., 1801 Pittsburgh Ave., Erie, Pa. 16512

Hose, exhaust

Aero Marine Div., Aeroceanic Corp., 6737 E. Washington Blvd., El Monte, Calif. 91731

Flexaust Co., Div., Callahan Mining Corp., 277 Park Ave., New York, N.Y. 10017

Kenyon Marine, Guilford, Conn. 06437

Phillips Hardware Co., 490 N. W. S. River Dr., Corner N.W. 9th Ave. and 5th St., Miami, Fla. 33128

Raybestos-Manhattan, Inc., 205 Middle St., Bridgeport, Conn. 06603

M. L. Snyder and Son, Inc., 2420 N. Jasper St., Philadelphia, Pa. 19100

Wilcox-Crittenden Div., Gulf and Western Co., Dept. 8, Middletown, Conn. 06457

Hose, flexible-metal

Allan Marine, 91 Industry Ct., Deer Park, N.Y. 11729

Buck-Algonquin Marine Hardware Div., Dixon Valve and Coupling Co., Second and Columbia, Philadelphia, Pa. 19122

Carlisle Tire and Rubber Div., Carlisle Corp., Carlisle, Pa. 17013

Flexaust Co., Div., Callahan Mining Corp., 277 Park Ave., New York, N.Y. 10017

Alva T. Smith Div., Western Industries, Inc., 300 Breed St., Chilton, Wis. 53014

Zurn Industries, Inc., Marine Div., 1801 Pittsburgh Ave., Erie, Pa. 16512

Hose, neoprene

Ace Lite Step Co., 1516 S. Wabash Ave., Chicago, Ill. 60605

Minisink Rubber Co., Inc., Unionville, N.Y. 10988

Mirax Chemical Products Corp., Marine Products Div., 4999 Fyler Ave., St. Louis 37, Mo. 63137

Ohio Rubber Co., Ben-Hur Ave., Willoughby, O. 44094

Preferred Electric and Wire Corp., 68 33rd St., Brooklyn, N.Y. 11232

Salisbury Rubber Products, W. H. Salisbury and Co., 410 N. Morgan St., Chicago, Ill. 60600

Sierra Supply Co., P.O. Box 596, McHenry, Ill. 60058

M. L. Snyder and Son, Inc., 2420 N. Jasper St., Philadelphia, Pa. 19100

Hose, plastic

Admiral Marine Prod., 2003 W. 8-Mile Rd., Detroit, Mich. 48203

Aero Marine Div., Aeroceanic Corp., 6737 E. Washington Blvd., El Monte, Calif. 91731

Cadillac Plastic Co., 15111 2nd Ave., Detroit, Mich. 48203

Crowell Designs, Inc., 2106 Bridge Ave., Point Pleasant, N.J. 08743

DeVilbiss Co., P.O. Box 913, 300 Phillips Ave., Toledo, O. 43601

Geauga Industries Co., Old State Rd., Middlefield, O. 44062

Industrial Plastics Corp., 816 W. Beardsley Ave., Elkhart, Ind. 46514

Johnson Rubber Co., 111 Vine St., Middlefield, O. 44062

Kenyon Marine, Guilford, Conn. 06437

Preferred Electric and Wire Corp., 68 33rd St., Brooklyn, N.Y. 11232

Raybestos-Manhattan, Inc., 205 Middle St., Bridgeport, Conn. 06603

Rule Industries, Inc., Cape Ann Industrial Park, Gloucester, Mass. 01930

W. S. Shamban and Co., 11543 West
Olympic Blvd., Los Angeles, Calif.
90064
Joseph B. Stinson Co., 406 Justice St.,
Fremont, O. 44820
Supplex Div., Amerace-Esna Corp.,
Bucyrus, O. 44820
Zurn Industries, Inc., Marine Div.,
1801 Pittsburgh Ave., Erie, Pa.
16512

Hose, rubber

Ace Lite Step Co., 1516 S. Wabash
Ave., Chicago, Ill. 60605
DeVilbiss Co., P.O. Box 913, 300
Phillips Ave., Toledo, O. 43601
Goodyear Tire and Rubber Co., In-
dustrial Products Div., 1144 E.
Main St., Akron, O. 44316
Kenyon Marine, Guilford, Conn.
06437
Minisink Rubber Co., Inc., Orange
County, Unionville, N.Y. 10988
Preferred Electric and Wire Corp.,
68 33rd St., Brooklyn, N.Y. 11232
Raybestos-Manhattan, Inc., 205 Mid-
dle St., Bridgeport, Conn. 06603
M. L. Snyder and Son, Inc., 2420 N.
Jasper St., Philadelphia, Pa. 19125
Supplex Div., Amerace-Esna Corp.,
Bucyrus, O. 44820
Zurn Industries, Inc., Marine Div.,
1801 Pittsburgh Ave., Erie Pa.
16512

Ice-melting systems, boat

Hinde Engineering Co., 654 Deer-
field Rd., Highland Park, Ill. 60035
Marine Power Products, Inc., 4 Rose-
dale Ave., Barrington, R.I. 02806
Schramm, Inc., 602 N. Garfield Ave.,
West Chester, Pa. 19380

Ignition kits, inboard

Bendix Automotive Service Div., 1217
S. Walnut St., South Bend, Ind.
46620
Bendix Corp., Electrical Components
Div., Delaware Ave., Sidney, N.Y.
13838
Preferred Electric and Wire Corp., 68
33rd St., Brooklyn, N.Y. 11232
Sydmur Electronic Specialties, 1268
E. 12th St., Brooklyn, N.Y. 11230
Tungsten Contact Mfg., Inc., 7311
Cottage Ave., North Bergen, N.J.
07040

Ignition kits, outboard

Bendix Automotive Service Div., 1217
S. Walnut St., South Bend, Ind.
46620
Bendix Corp., Electrical Components
Div., Delaware Ave., Sidney, N.Y.
13838
R. E. Phelon Co., Inc., 70 Maple St.,
East Longmeadow, Mass. 01028
Preferred Electric and Wire Corp., 68
33rd St., Brooklyn, N.Y. 11232
Sierra Supply Co., P.O. Box 596, Mc-
Henry, Ill. 60050
Sydmur Electronic Specialties, 1268
E. 12th St., Brooklyn, N.Y. 11230
Tungsten Contact Mfg. Co., Inc.,
7311 Cottage Ave., North Bergen,
N.J. 07040

Ignition-starting aids

Bendix Automotive Service Div., 1217
S. Walnut St., South Bend, Ind.
46620
Cole-Hersee Co., 20 Old Colony Ave.,
Boston, Mass. 02127
Goodall Mfg. Corp., 4570 W. 77th
St., Minneapolis, Minn. 55435

HLS, Inc., 2576 Lafayette St., Santa Clara, Calif. 95050

Richardson Controls Corp., 410 Tidewater Dr., Warwick, R.I. 02889

Schauer Mfg. Corp., 4538 Alpine Ave., Cincinnati, O. 45242

Sydmur Electronic Specialties, 1268 E. 12th St., Brooklyn, N.Y. 11230

Knives, caulking and putty

Allway Mfg. Co., Inc., 1513 Olmstead Ave., Bronx, N.Y. 10462

Russell Harrington Co., 44 River, Southbridge, Mass. 01550

Hyde Mfg. Co., 54 Eastford Rd., Southbridge, Mass. 01550

Millers Falls Co., 57 Wells St., Greenfield, Mass. 01301

R. Murphy Co., Inc., 13 Groton-Harvard Rd., Ayer, Mass. 01432

Letters and numbers, metal

Corbin Cabinet Lock Div., Emhart Corp., 225 Episcopal Rd., Berlin, Conn. 06037

Hy-Ko Products Co., 24001 Aurora Rd., Bedford Hts., O. 44146

Improved Methods Corp., P.O. Box 8419, Linden Lane, Shawnee Mission, Kans. 66207

Kraft's Boat Names Co., P.O. Box 22, Kansas City, Mo. 64141

LaFrance Precision Casting Co., Enterprise and Executive Aves., Philadelphia, Pa. 19153

Macklanburg-Duncan Co., P.O. Box 25188, Oklahoma City, Okla. 73125

Miller Falls Co., 57 Wells St., Greenfield, Mass. 01301

Premax Products Div., Chisholm-Ryder Co., Inc., Highland and College Ave., Niagara Falls, N.Y. 14305

Seton Name Plate Co., Inc., 592–B1 Boulevard, New Haven, Conn. 06519

Letters and numbers, plastic

Bernard Engraving Co., 5055 Stickney, Toledo, O. 43612

Denbro Plastics Co., Inc., 3320 Bishop St., Toledo, O. 43606

Florida Plastics, Inc., 904 Fourth St., St. Paul Park, Minn. 55071

Garrison Signs, 235 Pearl St., Adrian, Mich. 49221

Garrison-Wagner Co., 2018 Washington Ave., St. Louis, Mo. 63103

Hy-Ko Products Co., 24001 Aurora Rd., Bedford Hts., O. 44146

LaFrance Precision Casting Co., Enterprise and Executive Aves., Philadelphia, Pa. 19153

MSL Plastics Co., 10500 Seymour Ave., Franklin Park, Ill. 60131

Transfer Monogram Co., Inc., 2614 W. North Ave., Chicago, Ill. 60647

Letters and numbers, pressure-sensitive

Ace Flag and Pennant Co., Box 34, Woodmere, N.Y. 11590

Applebaum Tag and Label Co., 30–30 Northern Blvd., Long Island City, N.Y. 11101

Automatic Lettering Co., 178 E. Ninth St., St. Paul, Minn. 55101

Bernard Engraving Co., 5055 Stickney, Toledo, O. 43612

W. H. Brady Co., 727 W. Glendale Ave., Milwaukee, Wis. 53201

Demp-Nock Co., 21433 Mound Rd., Warren, Mich. 48090

Denbro Plastics Co., Inc., 3320 Bishop St., Toledo, O. 43606

Dyer Specialty Co., Inc., P.O. Box 2513, 9901 Alburtis Ave., Santa Fe Springs, Calif. 90570

Garelick Mfg. Co., 644 2nd St., St. Paul, Minn. 55110

Garrison Signs, 119 Maiden Lane, Adrian, Mich. 49221

Hy-Ko Products Co., 24001 Aurora Rd., Bedford Hts., O. 44146

Improved Methods Corp., 8419 Linden Lane, Shawnee Mission, Kans. 66207

LaFrance Precision Casting Co., Enterprise and Executive Aves., Philadelphia, Pa. 19153

Macklanburg-Duncan Co., P.O. Box 25188, Oklahoma City, Okla. 73125

Magix Div., Keyes-Davis Co., 74 14th St., Battle Creek, Mich. 49016

MSL Plastics, Inc., 10500 Seymour Ave., Franklin Park, Ill. 60131

Palm Brothers Co., 3736 Regent St., Cincinnati, O. 45212

Premium Marine Prod., 15 Clinton St., Yonkers, N.Y. 10701

Transfer Monogram Co., 2614 W. North Ave., Chicago, Ill. 60647

Wiljo Corp., 507 S. Main St., Galena, Ill. 61036

Lumber

M. L. Condon Co., Inc., 250 Ferris Ave., White Plains, N.Y. 10603

Chester B. Stem, Inc., Box 69 Grant Line Rd., New Albany, Ind. 47150

Thompson Mahogany Co., 7400 Edmund St., Philadelphia, Pa. 19136

United States Mahogany Comp., 152 W. 42nd St., New York, N.Y. 10036

Lumber, treated

Cross, Austin and Ireland Lumber Co., 1245 Grand St., Brooklyn, N.Y. 11211

Magnetos, inboard-engine

AMBAC Industries, Inc., American Bosch Marketing Div., 3664 Main St., Springfield, Mass. 01107

Bendix Corp., Electrical Components Div., Delaware Ave., Sidney, N.Y. 13838

Colt Industries, Inc., Fairbanks Morse, Inc., Engine Accessories Operations, 701 Lawton Ave., Beloit, Wis. 53511

Magnetos, outboard-motor

Bendix Corp., Electrical Components Div., Delaware Ave., Sidney, N.Y. 13838

Chrysler Marine and Industrial Opns., Box 2641, Detroit, Mich. 48231

Colt Industries, Inc., Fairbanks Morse, Inc., 701 Lawton Ave., Beloit, Wis. 53511

Preferred Electric and Wire Corp., 68 33rd St., Brooklyn, N.Y. 11232

Masks, dust

American Optical Corp., Mechanic St., Southbridge, Mass. 01550

Martindale Electric Co., 1364 Third Ave., Cleveland, O. 44107

Welsh Manufacturing Co., Div., Weishgard, 9 Magnolia St., Providence, R.I. 02909

Molding, plastic

Ashley Molded Products, Inc., 320 S. Wabash Ave., Ashley, Ind. 46705

Broadwater Boat Co., Box 135, Mayo, Md. 21106

Florida Plastics, Inc., 420 19th Ave., Palmetto, Fla. 33561

Gries Reproducer Co., Div., Coats and Clark, Inc., 61 Second St., New Rochelle, N.Y. 10801

J and B Plastics Co., Inc., West Stone Ave., Fairfield, Ia. 52556

W. S. Shamban and Co., 11543 W. Olympic Blvd., Los Angeles, Calif. 90064

Standard Products Co., Inc., 2130 W. 110th St., Cleveland, O. 44120

Stokes Molded Products Div., Electric Storage Battery Co., 813–B Taylor St., Trenton, N.J. 08638

Moldings, rubber

Belko Corp., Kingsville, Md. 21087

Griffith Rubber Mills, 2439 N.W. 22nd Ave., Portland, Ore. 97210

Ohio Rubber Co., Ben-Hur Ave., Willoughby, O. 44094

Perkins Marine Lamp and Hardware Corp., 16490 N.W. 13th Ave., P.O. Box D, Miami, Fla. 33164

Standard Products Co., Inc., 2130 W. 110th St., Cleveland, O. 44120

Wefco Rubber Mfg. Corp., 1655 Euclid St., Santa Monica, Calif. 90404

Oakum

New Bedford Cordage Co., 131 Court St., New Bedford, Mass. 02740

Phillips Hardware Co., 490 N.W. S. River Dr., Corner N.W. 9th Ave. and 5th St., Miami, Fla. 33128

Seaboard Twine and Cordage Co., Inc., 49 Murray St., New York, N.Y. 10007

Wall Rope Works, Beverly, N.J. 08010

Oar leathers

Auburn Mfg. Co., 200 Stack St., Middletown, Conn. 06457

Perkins Marine Lamp and Hardware Corp., P.O. Box D, 16490 N.W. 13th Ave., Miami, Fla. 33164

Phillips Hardware Co., 490 N.W. S. River Dr., Corner N.W. 9th Ave. and 5th St., Miami, Fla. 33128

Swanson Boat Oar Factory, Bradish Ave. and Walnut Ave., Albion, Pa. 16401

Oar tips

Perkins Marine Lamp and Hardware Corp., P.O. Box D, 16490 N.W. 13th Ave., Miami, Fla. 33164

Phillips Hardware Co., 490 N.W. South River Dr. Corner N.W. 9th Ave. and 5th St., Miami, Fla. 33128

Oil, marine-engine

Bray Oil Co., 1925 N. Marianna St., Los Angeles, Calif. 90032

Chevron Oil Co., 1200 State St., Perth Amboy, N.J. 08861

Dew-Coated Lubricants, P.O. Box 5755, Chicago, Ill. 60680

Gulf Oil Corp., P.O. Box 1519, Houston, Tex. 77001

Gumout Div., Pennsylvania Refining Co., 2868 Lisbon Rd., Cleveland, O. 44104

Humble Oil and Refining Co., P.O. Box 2180, Houston, Tex. 77001

Intercontinental Lubricants Corp., 19 Michael St., East Haven, Conn. 06512

Mercury Marine, Fond du Lac, Wis. 54935

Mobil Oil Co., Marine Retail Dept., 150 E. 42nd St., New York, N.Y. 10017

Phillips Petroleum Co., Bartlesville, Okla. 74003

Plowman Co., 6 Commercial Ave., Garden City, N.J. 11530

Quaker State Oil Refining Corp., P.O. Box 989, Oil City, Pa. 16301

Shell Oil Co., 50 W. 50th St., New York, N.Y. 10020

Texaco, Inc., 135 E. 42nd St., New York, N.Y. 10017

Valvoline Oil Co., Div., Ashland Oil and Refining Co., 1409 Winchester Ave., Ashland, Ky. 41101

White and Bagley Co., 100 Foster St., P.O. Box 1171, Worcester, Mass. 01601

Mobil Oil Co., Inc., Marine Retail Dept., 150 E. 42nd St., New York, N.Y. 10017

Phillips Petroleum Co., Bartlesville, Okla. 74003

Plowman Co., 6 Commercial Ave., Garden City, N.J. 11530

Quaker State Oil Refining Corp., P.O. Box 989, Oil City, Pa. 16301

RSA Products Co., 3450 Lovett St., Detroit, Mich. 48210

Texaco, Inc. 135 E. 42nd St., New York, N.Y. 10017

Valvoline Oil Co., Div., Ashland Oil and Refining Co., 1409 Winchester Ave., Ashland, Ky. 41101

White and Bagley Co., 100 Foster St., P.O. Box 1171, Worcester, Mass. 01601

Oil, outboard-motor

Bardahl Mfg. Corp., 1400 N.W. 52nd St., Seattle, Wash. 98107

Bray Oil Co., 1925 N. Marianna St., Los Angeles, Calif. 90032

Chevron Oil Co., 1200 State St., Perth Amboy, N.J. 08861

Dew-Coated Lubricants, P.O. Box 5755, Chicago, Ill. 60680

Gulf Oil Corp., P.O. Box 1519, Houston, Tex. 77001

Gumout Div., Pennsylvania Refining Co., 1868 Lisbon Road, Celveland, O. 44104

Intercontinental Lubricants Corp., 19 Michael St., East Haven, Conn. 06512

Mercury Marine, Fond du Lac, Wis. 54935

Lubriplate Div., Fiske Bros. Refining Co., 129 Lockwood St., Newark, N.J. 07105

Micro-Lube, Inc., 8505 Directors Row, Dallas, Tex. 75247

Paint, aluminum

Adelphi Paint and Color Works, Inc., 86–00 Dumont Ave., Ozone Park, N.Y. 11417

Armstrong Paint and Varnish Works, Inc., 1330 S. Kilbourn Ave., Chicago, Ill. 60623

Atlantic Varnish and Paint Co., Inc., 3000 N. Boulevard, Richmond, Va. 23230

Andrew Brown Co., 5431 District Blvd., P.O. Box 22066, Los Angeles, Calif. 90022

Coopers Creek Chemical Corp., 28 River Ave., West Conshohocken, Pa. 19428

Ditzler Automotive Finishes, PPG Industries, 8000 W. Chicago, Detroit, Mich. 48204

Dolphin Paint and Chemical Co., 922 Locust St., P.O. Box 1927 Central Station, Toledo, O. 43603

Gillespie Varnish Co., 131 Dey St., Jersey City, N.J. 07306

Gloucester Paints Inc., 129 Duncan St., Gloucester, Mass. 01930

International Paint Co., Inc., 21 West St., New York, N.Y. 10006

Maas and Waldstein Co., 2121 Mc-Carter Hwy., Newark N.J. 07104

Pettit Paint Co., Inc., 507 Main St., Rockaway, N.J. 07866

SPC, Inc., 2213 15th Ave. West, Seattle, Wash. 98119

Valspar Corp., Marine Div., 200 Sayre St., Rockford, Ill. 61101

Western Prods., Div., Mount Vernon Mills, Inc., 1015 River St., Haverhill, Mass. 01830

Wisconsin Protective Coating Corp., P.O. Box 3396, Green Bay, Wis. 54303

Woolsey Marine Industries, 201 E. 42nd Street, New York, N.Y. 10017

Paint, anti-electrolysis

Dolphin Paint and Chemical Co., 922 Locust St., P.O. Box 1927 Central Station, Toledo, O. 43603

International Paint Co., 21 West St., New York, N.Y.10006

Maas and Waldstein Co., 2121 Mc-Carter Hwy., Newark, N.J. 07104

SPC, Inc., 2213 15th Ave. West, Seattle, Wash. 98119

Valspar Corp., Marine Div., 200 Sayre St., Rockford, Ill. 61101

Wisconsin Protective Coating Corp., P.O. Box 3396, Green Bay, Wis. 54303

Woolsey Marine Industries, 201 E. 42nd St., New York, N.Y. 10017

Paint, antifouling

Adelphi Paint and Color Works, Inc., 86-00 Dumont Ave., Ozone Park, N.Y. 11417

Armstrong Paint and Varnish Works, Inc., 1330 S. Kilbourn Ave., Chicago, Ill. 60623

Atlantic Varnish and Paint Co., Inc., 3000 N. Blvd., Richmond, Va. 23230

Baltimore Copper Paint Co., 501 Key Hwy., Baltimore, Md. 21230

BoatLIFE Div., Flo-Paint, Inc., 5-45 49th Ave., Long Island City, N.Y. 11101

Andrew Brown Co., 5431 District Blvd., P.O. Box 22066, Los Angeles, Calif. 90022

Carboline Co., 328 Hanley Ind. Ct., St. Louis, Mo. 63144

Chilton Paint Co., 109-09 15th Ave., College Point, N.Y. 11356

Coopers Creek Chemical Corp., 28 River Ave., West Conshohocken, Pa. 19428

Dolphin Paint and Chemical Co., 922 Locust St., P.O. Box 1927 Central Station, Toledo, O. 43603

Gillespie Varnish Co., 131 Dey St., Jersey City, N.J. 07306

Gloucester Paints Inc., 129 Duncan St., Gloucester, Mass. 01930

Intercoastal Corp., Dundalk P.O., Baltimore, Md. 21222

International Paint Co., Inc., 21 West St., New York, N.Y. 10006

Jewel Paint and Varnish Co., 395 N. Western Ave., Chicago, Ill. 60612

Pettit Paint Co., Inc., 507 Main St., Rockaway, N.J. 07866

Red Hand Compositions Co., Inc., 1 Broadway, New York, N.Y. 10004

Sudbury Laboratory, Dutton Rd., Sudbury, Mass. 01776

U. S. Marine Coatings, Inc., P.O. Box 3318, Sarasota, Fla. 33578

Valspar Corp., Marine Div., 200 Sayre St., Rockford, Ill. 61101

Woolsey Marine Industries, 201 E. 42nd St., New York, N.Y. 10017

Paint, bilge

Coopers Creek Chemical Corp., 28 River Ave., West Conshohocken, Pa. 19428

Dolphin Paint and Chemical Co., 922 Locust St., P.O. Box 1927 Central Station, Toledo, O. 43603

Gillespie Varnish Co., 131 Dey St., Jersey City, N.J. 07306

International Paint Co., Inc., 21 West St., New York, N.Y. 10006

Pettit Paint Co., Inc., 507 Main St., Rockaway, N.J. 07866

SPC, Inc., 2213 15th Ave. West, Seattle, Wash. 98119

Valspar Corp., Marine Div., 200 Sayre St., Rockford, Ill. 61101

Woolsey Marine Industries, 201 E. 42nd St., New York, N.Y. 10017

Paint, deck

Adelphi Paint and Color Works, Inc., 86–00 Dumont Ave., Ozone Park, N.Y. 11417

Armstrong Paint and Varnish Works, Inc., 1330 S. Kilbourn Ave., Chicago, Ill. 60623

Atlantic Varnish and Paint Co., Inc., 3000 N. Boulevard, Richmond, Va. 23230

Andrew Brown Co., 5431 District Blvd., P.O. Box 22066, Los Angeles, Calif. 90022

Samuel Cabot, Inc., 246 Sumner St., Boston, Mass. 02128

Carboline Co., 328 Hanley Ind. Ct., St. Louis, Mo. 63144

Chilton Paint Co., 109–09 15th Ave., College Point, N.Y. 11356

Debevoise Co., 74 20th St., Brooklyn, N.Y. 11232

Dolphin Paint and Chemical Co., 922 Locust St., P.O. Box 1927 Central Station, Toledo, O. 43603

Falcon Safety Products, Inc., 1137 Rt. 22, Mountainside, N.J. 07092

Gillespie Varnish Co., 131 Dey St., Jersey City, N.Y. 07306

International Paint Co., Inc., 21 West St., New York, N.Y. 10006

Jewel Paint and Varnish Co., 345 N. Western Ave., Chicago, Ill. 60612

Pettit Paint Co., Inc., 507 Main St., Rockaway, N.J. 07866

Plasticover, Inc., 72 Commerce St., Brooklyn, N.Y. 11231

Red Hand Compositions Co., Inc., 1 Broadway, New York, N.Y. 10004

SPC, Inc., 2213 15th Ave. West, Seattle, Wash. 98119

Stay-Tite Products Co., Inc., 2889 E. 83rd St., P.O. Box 20130, Cleveland, O. 44120

U. S. Yacht Paint Co., Box 525, Roseland, N.J. 07068

Valspar Corp., Marine Div., 200 Sayre St., Rockford, Ill. 61101

J. C. Whitlam Mfg. Co., Box 71, Wadsworth, O. 44281

Wisconsin Protective Coating Corp., P.O. Box 3396, Green Bay, Wis. 54303

Woolsey Marine Industries, 201 E. 42nd St., New York, N.Y. 10017

Paint, engine

Adelphi Paint and Color Works, Inc., 86–00 Dumont Ave., Ozone Park, N.Y. 11417

Atlantic Varnish and Paint Co., Inc., 3000 N. Boulevard, Richmond, Va. 23230

Borden Chemical, Div., Borden, Inc., 350 Madison Ave., New York, N.Y. 10017

Andrew Brown Co., 5431 District Blvd., P.O. Box 22066, Los Angeles, Calif. 90022

Chrysler Corp., Chemical Div., 5437 West Jefferson, Trenton, Mich. 48183

Debevoise Co., 74 20th St., Brooklyn, N.Y. 11232

Gillespie Varnish Co., 131 Dey St., Jersey City, N.J. 07306

International Paint Co., Inc., 21 West St., New York, N.Y. 10006

Maas and Waldstein Co., 2121 McCarter Hwy., Newark, N.J. 07104

Pettit Paint Co., Inc., 507 Main St., Rockaway, N.J. 07866

Valspar Corp., Marine Div., 200 Sayre St., Rockford, Ill. 61101

Wisconsin Protective Coating Corp., P.O. Box 3396, Green Bay, Wis. 54303

Woolsey Marine Industries, 201 E. 42nd St., New York, N.Y. 10017

Chrysler Corp., Chemical Div., 5437 West Jefferson, Trenton, Mich. 48183

Debevoise Co., 74 20th St., Brooklyn N.Y. 11232

Gloucester Paints, Inc., 129 Duncan St., Gloucester, Mass. 01930

C. J. Hendry Co., 189 Townsend St., San Francisco, Calif. 94107

Kristal Kraft, Inc., 900 4th St., Palmetto, Fla. 33561

Maas and Waldstein Co., 2121 McCarter Hwy., Newark, N.J. 07104

Pettit Paint Co. Inc., 507 Main St., Rockaway, N.J. 07866

Ram Chemicals, 210 E. Alondra Blvd., Gardena, Calif. 90247

U. S. Yacht Paint Co., Box 525, Roseland, N.J. 07068

Valspar Corp., Marine Div., 200 Sayre St., Rockford, Ill. 61101

Woolsey Marine Industries, 201 E. 42nd St., New York, N.Y. 10017

Paint, epoxy

Adelphi Paint and Color Works, Inc., 86–00 Dumont Ave., Ozone Park, N.Y. 11417

Allied Resin Products Corp., Weymouth Ind. Park, Pleasant St., East Weymouth, Mass. 02189

American Petrochemical Corp., 3134 California St., N.E., Minneapolis, Minn. 55418

Andrew Brown Co., 5431 District Blvd., P.O. Box 22066, Los Angeles, Calif. 90022

Canadian Pittsburgh Industries, Ltd., 3730 Lakeshore Blvd., West Long Branch, Ont., Canada

Carboline Co., 328 Hanley Ind. Ct., St. Louis, Mo. 63144

Paint, fire-retardant

Maas and Waldstein Co., 2121 McCarter Hwy., Newark, N.J. 07104

Sav-Cote Chemical Laboratories, 20 S. Dove St., P.O. Box 2128 Potomac Station, Alexandria, Va. 22301

Valspar Corp., Marine Div., 200 Sayre St., Rockford, Ill. 61101

Paint, fluorescent and luminous

Day-Glo Color Corp., 4732 St. Clair Ave., Cleveland, O. 44103

Valspar Corp., Marine Div., 200 Sayre St., Rockford, Ill. 61101

Paint, hull

Adelphi Paint and Color Works, Inc., 86–00 Dumont Ave., Ozone Park, N.Y. 11417

Armstrong Paint and Varnish Works, Inc., 1330 S. Kilbourn Ave., Chicago, Ill. 60623

Atlantic Varnish and Paint Co., Inc., 3000 N. Boulevard, Richmond, Va. 23230

Baltimore Copper Paint Co., 501 Key Hwy., Baltimore, Md. 21230

BoatLIFE Div., Flo-Paint, Inc., 5–45 49th Ave., Long Island City, N.Y. 11101

Andrew Brown Co., 5431 District Blvd., P.O. Box 22066, Los Angeles, Calif. 90022

Samuel Cabot, Inc., 246 Sumner St., Boston, Mass. 02128

Carboline Co., 328 Hanley Ind. Ct., St. Louis, Mo. 63144

Chilton Paint Co., 109–09 15th Ave., College Point, N.Y. 11356

Debevoise Co., 74 20th St., Brooklyn, N.Y. 11232

Dolphin Paint and Chemical Co., 922 Locust St., P.O. Box 1927 Central Station, Toledo, O. 43603

Gloucester Paints, Inc., 129 Duncan St., Gloucester, Mass. 01930

International Paint Co., Inc., 21 West St., New York, N.Y. 10006

Jewel Paint and Varnish Co., 345 N. Western Ave., Chicago, Ill. 60612

Kyanize Paints, Inc., 2nd and Boston Sts., Everett, Mass. 02149

H. B. Fred Kuhls, 49 Sumner St., Milford, Mass. 01757

Pettit Paint Co., Inc. 507 Main St., Rockaway, N.J. 07866

Red Hand Compositions Co., Inc., 1 Broadway, New York, N.Y. 10004

SPC, Inc., 2213 15th Ave. West, Seattle, Wash. 98119

Stay-Tite Products Co., Inc. 2889 E. 83rd St., P.O. Box 20130, Cleveland, O. 44120

U. S. Yacht Paint Co., Box 525, Roseland, N.J. 07068

Valspar Corp., Marine Div., 200 Sayre St., Rockford, Ill. 61101

J. C. Whitlam Mfg. Co., Box 71, Wadsworth, O. 44281

Woolsey Marine Industries, 201 E. 42nd St., New York, N.Y. 10017

Paint, interior

Armstrong Paint and Varnish Works, Inc., 1330 S. Kilbourn Ave., Chicago, Ill. 60623

Carboline Co., 328 Hanley Ind. Ct., St. Louis, Mo. 63144

Debevoise Co., 74 20th St., Brooklyn, N.Y. 11232

Dolphin Paint and Chemical Co., 922 Locust St., P.O. Box 1927 Central Station, Toledo, O. 43603

International Paint Co., Inc., 21 West St., New York, N.Y. 10006

Pettit Paint Co., Inc., 507 Main St., Rockaway, N.J. 07866

Red Hand Compositions Co., Inc., 1 Broadway, New York, N.Y. 10004

SPC, Inc., 2213 15th Ave. West, Seattle, Wash. 98119

Valspar Corp., Marine Div., 200 Sayre St., Rockford, Ill. 61101

Woolsey Marine Industries, 201 E. 42nd St., New York, N.Y. 10017

Paint, nonskid

Andrew Brown Co., 5431 District Blvd., P.O. Box 22066, Los Angeles, Calif. 90022

Debevoise Co., 74 20th St., Brooklyn, N.Y. 11232

Falcon Safety Products, Inc., 1137 Rt. 22, Mountainside, N.J. 07092

Gillespie Varnish Co., 131 Dey St., Jersey City, N.J. 07306

Gloucester Paints, Inc., 129 Duncan St., Gloucester, Mass. 01930

International Paint Co., Inc., 21 West St., New York, N.Y. 10006

Lewbill Industries, Inc., P.O. Box 221, Scottdale, Pa. 15683

Miracle Adhesives Corp., 250 Pettit Ave., Bellmore, N.Y. 11710

Pettit Paint Co., Inc., 507 Main St., Rockaway, N.J. 07866

Valspar Corp., Marine Div., 200 Sayre St., Rockford, Ill. 61101

Woolsey Marine Industries, 201 E. 42nd St., New York, N.Y. 10017

Wooster Products, Inc., Spruce St., Wooster, O. 44691

Paint, polyurethane

Baltimore Copper Paint Co., 501 Key Hwy., Baltimore, Md. 21230

Valspar Corp., Marine Div., 200 Sayre St., Rockford, Ill. 61101

Paint, self-spraying

Borden Chemical Div., Borden, Inc., 350 Madison Ave., New York, N.Y. 10017

G. C. Electronics Co., 400 S. Wyman St., Rockford, Ill. 61101

Pettit Paint Co., Inc., 507 Main St., Rockaway, N.J. 07866

Tempo Products Co., 6200 Cochran Rd., Cleveland, O. 44139

Valspar Corp., Marine Div., 200 Sayre St., Rockford, Ill. 61101

Woolsey Marine Industries, 201 E. 42nd St., New York, N.Y. 10017

Paint, topside

Armstrong Paint and Varnish Works, Inc., 1330 S. Kilbourn Ave., Chicago, Ill. 60623

Atlantic Varnish and Paint Co., Inc., 3000 N. Boulevard, Richmond, Va. 23230

BoatLIFE Div., Flo-Paint, Inc., 5–45 49th Ave., Long Island City, N.Y. 11101

Andrew Brown Co., 5431 District Blvd., P.O. Box 22066, Los Angeles, Calif. 90022

Samuel Cabot, Inc., 246 Sumner St., Boston, Mass. 02128

Carboline Co., 328 Hanley Ind. Ct., St. Louis, Mo. 63144

Chilton Paint Co., 109–09 15th Ave., College Point, N.Y. 11356

Ditzler Automotive Finishes, PPG Industries, 8000 W. Chicago, Detroit, Mich. 48204

Dolphin Paint and Chemical Co., 922 Locust St., P.O. Box 1927 Central Station, Toledo, O. 43603

Epfanes Marine Finishes, 17–12 River Rd., Fairlawn, N.J. 07410

Gillespie Varnish Co., 131 Dey St., Jersey City, N.J. 07306

Gloucester Paints, Inc., 129 Duncan St., Gloucester, Mass. 01930

International Paint Co., 21 West St., New York, N.Y. 10006

Jewel Paint and Varnish Co., 345 N. Western Ave., Chicago, Ill. 60612

Lowe Brothers Co., 424 E. 3rd St., Dayton, O. 45011

Pettit Paint Co., Inc., 507 Main St., Rockaway, N.J. 07866

Red Hand Compositions Co., Inc. 1 Broadway, New York, N.Y. 10004

SPC, Inc. 2213 15th Ave. West, Seattle, Wash. 98119

Valspar Corp., Marine Div., 200 Sayre St., Rockford, Ill. 61101

J. C. Whitlam Mfg. Co., Box 71, Wadsworth, O. 44281

Woolsey Marine Industries, 201 E. 42nd St., New York, N.Y. 10017

Paint, touch-up, brush and spray

International Paint Co., Inc., 21 West St., New York, N.Y. 10006

Mercury Marine, Fond du Lac, Wis. 54935

Pettit Paint Co., Inc., 507 Main St., Rockaway, N.J. 07866

Valspar Corp., Marine Div., 200 Sayre St., Rockford, Ill. 61101

Woolsey Marine Industries, 201 E. 42nd St., New York, N.Y. 10017

Paint, vinyl plastic

Baltimore Copper Paint Co., 501 Key Hwy., Baltimore, Md. 21230

Bristol Marine Products, Inc., 147 10th Ave., Flushing, N.Y. 11357

Dolphin Paint and Chemical Co., 922 Locust St., P.O. Box 1927 Central Station, Toledo, O. 43603

Ferro Corporation, 4150 E. 56th St., Cleveland, O. 44105

Plasticover, Inc., 72 Commerce St., Brooklyn, N.Y. 11231

Paint primers, fiberglass

American Petrochemical Corp., 3134 California St., N.E., Minneapolis, Minn. 55418

Andrew Brown Co., 5431 District Blvd., P.O. Box 22066, Los Angeles, Calif. 90022

Canadian Pittsburgh Industries, Ltd., 3730 Lakeshore Blvd., West Long Branch, Ont., Canada

Dolphin Paint and Chemical Co., 922 Locust St., P.O. Box 1927 Central Station, Toledo, O. 43603

International Paint Co., Inc., 21 West St., New York, N.Y. 10006

Jewel Paint and Varnish Co., 345 N. Western Ave., Chicago, Ill. 60612

Pettit Paint Co., Inc., 507 Main St., Rockaway, N.J. 07866

SPC, Inc., 2213 15th Ave. West, Seattle, Wash. 98119

Valspar Corp., Marine Div., 200 Sayre St., Rockford, Ill. 61101

Woolsey Marine Industries, 201 E. 42nd St., New York, N.Y. 10017

X-I-M Products, Inc., 1169 Bassett Road, Westlake, O. 44091

Paint primers, metal

Adelphi Paint and Color Works, Inc., 86–00 Dumont Ave., Ozone Park, N.Y. 11417

American Petrochemical Corp., 3134 California St., N.E., Minneapolis, Minn. 55418

Armstrong Paint and Varnish Works, Inc., 1330 S. Kilbourn Ave., Chicago, Ill. 60623

Andrew Brown Co., 5431 District Blvd., P.O. Box 22066, Los Angeles, Calif. 90022

Canadian Pittsburgh Industries, Ltd., 3730 Lakeshore Blvd., West Long Branch, Ont., Canada

Carboline Co., 328 Hanley Ind. Ct., St. Louis, Mo. 63144

Chilton Paint Co., 109–09 15th Ave., College Point, N.Y. 11356

Dolphin Paint and Chemical Co., 922 Locust St., P.O. Box 1927 Central Station, Toledo, O. 43603

International Paint Co., Inc., 21 West St., New York, N.Y. 10006

Jewel Paint and Varnish Co., 345 N. Western Ave., Chicago, Ill. 60612

Maas and Waldstein Co., 2121
McCarter Hwy., Newark, N.J.
07104

Pettit Paint Co., Inc., 507 Main St.,
Rockaway, N.J. 07866

Red Hand Composition Co., Inc.,
1 Broadway, New York, N.Y. 10004

Rusticide Products Co., 3125 Perkins
Ave., Cleveland, O. 44114

Rust-Oleum Corp., 2425 Oakton St.,
Evanston, Ill. 60202

SPC, Inc., 2213 15th Ave. West. Seattle, Wash. 98119

Valspar Corp., Marine Div., 200
Sayre St., Rockford, Ill. 61101

Woolsey Marine Industries, 201 E.
42nd St., New York, N.Y. 10017

X-I-M Products, Inc., 1169 Bassett
Road, Westlake, O. 44091

Paint primers, plywood

Armstrong Paint and Varnish Works,
Inc., 1330 S. Kilbourn Ave., Chicago, Ill. 60623

Andrew Brown Co., 5431 District
Blvd., P.O. Box 22066, Los Angeles, Calif. 90022

Canadian Pittsburgh Industries, Ltd.,
3730 Lakeshore Blvd., West Long
Branch, Ont., Canada

Dolphin Paint and Chemical Co., 922
Locust St., P.O. Box 1927 Central
Station, Toledo, O. 43603

International Paint Co., Inc., 21 West
St., New York, N.Y. 10006

Pettit Paint Co., Inc., 507 Main St.,
Rockaway, N.J. 07866

SPC, Inc., 2213 15th Ave. West, Seattle, Wash. 98119

Valspar Corp., Marine Div., 200
Sayre St., Rockford, Ill. 61101

Woolsey Marine Industries, 201 E.
42nd St., New York, N.Y. 10017

X-I-M Products, Inc., 1169 Bassett
Road, Westlake, O. 44091

Paint primers, wood

Adelphi Paint and Color Works, Inc.,
86–00 Dumont Ave., Ozone Park,
N.Y. 11417

Armstrong Paint and Varnish Works,
Inc., 1330 S. Kilbourn Ave., Chicago, Ill. 60623

Andrew Brown Co., 5431 District
Blvd., P.O. Box 22066, Los Angeles, Calif. 90022

Canadian Pittsburgh Industries, Ltd.,
3730 Lakeshore Blvd., West Long
Branch, Ont., Canada

Carboline Co., 328 Hanley Ind. Ct.,
St. Louis, Mo 63144

Dolphin Paint and Chemical Co., 922
Locust St., P.O. Box 1927 Central
Station, Toledo, O. 43603

Glass Plastics/Valspar Corp., 200
Sayre St., Rockford, Ill. 61101

International Paint Co., Inc., 21 West
St., New York, N.Y. 10006

Jewel Paint and Varnish Co., 345 N.
Western Ave., Chicago, Ill. 60612

Pettit Paint Co., Inc., 507 Main St.,
Rockaway, N.J. 07866

SPC, Inc., 2213 15th Ave. West, Seattle, Wash. 98119

Valspar Corp., Marine Div., 200
Sayre St., Rockford, Ill. 61101

Woolsey Marine Industries, 201 E.
42nd St., New York, N.Y. 10017

X-I-M Products, Inc., 1169 Bassett
Road, Westlake, O. 44091

Paint and varnish removers

American Petrochemical Corp., 3134
California St., N.E., Minneapolis,
Minn. 55418

Atlantic Varnish and Paint Co., Inc.,
3000 N. Boulevard, Richmond, Va.
23230

Baltimore Copper Paint Co., 501 Key
Hwy., Baltimore, Md. 21320

Beck Equipment and Chemical Co., 3350 W. 137th St., Cleveland, O. 44111

Andrew Brown Co., 5431 District Blvd., P.O. Box 22066, Los Angeles, Calif. 90022

H. A. Calahan, Inc., 859 Mamaroneck Ave., Mamaroneck, N.Y. 10543

Chemical Products Co., Inc., P.O. Box 111, Aberdeen, Md. 21101

Darworth, Inc., Chemical Products Div., Simsbury, Conn. 06070

James B. Day and Co., 1872 Clybourn Ave., Chicago, Ill. 60614

Dolphin Paint and Chemical Co., 922 Locust St., P.O. Box 1927 Central Station, Toledo, O. 43603

Gillespie Varnish Co., 131 Dey St., Jersey City, N.J. 07306

International Paint Co., Inc., 21 West St., New York, N.Y. 10006

Jasco Chemical Corp., P.O. Drawer "J," Mountain View, Calif. 94111

H. B. Fred Kuhls, 100 Halladay St., Jersey City, N.J. 07304

Pettit Paint Co., Inc., 507 Main St., Rockaway, N.J. 07866

Savogran Co., P.O. Box 58, Norwood, Mass. 02062

SPC, Inc., 2213 15th Ave. West, Seattle, Wash. 98119

Sta-Lube, Inc., 3039 Ana St., Compton, Calif. 90221

Valspar Corp., Marine Div., 200 Sayre St., Rockford, Ill. 61101

Woolsey Marine Industries, 201 E. 42nd St., New York, N.Y. 10017

M. L. Condon Co., Inc., 250 Ferris Ave., White Plains, N.Y. 10603

J. H. Monteath Co., 2506 Park Ave., Bronx, N.Y. 10451

Simpson Timber Co., 2000 Washington Bldg., Seattle, Wash. 98101

U. S. Plywood Div., U. S. Plywood-Champion Paper, Inc., 777 3rd Ave., New York, N.Y. 10017

Preservatives, canvas

Baltimore Canvas Products, Inc., 2861 W. Franklin St., Baltimore, Md. 21223

John Boyle and Co., Inc., 112–14 Duane St., New York, N.Y. 10007

Marty Gilman, Inc., Marine Products Div., Gilman, Conn. 06336

International Paint Co., Inc., 21 West St., New York, N.Y. 10006

H. B. Fred Kuhls, 100 Halladay St., Jersey City, N.J. 07304

Lan-O-Sheen, Inc., 1 W. Water, St. Paul, Minn. 55107

Pettit Paint Co., Inc., 507 Main St., Rockaway, N.J. 07866

SPC, Inc., 2213 15th Ave. West, Seattle, Wash. 98119

Speco, Inc., 7308 Associate Ave., Cleveland, O. 44109

Valspar Corp., Marine Div., 200 Sayre St., Rockford, Ill. 61101

Watco Dennis Corp., 1756 22nd St., Santa Monica, Calif. 90404

Plywood, marine

American Plywood Association, 1119 "A" St., Tacoma, Wash. 98401

Bryne Plywood Co., 2400 Cole St., P.O. Box 504, Birmingham, Mich. 48008

Preservatives, rope

International Paint Co., Inc., 21 West St., New York, N.Y. 10006

H. B. Fred Kuhls, 100 Halladay St., Jersey City, N.J. 07304

Pettit Paint Co., Inc., 507 Main St., Rockaway, N.J. 07866

Preservatives, wood

Baltimore Copper Paint Co., 501 Key Hwy., Baltimore, Md. 21230

BoatLIFE Div., Flo-Paint, Inc., 5-45 49th Ave., Long Island City, N.Y. 11101

Andrew Brown Co., 5431 District Blvd., P.O. Box 22066, Los Angeles, Calif. 90022

H. A. Calahan, Inc., 859 Mamaroneck Ave., Mamaroneck, N.Y. 10543

Coopers Creek Chemical Corp., 28 River Ave., West Conshohocken, Pa. 19428

Darworth, Inc., Chemical Products Div., Simsbury, Conn. 06070

Dolphin Paint and Chemical Co., 922 Locust St., P.O. Box 1927 Central Station, Toledo, O. 43603

International Paint Co., Inc., 21 West St., New York, N.Y. 10006

Jasco Chemical Corp., P.O. Drawer "J," Mountain View, Calif. 94111

Pettit Paint Co., Inc., 507 Main St., Rockaway, N.J. 07866

United States Plywood Corp., 777 Third Ave., New York, N.Y. 10017

Valspar Corp., Marine Div., 200 Sayre St., Rockford, Ill. 61101

Woolsey Marine Industries, 201 E. 42nd St., New York, N.Y. 10017

Putty, epoxy

Dolphin Paint and Chemical Co., 922 Locust St., P.O. Box 1927 Central Station, Toledo, O. 43603

International Paint Co., Inc., 21 West St., New York, N.Y. 10006

R. E. Phelon Co., Inc., 70 Maple St., East Longmeadow, Mass. 01028

Red Hand Compositions Co., Inc., 1 Broadway, New York, N.Y. 10004

Ren Plastics, Inc., 5656 S. Cedar, Lansing, Mich. 48909

W. J. Ruscoe Co., 483 Kenmore Blvd., Akron, O. 44301

Valspar Corp., Marine Div., 200 Sayre St., Rockford, Ill. 61101

Willhold Glues, Inc., 8707 Millergrove Dr., Santa Fe Springs, Calif. 90670

Putty, fiberglass and plastic

Also see Compounds, plastic putty

Glas-Mate Div., Ransburg Electro-Coating Corp., 2959 N.E. Twelfth Terrace, Fort Lauderdale, Fla. 33307

Interplastics Corp., Commercial Resins Div., 2015 N.E. Broadway, Minneapolis, Minn. 55413

Pettit Paint Co., Inc., 507 Main St., Rockaway, N.J. 07866

Plastics Sales and Mfg. Co., Inc., 3030 McGee Trafficway, Kansas City, Mo. 64116

Presto Chemicals, Inc., 9346 Glenoaks Blvd., Sun Valley, Calif. 91352

Valspar Corp., Marine Div., 200 Sayre St., Rockford, Ill. 61101

Putty, polyester

Andrew Brown Co., 5431 District Blvd., Box 22066, Los Angeles, Calif. 90022

Valspar Corp., Marine Div., 200 Sayre St., Rockford, Ill. 61101

Putty, wood

Also see Compounds, deck and seam-filling

DAP, Inc., 5800 Huberville Ave., Dayton, O. 45431

Dolphin Paint and Chemical Co., 922 Locust St., P.O. Box 1927 Central Station, Toledo, O. 43603

Magic American Chemical Corp., 14215 Caine Ave., Cleveland, O. 44128

Pettit Paint Co., Inc., 507 Main St., Rockaway, N.J. 07866

Valspar Corp., Marine Div., 200 Sayre St., Rockford, Ill. 61101

Regulators, voltage

Robert Bosch Corp., 2800 S. 25th Ave., Broadview, Ill. 60153

Leece-Neville Co., 1374 E. 51st St., Cleveland, O. 44114

C. E. Neihoff and Co., 4925 Lawrence Ave., Chicago, Ill. 60630

Preferred Electric and Wire Corp., 68 33rd St., Brooklyn, N.Y. 11232

Prestolite Co., 511 Hamilton St., Toledo, O. 43601

Standard Motor Products, Inc., 37–18 Northern Blvd., Long Island City, N.Y. 11101

United Motors Service Div., General Motors Corp., 3044 West Grand Blvd., Detroit, Mich. 48202

Resin additives

Berton Plastics, Inc., 170 Wesley St., South Hackensack, N.J. 07606

Borden, Inc., Chemical Div., 350 Madison Ave., New York, N.Y. 10017

Lucidol Div., Wallace and Tiernan, Inc., 1740 Military Rd., Buffalo, N.Y. 14240

Pettit Paint Co., Inc., 507 Main St., Rockaway, N.J. 07866

Uniglass Industries, Div. Glascoat, 150 N.W. 176th St., Miami, Fla. 33169

Valspar Corp., Marine Div., 200 Sayre St., Rockford, Ill. 61101

Western Prods., Div., Mount Vernon Mills, Inc., 1015 River St., Haverhill, Mass. 01830

Resin catalysts

Berton Plastics, Inc., 170 Wesley St., South Hackensack, N.J. 07606

Cadillac Plastic Co., 15111 2nd Ave., Detroit, Mich. 48203

Clausen Co., 1055 King George Rd., Fords, N.J. 08863

International Paint Co., Inc., 21 West St., New York, N.Y. 10006

McKesson Chemical Co., 155 E. 44th St., New York, N.Y. 10017

Ram Chemicals, 210 E. Alondra Blvd., Gardena, Calif. 90247

Valspar Corp., Marine Div., 200 Sayre St., Rockford, Ill. 61101

Resin solvents

Berton Plastics, Inc., 170 Wesley St., South Hackensack, N.J. 07606

Cadillac Plastic Co., 15111 2nd Ave., Detroit, Mich. 48203

International Paint Co., Inc., 21 West St., New York, N.Y. 10006

Pettit Paint Co., Inc., 507 Main St., Rockaway, N.J. 07866

Ram Chemicals, 210 E. Alondra Blvd., Gardena, Calif. 90247

Valspar Corp., Marine Div., 200 Sayre St., Rockford, Ill. 61101

Resins, epoxy

Allan Marine, P.O. Box 120, Industry Ct., Deer Park, N.Y. 11729

Allied Resin Products Corp., Weymouth Ind. Park, Pleasant St., East
Weymouth, Mass. 02189

Berton Plastics, Inc., 170 Wesley St.,
South Hackensack, N.J. 07606

BoatLIFE Div., Flo-Paint, Inc., 5–45
49th Ave., Long Island City, N.Y.
11101

Cadillac Plastic Co., 15111 2nd Ave.,
Detroit, Mich. 48203

Defender Industries, Inc., 384 Broadway, New York, N.Y. 10013

Fiberglass-Evercoat Co., Inc., 6600
Cornell Ave., Cincinnati, O. 45242

Kristal Kraft, Inc., 900 4th St., Palmetto, Fla. 33561

Marblette Corp., 37–31 30th St.,
Long Island City, N.Y. 11101

Miracle Adhesives Corp., 250 Pettit
Ave., Bellmore, N.Y. 11710

Pettit Paint Co., Inc., 507 Main St.,
Rockaway, N.J. 07866

R. E. Phelon Co., Inc., 70 Maple St.,
East Longmeadow, Mass. 40128

Ram Chemicals, 210 E. Alondra Blvd.,
Gardena, Calif. 90247

Reichhold Chemicals, Inc., 525 N.
Broadway, White Plains, N.Y.
10603

Ren Plastics, Inc., 5656 S. Cedar,
Lansing, Mich. 48909

Resin Coatings Corp., 3595 N.W.
74th St., Miami, Fla. 33147

Smooth-On, Inc., 1000 Valley Rd.,
Stirling, N.J. 07933

Tra-Con, Inc., Resin Systems Div.,
55 North St., Medford, Mass. 02155

Travaco Laboratories, 345 Eastern
Ave., Chelsea, Mass. 02150

Uniglass Industries, Div., Glascoat,
150 N.W. 176th St., Miami, Fla.
33169

Valspar Corp., Marine Div., 200
Sayre St., Rockford, Ill. 61101

Woodhill Chemical Sales Corp.,
18731 Cranwood Pkwy., Cleveland, O. 44128

Resins, marine

Borden, Inc., Chemical Div., 350
Madison Ave., New York, N.Y.
10017

Valspar Corp., Marine Div., 200
Sayre St., Rockford, Ill. 61101

Resins, polyester

Allied Resin Products Corp., Weymouth Ind. Park, Pleasant St., East
Weymouth, Mass. 02189

American Cyanamid Co., Plastics
Div., Wallingford, Conn. 06492

American Petrochemical Corp., 3134
California St., N.E., Minneapolis,
Minn. 55418

Berton Plastics, Inc., 170 Wesley St.,
South Hackensack, N.J. 07606

Cadillac Plastic Co., 15111 2nd Ave.,
Detroit, Mich. 48203

Canadian Pittsburgh Industries, Ltd.,
3730 Lakeshore Blvd., Long
Branch, Ont., Canada

Defender Industries, Inc., 384 Broadway, New York, N.Y. 10013

Durez Plastics Div., Hooker Chemical
Corp., 1932 Walck Rd., North
Tonawanda, N.Y. 14121

Freeman Chemical Corp., 222 Main
St., Port Washington, Wis. 53074

Glas-Mate Div., Ransburg Electro-
Coating Corp., 2959 N.E. 12th Terrace, Fort Lauderdale, Fla. 33307

International Paint Co., Inc., 21 West
St., New York, N.Y. 10006

Interplastics Corp., Commercial Resins
Div., 2015 N.E. Broadway, Minneapolis, Minn. 55413

Kristal Kraft, Inc., 900 4th St., Palmetto, Fla. 33561

J. M. McGivney, Inc., 214 N.W. 73rd
St., Miami, Fla. 33150

Pettit Paint Co., Inc., 507 Main St.,
Rockaway, N.J. 07866

Plastic Engineering and Chemical Co., 3501 N.W. Ninth Ave., Fort Lauderdale, Fla. 33309

PPG Industries, Inc., Plastic Sales, Bldg. 1, Gateway Center, Pittsburgh, Pa. 15222

Ram Chemicals, 210 E. Alondra Blvd., Gardena, Calif. 90247

Reichhold Chemicals, Inc., 525 N. Broadway, White Plains, N.Y. 10603

Rohm and Haas, Independence Mall West, Philadelphia, Pa. 19105

Tra-Con Inc., Resin Systems Div., 55 North St., Medford, Mass. 02155

Uniglass Industries, Div., Glascoat, 150 N.W. 176th St., Miami, Fla. 33169

Resins, polyurethane

Defender Industries, Inc., 384 Broadway, New York, N.Y. 10013

Durez Plastics Div., Hooker Chemical Corp., 1932 Walck Rd., North Tonawanda, N.Y. 14121

Freeman Chemical Corp., 222 Main St., Port Washington, Wis. 53074

Interplastics Corp., Commercial Resins Div., 2015 N.E. Broadway, Minneapolis, Minn. 55413

Kristal Kraft, Inc., 900 4th St., Palmetto, Fla. 35561

PPG Industries, Inc., Plastic Sales, Bldg. 1, Gateway Center, Pittsburgh, Pa. 15222

Reichhold Chemicals, Inc., 525 N. Broadway, White Plains, N.Y. 40603

Tra-Con, Inc., Resin Systems Div., 55 North St., Medford, Mass. 02155

Uniglass Industries, Div., Glascoat, 150 N.W. 176th St., Miami, Fla. 33169

Valspar Corp., Marine Div., 200 Sayre St., Rockford, Ill. 61101

Sanders, belt

Arco Mfg. Co., 1701 13th Ave. N., P.O. Box 817, Grand Forks, N.D. 58201

Dotco, Inc., Hicksville, O. 43526

Rockwell Tools, The Thomas Flynn Highway, Pittsburgh, Pa.

Skil Corp., 5033 Elston Ave., Chicago, Ill. 60630

Thor Power Tool Co., 175 N. State St., Aurora, Ill. 60507

Sanders, orbital

Clarke Floor Machines Div., Studebaker Corp., 1796-70 E. Clay Ave., Muskegon, Mich. 49443

Clausen Co., 1055 King George Rd., Fords, N.J. 08863

D. S. M. Co., 7586 Dixie Hwy., Lake Worth, Fla. 33460

Millers Falls Co., 57 Wells, Greenfield, Mass. 01301

National-Detroit, Inc., 2810 Auburn St., Rockford, Ill. 61103

Rockwell Tools, The Thomas Flynn Highway, Pittsburgh, Pa.

Skil Corp., 5033 Elston Ave., Chicago, Ill. 60603

Thor Power Tool Co., 175 N. State St., Aurora, Ill. 60507

Sanders, rotary and disk

Clarke Floor Machines Div., Studebaker Corp., 1796-70 E. Clay Ave., Muskegon, Mich. 49443

Dotco, Inc., Hicksville, O. 43526

D. S. M. Co., 7586 S. Dixie Hwy., Lake Worth, Fla. 33460

Milwaukee Electric Tool Corp., 13135
W. Lisbon Rd., Brookfield, Wis.
53005

National-Detroit, Inc., 2810 Auburn
St., Rockford, Ill. 61103

Rockwell Tools, The Thomas Flynn
Highway, Pittsburgh, Pa.

Superior Pneumatic and Mfg., Inc.,
P.O. Box 9667, Cleveland, O. 44140

Carborundum Co., Merchandising
Sales, Box 477, Niagara Falls, N.Y.
14302

Coastal Abrasive and Tool Co., Inc.,
P.O. Box 337, Merritt Industrial
Park, Trumbull, Conn. 06611

Norton Co., Coated Abrasive and
Tape Div., Dept. 6956, Troy, N.Y.
12181

Sanders, rotary-brush

Coastal Abrasive and Tool Co., Inc.,
P.O. Box 337, Merritt Industrial
Park, Trumbull, Conn. 06611

Rockwell Tools, The Thomas Flynn
Highway, Pittsburgh, Pa.

Sanding blocks

Carborundum Co., Merchandising
Sales, Box 477, Niagara Falls, N.Y.
14302

Carter Products Co., P.O. Box 1924,
Columbus, O. 43216

Millers Falls Co., 57 Wells, Greenfield, Mass. 01301

Norton Co., Coated Abrasive and
Tape Div., Dept. 6956, Troy, N.Y.
12181

Sanding pads

Carborundum Co., Merchandising
Sales, Box 477, Niagara Falls, N.Y.
14302

Coastal Abrasive and Tool Co., Inc.,
P.O. Box 327, Merritt Industrial
Park, Trumbull, Conn. 06611

Sandpaper and disks

Also see Abrasives

Spark plugs

AC Spark Plug Div., General Motors
Corp., 1300 N. Dort Hwy., Flint,
Mich. 48556

Robert Bosch Corp., 2800 S. 25th
Ave., Broadview, Ill. 60153

Champion Spark Plug Co., 900 Upton Ave., Toledo, O. 43601

Gale Products Div., Outboard Marine
Corp., Galesburg, Ill. 61401

Mercury Marine, Fond du Lac, Wis.
54935

Nisonger Corp., 125 Main St., New
Rochelle, N.Y. 10801

Prestolite Co., 511 Hamilton St.,
Toledo, O. 43601

Smiths Industries North America,
Ltd., 105 Scarsdale Rd., Don Mills,
Ont., Canada

Spark plugs, resistor-type

AC Spark Plug Div., General Motors
Corp., 1300 N. Dort Hwy., Flint,
Mich. 48556

Champion Spark Plug Co., 900 Upton
Ave., Toledo, O. 43601

Leonard Spark Plug Co., Inc., 23
Centerway, E. Orange, N.J. 07017

Sponges, cellulose and rubber

American Sponge and Chamois Co.,
Inc., 4700 34th St., Long Island
City, N.Y. 11101
Commodore Nautical Supplies, 396
Broadway, New York, N.Y. 10013
Garelick Mfg. Co., 644 2nd St., St.
Paul Park, Minn. 55071
Gulf and West Indies Co., Inc., 141
Front St., New York, N.Y. 10005
Phillips Hardware Co., 490 N.W. S.
River Dr., Corner N.W. 9th Ave.
and 5th St., Miami, Fla. 33128

Sponges, natural

American Sponge and Chamois Co.,
Inc., 4700 34th St., Long Island
City, N.Y. 10011
Garelick Mfg. Co., 644 2nd St., St.
Paul Park, Minn. 55071
Gulf and West Indies Co., Inc., 141
Front St., New York, N.Y. 10005

Sponges, plastic

Gulf and West Indies Co., Inc., 141
Front St., New York, N.Y. 10005

Sprayers, paint

DeVilbiss Co., P.O. Box 913, 300
Phillips Ave., Toledo, O. 43601
Glas-Mate Div., Ransburg Electro-
Coating Corp., 2959 N.E. 12th Ter-
race, Fort Lauderdale, Fla. 33307
SPC, Inc., 2213 15th Ave. West, Se-
attle, Wash. 98119

Tapes, masking

Alvin and Co., Inc., 611 Palisade Ave.,
Windsor, Conn. 06095

Arno Adhesive Tapes, Inc., U.S. 20
at Ohio St., Michigan City, Ind.
46360
Fedtro, Inc., Federal Electronics
Building, Rockville Centre, N.Y.
11571
Griffolyn Co., Inc., P.O. Box 33248,
Houston, Tex. 77033
Iroquois Paper, Marine Prods, Div.,
2220 W. 56th St., Chicago, Ill.
60636
3M Co., 3M Center, St. Paul, Minn.
55101
Phillips Hardware Co., 490 N.W. S.
River Dr., Corner N.W. 9th Ave.
and 5th St., Miami, Fla. 33128
Preferred Electric and Wire Corp.,
68 33rd St., Brooklyn, N.Y. 11232
W. S. Shamban and Co., 11543 West
Olympic Blvd., Los Angeles, Calif.
90064
Ward International, Inc., P.O. Box
1377, Studio City, Calif. 91604
J. C. Whitlam Mfg. Co., Box 71,
Wadsworth, O. 44281

Tarpaulins, canvas

Baltimore Canvas Products, Inc., 2861
W. Franklin St., Baltimore, Md.
21207
Burch Mfg. Co., Inc., 618 1st Ave. N.,
Fort Dodge, Ia. 50501
Manart Textile Co., 116 Franklin St.,
New York, N.Y. 10013

Tarpaulins, plastic

Boyle, John and Co., Inc., 112 Duane
St., New York, N.Y. 10007
Burch Mfg. Co., Inc., 618 1st Ave. N.,
Fort Dodge, Ia. 50501
Fabrico Mfg. Corp., 1300 W. Ex-
change Ave., Chicago, Ill. 60609
Griffolyn Co., Inc., P.O. Box 33248,
Houston, Tex. 77033

Van Brode Sales Co., 20 Cameron St., Clinton, Mass. 01510

Teak oil

H. B. Fred Kuhls Co., 49 Sumner St., Milford, Mass. 01757
Watco Dennis Corp., 1756 22nd St., Santa Monica, Calif. 90404

Tie-downs, cover

Griffolyn Co., Inc., P.O. Box 33248, Houston, Tex. 77033

Tools, engine service

Channellock, Inc., S. Main St., Meadville, Pa. 16335
Jonard Industries Corp., 3047 Tibbett Ave., Bronx, N.Y. 10463
Kedman Co., 762 S. Redwood Rd., P.O. Box 267, Salt Lake City, Utah 84110
Bob Kerr's Marine Tool Co., P.O. Box 1135, Winter Garden, Fla. 32787
Snap-On Tools Corp., 8028 28th Ave., Kenosha, Wis. 53140

Tools, paint-stripping

Allway Mfg. Co., Inc., 1513 Olmstead Ave., Bronx, N.Y. 10462
Aurand Mfg. and Equipment Co., 1350 Ellis St., Cincinnati, O. 45223
BernzOmatic Corp., 740 Driving Park Ave., Rochester, N.Y. 14613

Tools, woodworking

Ashley Molded Products, Inc., 320 S. Wabash Ave., Ashley, Ind. 46705

Black and Decker Mfg. Co., 701 E. Joppa Rd., Towson, Md. 21204
Container Stapling Corp., 100 S. 27th St., Herrin, Ill. 62948
Gordon Associates, Inc., Derby, Conn. 06418
Rockwell Tools, The Thomas Flynn Highway, Pittsburgh, Pa.
Stanley Tooks, 600 Myrtle St., New Britain, Conn. 06053
Ullman Devices Corp., P.O. Box 398, Ridgefield, Conn. 06877

Tubing, copper

Anaconda American Brass Co., 414 Meadow St., Waterbury, Conn. 06720
Cerro Copper and Brass Div., Cerro Corp., 16600 St. Clair Ave., Cleveland, O. 44110
Clendenin Bros., Inc., 4309 Erdman Ave., Baltimore, Md. 21213
Preferred Electric and Wire Corp., 68 33rd St., Brooklyn, N.Y. 11232
Revere Copper and Brass, Inc., 230 Park Ave., New York, N.Y. 10017

Tubing, flexible-metal

Anaconda American Brass Co., 414 Meadow St., Waterbury, Conn. 06720
Russell Industries, Inc., 96 Station Plaza, Lynbrook, N.Y. 11563

Tubing, plastic

Backstay Welt Co., Inc., 409 W. Oak St., Union City, Ind. 17390
Beckson Mfg., Inc., P.O. Box 3336, Bridgeport, Conn. 06605
Detroit Marine Engineering, 227 Adair, Detroit, Mich. 48207

GC Electronics Co., 400 S. Wyman St., Rockford, Ill. 61101

Geauga Industries Co., Old State Rd., Middlefield, O. 44062

Glass Laboratories, Inc., 863 65th St., Brooklyn, N.Y. 11220

DeVilbiss Co., P.O. Box 913, 300 Phillips Ave., Toledo, O. 43601

Industrial Plastics Corp., 816 W. Beardsley Ave., Elkhart, Ind. 46514

J and B Plastics Co., Inc., West Stone Ave., Fairfield, Ia. 52556

Johnson Rubber Co., 111 Vine St., Middlefield, O. 44062

Kenyon Marine Corp., Guilford, Conn. 06437

Manart Textile Co., 116 Franklin St., New York, N.Y. 10013

Minnesota Mining and Mfg. Co., 3M Center, St. Paul, Minn. 55101

Moeller Mfg. Co., Inc., P.O. Box 1318, Greenville, Miss. 38701

Plastic Sales and Mfg. Co., Inc., 3030 McGee Trafficway, Kansas City, Mo. 64116

Ren Plastics, Inc., 5656 S. Cedar, Lansing, Mich. 48909

Rule Industries, Inc., Cape Ann Industrial Park, Gloucester, Mass. 09130

W. S. Shamban and Co., 11543 West Olympic Blvd., Los Angeles, Calif. 90064

Zurn Industries, Inc., Marine Div., 1801 Pittsburgh Ave., Erie, Pa. 16512

Tubing, rubber

Amerace Corp., Molded Products Div., Ace Rd., Butler, N.J. 07405

Auburn Mfg. Co., 200 Stack St., Middletown, Conn. 06457

Byron Jackson, Inc., 1900 E. 65th St., Los Angeles, Calif. 90001

Geauga Industries Co., Old State Rd., Middlefield, O. 44062

Johnson Rubber Co., 111 Vine St., Middlefield, O. 44062

Lake Rubber, Inc., Box 547, Willoughby, O. 44094

Minisink Rubber Co., Inc., Orange County, Unionville, N.Y. 10988

Ohio Rubber Co., Ben-Hur Ave., Willoughby, O. 44094

Preferred Electric and Wire Corp., 68 33rd St., Brooklyn, N.Y. 11232

Upholstery material

AMXCO, Inc., 850 Ave. H East, Arlington, Tex. 16010

Cruis-Tops, Inc., 617 Farnsworth, Oconto, Wis. 54153

Douglass Fabrics, Marine Div., 186 N. Main St., Pleasantville, N.J. 08232

General Tire and Rubber Co., Chemical/Plastics Div., P.O. Box 875, Toledo, O. 43601

Goodall Vinyl Fabrics Div., Burlington Industries, 846GH Merchandise Mart, Chicago, Ill. 60654

International Cushion Co., 1110 N. E. 8th Ave., Fort Lauderdale, Fla. 33304

Manart Textile Co., 116 Franklin St., New York, N.Y. 10013

Masland Duraleather Co., Amber and Willard Sts., Philadelphia, Pa. 19134

Reeves Bros., Inc., 1071 6th Ave., New York, N.Y. 10018

Sackner Products, Inc., 901 Ottawa Ave., N.W., Grand Rapids, Mich. 49502

Sportsmen's Industries, Inc., 7878 N.W. 103rd St., Hialeah Gardens, Fla. 33012

Weymouth Art Leather Co., Inc., 180 Pearl St., South Braintree, Mass. 02185

Varnish, polyurethane

Andrew Brown Company, 5431 District Blvd., P.O. Box 22066, Los Angeles, Calif. 90022

Chilton Paint Co., 109–09 15th Ave., College Point, N.Y. 11356

Chrysler Corp., Chemical Div., 5437 W. Jefferson, Trenton, Mich. 48183

Jewel Paint and Varnish Co., 345 N. Western Ave., Chicago, Ill. 60612

Kristal Kraft, Inc., 900 4th St., Palmetto, Fla. 33561

Valspar Corp., Marine Div., 200 Sayre St., Rockford, Ill. 61101

Varnish, spar

Adelphi Paint and Color Works, Inc., 86–00 Dumont Ave., Ozone Park, N.Y. 11417

Baltimore Copper Paint Co., 501 Key Hwy., Baltimore, Md. 21230

Andrew Brown Co., 5431 District Blvd., P.O. Box 22066, Los Angeles, Calif. 90022

H. A. Calahan, Inc., 859 Mamaroneck Ave., Mamaroneck, N.Y. 10543

Chilton Paint Co., 109–09 15th Ave., College Point, N.Y. 11356

Debevoise Co., 74 20th St., Brooklyn, N.Y. 11232

Dolphin Paint and Chemical Co., 922 Locust St., P.O. Box 1927 Central Station, Toledo, O. 43603

Gillespie Varnish Co., 131 Dey St., Jersey City, N.J. 07306

International Paint Co., Inc., 21 West St., New York, N.Y. 10006

Jewel Paint and Varnish Co., 345 N. Western Ave., Chicago, Ill. 60612

Kyanize Paints, Inc., 2nd and Boston Sts., Everett, Mass. 02149

Pettit Paint Co., Inc., 507 Main St., Rockaway, N.J. 07866

U. S. Yacht Paint Co., P.O. Box 525, Roseland, N.J. 07068

Valspar Corp., Marine Div., 200 Sayre St., Rockford, Ill. 61101

J. C. Whitlam Mfg. Co., Box 71, Wadsworth, O. 44281

Woolsey Marine Industries, Inc., 201 E. 42nd St., New York, N.Y. 10017

Ventilation kits

Mercury Marine, Fond du Lac, Wis. 54935

Voltmeters

C. B. Archibald and Co., 134 Old Black Point Rd., Niantic, Conn. 06357

Dixson, Inc., P.O. Box 1449, Grand Junction, Colo. 81501

Fox Valley Instruments Co., 8627 Straits Hwy., Cheboygan, Mich. 49721

Medallion Instruments, Inc., 917 W. Savidge St., Spring Lake, Mich. 49456

Preferred Electric and Wire Corp., 68 33rd St., Brooklyn, N.Y. 11232

Wax, boat

Craft Plastics Corp., Box 33, Parcel Post St., Worcester, Mass. 01604

Fuller Brush Co., Marine Div., East Hartford, Conn. 06108

Winterizing compounds

Olson Industries, Inc., P.O. Box 2520, Sarasota, Fla. 33578

Protect-A-Systems, Inc., 73 Ruth Ann Terr., Milford, Conn. 06460

The manufacturers listed in this directory are among those included in the appropriate manufacturing categories. There has been no attempt, nor is there any intent, to interpret this listing as an exclusive and totally complete one. It is as complete as the author of this book could make it, but there are doubtless a number of other manufacturers who could have been included. No insertion fees or commissions were charged those manufacturers listed.

INDEX

Abrasives, 145. *See also* Sanding
Acetone, avoiding, on vinyl, 32
Additives
    gas and oil, 145–47
    resin, 193
Air filters, 173
Aluminum boats
    bottom paint on, 16–19
    choosing, 3, 4
    fall maintenance of, 81–84
    repairing, 123–26
        dents, 123–24
        punctures and skin fractures,
          126
        riveting, 125–26
        structural damage, 124–25
    season maintenance of painted, 65
    season maintenance of unpainted
        marine, 68–69
    topside spring maintenance of, 26–
        27
    and torching, 137
Aluminum outboard motors, antifoul-
    ing paints on, 74
Aluminum paint, 183–84
Anchor and chain, spring checking of,
    53–54
Anti-electrolysis paint, 184
Antifouling compounds, 159
Antifouling paints
    for aluminum boats, 16–19
    for fiberglass boats, 13–16
    modern synthetic, 15–16
    on outboards, 74
    traditional, 15, 16
    where to find, 184
    for wood boats, 24
Antiskid compounds, 162–63

Antiskid paint, 187–88
Antiskid surfacing material, 147–48
Arsenic and bottom painting alumi-
    num boats, 18

Batteries, winterizing, 100
Bedding compounds, 159–60
Belt sanders, 195
Bilge cleaners, 151–52
Bilge paint, 185
Bimetallic couple, corrosion of
        aluminum in, 17
Bird droppings, 61
Bits, drill, 147
Bleach, wood, 147
Blind holes, repairing, in fiberglass,
    117–22
Board, fiberglass, 170
Boat ice-melting systems, 179
Boating Industry Association, 3, 47
Boom, storing of, 52
Boottop stripe, applying, 28–29
Bottom
    of carvel-planked boats, 20
    fall maintenance of wood, 84–85,
        89–90
Bottom cleaners, 152
Bottom paint
    on aluminum boats, 16–19
    on fiberglass boats, 13–16
    modern synthetic, 15–16
    traditional, 15, 16
Brass, cleaning, 70
Breaks, repairing, in fiberglass, 117–
    22
Brightwork, defined, 32
Brokers, in shopping for used boats,
    4–5